Collaborative, Competency-Based Counseling and Therapy

Collaborative, Competency-Based Counseling and Therapy

Bob Bertolino

Therapeutic Collaborations Consultation & Training

Youth In Need, Inc.

Bill O'Hanlon

Possibilities

Allyn and Bacon

Boston ▪ London ▪ Toronto ▪ Sydney ▪ Tokyo ▪ Singapore

Series Editor: *Patricia Quinlin*
Editor-in-Chief, Social Sciences: *Karen Hanson*
Series Editorial Assistant: *Alyssa Pratt*
Marketing Manager: *Jacqueline Aaron*
Production Editor: *Christopher H. Rawlings*
Editorial-Production Service: *Omegatype Typography, Inc.*
Composition and Prepress Buyer: *Linda Cox*
Manufacturing Manager: *Suzanne Lareau*
Cover Administrator: *Kristina Mose-Libon*
Electronic Composition: *Omegatype Typography, Inc.*

A Pearson Education Company
160 Gould Street
Needham Heights, MA 02494

Internet: www.ablongman.com

Library of Congress Cataloging-in-Publication Data

Bertolino, Bob
Collaborative, competency-based counseling and therapy / Bob Bertolino, Bill O'Hanlon.
p. cm.
Includes bibliographical references and index.
ISBN 0-205-32605-6
1. Counseling. 2. Psychotherapy. I. O'Hanlon, William Hudson. II. Title.

BF637.C6 B443 2002
616.89—dc21

00-067629

Printed in the United States of America
10 9 8 7 6 5 4 3 2 1 06 05 04 03 02 01

To my wife, Christine, and my daughter, Morgan.
You are the loves of my life.

And to the late Dr. John DiTiberio. Thank you for your kindness
and selfless dedication. Your spirit is present in this book.
We miss you very much.

—Bob

To Steffanie, who is my friend and collaborator. Thank you for finding my
strengths and for accepting my flaws.

—Bill

CONTENTS

PREFACE

"If you want truly to understand something, try to change it."
—Kurt Lewin

In early 1997 we began talking about writing a book that would begin to move competency-based ideas into counseling, marriage, family, social work, and psychology programs. Although we both became involved in a variety of other projects, including a few together, this particular one was never far from our thoughts. For Bob this book became especially important when he found himself teaching graduate courses in four different departments at three different universities. Although there has been a plethora of books published on traditional counseling theories and family therapy approaches, there was nothing available to students that brought collaborative, competency-based ideas into one succinct volume. This made the writing of this book not only important for the field, but also a practicality in terms of training others to work in what we consider to be respectful and effective ways.

As with traditional thinkers, unfortunately there are turf issues among competency-based theorists. For example, there continues to be a split between solution-based and narrative thinkers. This was no more apparent than in 1996 at the Therapeutic Conversations conference held in Denver, Colorado. Although touted as a collaborative conference, the split between solution-based and narrative thinkers left many attendees feeling as if one theory was better than another or that they had to choose sides (Bertolino & O'Hanlon, 1998).

During one of the group conversational processes that ended each day of the conference, a woman stood up and said that she had decided that the conference wasn't for her. She had told people in her small group that she did long-term therapy, and they began to tell her how incorrect that was. They made her feel that what she was doing was bad and that she was wrong. Bill was very upset at hearing this and told her that even though he had an international reputation as a brief therapist, he had seen at least one client for twelve years. Interestingly, the dogmatic idea that had plagued therapy for years had invaded a collaborative conference and in the process had alienated some of its participants.

One of the ways we chose to address this concern was to find how therapy approaches were similar and complemented one another as opposed to what made them distinctly different. In addition, we made it a mission to support our ideas with current research on therapy outcomes. We believe all mental health professionals should be interested in knowing whether what they do in treatment contributes to positive outcomes.

We also formulated a mission statement that we would like to share with you. It reflects all that we do in clinical practice, teaching, training, and research:

> We vow to support and promote effective and respectful approaches to counseling and psychotherapy and stand opposed to those approaches that are ineffective and disrespectful.

Notice that this mission statement does not reflect any single approach or theory. It does not suggest that we are this or that. What it does do is promise that whatever we do as clinicians, teachers, or researchers will be respectful of our clients and others. It also states that we will do our best to study the outcomes of our ideas and methods in order to determine how we can be most effective with our clients.

Throughout this text we will offer collaborative, competency-based ideas that directly reflect our mission statement. Some of these ideas are based in empirical research, and some are based more on our observation of clinical results and anecdotal responses from clients and others we have taught. We fully expect that time, more research, and more experience will alter our articulation of these ideas and methods. However, we do not expect to alter our basic desire to be respectful and effective.

How This Book Is Arranged

We begin with an introductory chapter on the three waves of psychotherapy. We believe it is important to briefly reorient readers with the general roots of psychotherapy to gain an understanding of how collaborative, competency-based approaches developed. Following this introduction are nine chapters organized in four parts. Each part emphasizes a particular aspect of collaborative and competency-based theory.

Part One, "Creating a Context for Change through Collaboration," begins with two chapters that set the tone for the entire book. Chapter 1 is "Foundations of a Collaborative, Competency-Based Approach to Counseling and Therapy." In this chapter we explore the implications of outcome research, guiding ideas, and four areas to create change. "Creating Collaborative Relationships through Attending, Listening, and Language" is the second chapter. Here we introduce ways that therapists can begin to form collaborative relationships prior to the start of formal therapy. We also discuss the importance of acknowledgment and show how therapists can use subtle changes in language to begin to create possibilities for change.

Part Two, "Clarifying Concerns, Complaints, Goals, and Preferred Outcomes," also is divided into two chapters. In Chapter 3, "Creating Change through Collaborative, Competency-Based Conversations," we continue to explore how language can be utilized as a vehicle for creating change. In addition, we discuss how therapists' biases can affect therapy, the role of psychiatric diagnosis, and the use of formal assessment procedures. "Creating and Clarifying Preferences, Goals, and Preferred Outcomes" is Chapter 4. Here we investigate ways of collaborating with clients on their conversational and relational preferences, goals, and outcomes.

In Part Three, "Creating Change in the Realms of Viewing, Action, and Context," we explore different areas of intervention by devoting a chapter to each of three realms. Chapter 5, "Changing the Viewing of Problems," gets us started as we define ways of helping clients change their patterns of attention and the stories they hold. "Changing the Doing of Problems" follows. This chapter focuses on ways of getting clients to change patterns of action and interaction involved with problems. Chapter 7, "Changing Contextual Propensities Associated with Problems" rounds out Part Three. Here we explore a variety of different influences that contribute to problematic patterns as well as solution patterns.

Part Four is "Evaluating Progress, Planning Next Steps, and Ending Therapy." We begin with Chapter 8, "Identifying, Amplifying, and Extending Change in Future Sessions." In this chapter we discuss how to identify and build on small changes and how to extend those changes into the future. We also describe ways of working with clients when things do not seem to be progressing in preferred directions. Chapter 9, "Planning for the End from the Beginning," is next. Here we offer ways of managing setbacks, negotiating hurdles and perceived barriers, and ending therapy.

We round out the book with a brief epilogue, "Toward a Personalized Theory of Counseling and Therapy." Here we discuss the importance of remaining client-informed and how theoretical perspectives can facilitate burnout or personal change.

Throughout this book we include case examples, stories, and anecdotes as a way of enhancing your learning experience. In addition, although there are differing opinions on the matter, we use the terms *counseling* and *psychotherapy*, and *counselor, therapist*, and *clinician* interchangeably. We also periodically use the term *mental health professional*. We are referring to those people who are engaged in facilitating change in human beings and relationships. We've also changed clients' and others' names to protect their confidentiality.

We hope you will enjoy your journey through the world of collaboration and competency in counseling and therapy!

Acknowledgments

We would like to thank Christine Bertolino, Silvia Bobadilla, Adrian Blow, Karen Caldwell, Tom Conran, John Jaeger, Jay Memmott, Nancy Morrison, and Steffanie O'Hanlon for their helpful comments, suggestions, and encouraging words during the writing of the manuscript.

We would also like to thank the staff at Allyn and Bacon, especially Alyssa Pratt and Karen Hanson, for their assistance throughout the project, and Judy Fifer for her vision of this book as a major contribution to the field. We are grateful to the following reviewers: Marsha Carolan, Michigan State University, and Doug Fleischer, Walla Walla College.

From Bob: Thanks to Bill for another wonderfully collaborative effort. Thank you to the faculty in the Departments of Counseling and Family Therapy and Social Work at St. Louis University and Professional Counseling at Lindenwood University for your support and feedback. To my colleagues at Youth In Need, Inc., thank you for being so supportive and genuine. To my students, thank you for the collaborative learning experiences. To my colleagues at the Institute for the Study of Therapeutic Change (ISTC), thanks for your hard work, persistence, and support. Thanks to Don and Belinda Willis for sharing my passion for these ideas and for helping to spread the word. And to my clients, thank you for being such wonderful teachers—I hope that I have been, and will continue to be, a worthy student.

From Bill: Thanks to Bob for all your work in making this project come to fruition. And you didn't even need to send the cardboard cutout of yourself to stand over me at the computer to get me to focus!

Collaborative, Competency-Based Counseling and Therapy

INTRODUCTION

The Evolution of Collaborative, Competency-Based Therapies and the Third Wave

The field of psychotherapy has undergone significant changes since its inception in the early 1900s. As this field continues to evolve, we find ourselves rethinking previously held assumptions, ideas, and beliefs regarding our work with individuals, couples, and families. We view this rethinking or challenging of assumptions as movement into a third wave of psychotherapy. The third wave represents the heart and soul of this book—a collaborative, competency-based approach to counseling and therapy. To understand the significance of this shift, it's important to recognize where we've been during the first two waves. Let's take a moment to briefly review and revisit the roots of counseling and psychotherapy.

The First Wave: Intrapsychic, Pathology, and Past Focus

Prior to Sigmund Freud, mental illness was believed to be the result of physical causes (e.g., lesions on the brain) or demonic spirit possession. Although Freud maintained close linkage to biological thinking, he offered a different perspective, reframing the cause and cure of emotional maladjustment in psychological terms. Freud's work laid the foundation for the first wave in the field of psychotherapy.

Dominated by psychoanalysis, psychodynamic theories, and biological psychiatry, first-wave approaches were pathology-based. Mental illness was understood to be *intrapsychic,* or within the person. First-wave approaches helped shift the view of people from morally deficient to mentally ill. They also introduced stigmatizing labels and jargon that remain a central part of our language today. This is evidenced by the *Diagnostic and Statistical Manual of Mental Disorders (DSM)* (American Psychiatric Association, 1994) and mental health professionals' use of terms such as *borderline, narcissistic,* and *oppositional–defiant* to describe their clients and patients.

The psychoanalytic perspective represented a starting point and a testing ground for countless ideas. Much emphasis was placed on the role of professionals, primarily psychiatrists, as experts. There was a search for underlying pathology that could be uncovered by delving deeply into a patient's past, and then explained through experts' respective theories. Thus therapy was understood to be a process in which clients and patients revisited the past to discover, reexperience, and relive traumatic or painful events. It was believed that such cathartic rituals were necessary to bring about healing.

It was also during the first wave that behaviorism gained prominence and challenged the premises of analytical thinking. Based on principles associated with classical and operant conditioning, and offering a radical departure from psychoanalysis, behaviorists maintained that people were conditioned through external factors. Behaviorists downplayed psychological processes and viewed change as a result of the expertise of therapists who identified maladaptive behaviors and the contingencies of those behaviors. Therapists would then design programs and interventions to modify those behaviors.

Although initial forms of behaviorism brought about an alternative to psychoanalysis, therapists were still held as the only experts in the therapeutic milieu. In addition, behaviorism was criticized as inhumane, viewing human beings as machine-like. In spite of its criticisms, the contributions of behaviorism are numerous, and it served as a thread in connecting the first and second waves of psychotherapy.

The Second Wave: From Intrapsychic and Past to Interactional and Present

The second wave, which began in the 1950s, did not completely move away from the foundation created by the first wave. What did occur was a shift in focus. Instead of attending to pathology located in the past, second-wave theorists concurred with behaviorists and placed emphasis on the present, or here and now. Problem-focused approaches were developed and family therapy ideas brought to light new ways of conceptualizing and approaching problems. Systemic thinking defined problems as being within small systems and between people as opposed to within them. For family therapists, the term *intrapsychic* was replaced with *interactional*—the study of relationships. This meant that constructs such as personality were no longer sealed within the person, but were influenced by patterns of communication, family and social relationships, stimulus and response, and even "self-talk."

The expertise of the therapist remained at the forefront during the second wave. The therapist's role was to take responsibility for solving clients' problems by first determining the dysfunction within relationships by studying elements such as family structure, rules, roles, and boundaries and then prescribing interventions to alter, interrupt, and ultimately change patterns of action and interaction. Many new theoretical ideas were also introduced during this time, contributing to a new vocabulary of terms such as *enmeshment, hierarchy, homeostasis,* and *feedback loop.* This language became as influential as that of the first wave.

The first two waves dealt primarily with the discovery of pathology, and problems with reality being conceived as knowable by the therapist. This modernist template defined mental health professionals as experts who could somehow determine or find and possess truth through their respective theoretical explanations. In addition, commonalities were shared by first- and second-wave approaches, including:

- Focusing on problems and pathology instead of competency
- Focusing on therapist-generated explanations instead of possibilities and solutions
- Orienting clients toward what can't be changed—the past or personality characteristics
- Encouraging clients to view themselves as determined by childhood events, biology or genetics, family, or societal oppression
- Often creating new problems that clients didn't even know they had prior to the start of therapy

Although first- and second-wave approaches shared the above characteristics, various models competed with each other as to the right or correct ways of working with people. It was assumed that if the right method was determined, principles could be discovered to universally explain all human behavior.

The Third Wave: Collaborative, Competency-Based Approaches

The third wave began with what some have deemed a time of reexamination. In the late 1970s and early 1980s, mental health practitioners and, in particular, family therapists, began to take notice of their biases and blinders. Therapists were finding holes in their theories and prejudices (i.e., sexism and cultural biases) that had gone unacknowledged and without challenge for years. In particular, the feminist critique emphasized the importance of gender-related and sociocultural issues that had been discounted during the first 100 years of psychotherapy (Goldner, 1993; Hare-Mustin, 1978, 1994). Many first- and second-wave theories and practices marginalized women and minorities while all but avoiding the larger social context within which "problems" occurred. The feminist critique called on clinicians to conduct self-evaluations and challenge their traditional ideologies in order to do away with practices that were judgmental, pathologizing, and control- or power-oriented.

In addition to the feminist critique, other theoretical perspectives began to emerge during this time. These theories shared a common thread—competency.

O'Hanlon (1994) remarked, "We believed that the focus on problems often obscures the resources and solutions residing within clients.... We no longer saw the therapists as the source of the solution—the solutions rested in people and their social networks" (p. 23). With an emphasis on strengths, abilities, and resources, therapists no longer had to accept what their theories were saying—that clients were in some way damaged goods and/or incapable of positive change.

Accompanying the shift to more competency-based approaches were the ideas of *second-order cybernetics* or *cybernetics of cybernetics* and *postmodernism.* Although it is not our intention to engage in deep-seated philosophical discussions of either premise, we would like to situate their contributions in context. First, cybernetics of cybernetics represented a shift from viewing the therapist as an outside observer to one who is part of the therapeutic system. This way of thinking brought to light what many had already surmised—as clinicians we are in a continual process of influencing and being influenced. We affect clients and they affect us.

The second premise, postmodernism, essentially represented a shift away from attempting to develop a universal theory of knowing. It ushered in the idea that individuals' narratives and discourses are shaped by society, culture, and history. For mental health professionals, postmodernism brought attention to their role in both the creation and construction of problems and solutions. Perhaps for the first time, therapists began to identify ways in which problems could be a by-product of language and interaction. This was punctuated by *constructivism* and *social constructionism.*

Constructivism and Social Constructionism

Constructivism is a philosophical stance rooted in biology and the physical properties of individual perception (Maturana, 1978; von Foerster, 1984; von Glasersfeld, 1984; Watzlawick, 1984). From this perspective, the subjective constructions of the world that people hold aren't the same as the physical reality that is "out there." For counselors, this means that there are multiple ways of understanding the world with no single theory being more true or correct than another. A constructivist approach holds that there are as many realities as there are people in the world. It's a matter of finding what fits best with the environment given ethical and ecological factors including, but not limited to, age, sex, race, class, ethnicity, religion, and family background. Thus, therapists and clients can both have constructed realities or *stories* that are more or less useful depending on the situation, but no more or less true in any event.

Social constructionism is grounded in philosophy, relationships, and community and represents a wider domain of interpretation (Berger & Luckmann, 1966; Gergen, 1982, 1985, 1994). Social constructionists emphasize how meaning emerges through the complex webs of interaction, relationships, and social processes. The generation of meaning occurs as individuals interact and talk with others or talk with themselves. Consequently, meaning and therefore social realities are continually renegotiated and never truly set. Although there is a physical reality (e.g., if you touch fire, it will burn you), social realities are constantly created and recreated through language and interaction and are subject to change.

In regard to the idea of problems, Goolishian and Anderson (1987) stated, "Problems are no more than a socially created reality that is sustained by behavior and coordinated in language" (p. 532). Madsen (1999) discussed this idea in relation to the constructs of personality and self:

> Many individual psychology models assume that what we call the "self" consists of innate personality characteristics that represent the true essence of the person (e.g., Linda is a borderline). These models often take an ahistorical, acontextual approach that isolates individuals from their social context. Social constructionist approaches view "self" as constructed in social interaction (e.g., Linda would become a very different woman in different cultures and in different historical periods). (p. 49)

The assertion is that problems are in effect socially constructed, generated, and anchored in language and social interaction. Therefore, individual identities are continually being reformed through interaction with others.

Constructivist and social constructionist philosophies brought to light the role of language as the primary vehicle for creating meaning and change. Therapists learned that each therapeutic dialogue or interaction leads to the creation or recreation of something new—a *reauthoring* or *rewriting* of a new story for the client. This shift to focusing on the role of language in therapeutic processes was significant because it was the first time that theorists thoroughly studied the implications of language on the construction and resolution of problems.

The third wave also brought with it a challenge to the previously held notion of the counselor as single expert in the therapeutic process. Therapy was considered a more collaborative effort between therapists and clients with expertise being shared. This represents a significant shift from the first two eras.

Similar in Name, Not the Same: Varieties of Competency-Based Approaches

Today a variety of competency-based approaches are available to therapists. In this section we'll highlight a few of these perspectives and discuss their contributions to the approach offered in this book.

Milton H. Erickson and the Solution-Orientation

It took the third wave to bring about a major shift in the field of psychotherapy and for the masses to take notice. Ironically, years earlier others had presented the idea that clients' have the abilities, resources, and strengths to resolve their own problems. One of the first to highlight this idea was the psychiatrist Milton Erickson. In fact, we consider Erickson's contributions seminal to the evolution of a collaborative, competency-based approach.

Erickson was the ultimate competency-based therapist. He did not subscribe to any one theoretical perspective and did not believe that any single theory could explain or describe the complexity or continuum of human behavior. Instead, he relied on his keen sense of observation and open-mindedness in exploring possibilities with his patients. Havens (1985) remarked:

> [Erickson] did not sit in his office reading or thinking about how people operate—he watched them. He did not become immersed in theories which he then tried to apply to various patients—he noticed what his patients did and modified his thinking in response. Erickson's spectacular success was based upon his willingness to let people teach him what was real or true about themselves and not upon unique theoretical constructs. (p. 7)

Erickson was a master at evoking his patient's abilities, strengths, and resources. It was through these avenues that he would help them change. His utilization of what the patient brought to the therapeutic encounter was central to his way of doing therapy (O'Hanlon, 1987; Rossi, 1980a; Rossi & Ryan, 1983a, 1983b, 1983c; Rossi, Ryan, & Sharp, 1983). Erickson stated (1954a), "The purpose of psychotherapy should be the helping of the patient in that fashion most adequate, available, and acceptable. In rendering the patient aid, there should be full respect for and utilization of whatever the patient presents" (p. 127). He believed that people already possess what they need to resolve their problems within themselves or their social systems.

In a time when most approaches to therapy were oriented toward the past, Erickson focused on the present and the future. He remarked, "Emphasis should be placed more upon what the patient does in the present and will do in the future than upon a mere understanding of why some long-past event occurred" (1954a, p. 127). To help his patients to resolve their problems and develop a sense of the future he often used techniques such as pseudo-orientation in time, where he would have clients envision a future in which their problems were resolved (Erickson, 1954b). Erickson would help people to take action in the present in order to reach problem resolution and future goals.

Erickson also believed that people could change rapidly. He did not hold the adage, "If a problem took a long time to develop then it will take a long time to go away." In fact, he had many one-session cures (O'Hanlon & Hexum, 1990). He commented:

> Illness can come on all of a sudden; one can make a massive response all at once to a particular thing. I do not think we need to presuppose or propound some long, drawn-out causation and a long, drawn-out therapeutic process. You see, if illness can occur suddenly, then therapy can occur quite as suddenly. (quoted in Rossi, Ryan, & Sharp, 1983, p. 71)

Many former students and followers of Erickson meticulously studied his work in an effort to outline the underlying principles of what in the early 1980s became known as *Ericksonian therapy* (see Bandler & Grinder, 1975; Gilligan, 1987;

Grinder, DeLozier, & Bandler, 1977; Lankton & Lankton, 1983, 1986; O'Hanlon, 1987; Zeig, 1982, 1985a, 1985b, 1994; Zeig & Lankton, 1988). Despite such efforts, no consensus could be established as to what constituted Ericksonian therapy. The reason for this is that researchers focused primarily on Erickson's methods and techniques. In fact, the only common denominator in Erickson's work was the patient

Erickson's therapeutic approach was client-informed. His astute attention to communication enabled him to learn from his patients their ways of healing devoid of theoretical constructions and limitations. Erickson (1980) remarked:

> The therapist's task should not be a proselytizing of the patient with his own beliefs and understandings. No patient can really understand the understandings of his therapist nor does he need them. What is needed is the development of a therapeutic situation permitting the patient to use his own thinking, his own understandings, his own emotions in the way that best fits for him in his scheme of life. (p. 223)

What became clear in Erickson's work was the emphasis he placed on creating possibilities for change with his patients. To do so, he directed his attention to his patients and their respective theories as opposed to his own.

Solution-Oriented and Possibility Therapies: Bill O'Hanlon

Bill O'Hanlon is a former student of Milton Erickson and, along with Michele Weiner-Davis, is considered the co-developer of solution-oriented therapy (O'Hanlon & Weiner-Davis, 1989). He is also the creator of solution-oriented hypnosis and was the first to thoroughly discuss a possibility approach to therapy (O'Hanlon, 1993, 1999; O'Hanlon & Beadle, 1994, 1999). Both solution-oriented and possibility therapies emphasize the importance of clients' internal experience. Within this realm, O'Hanlon has stressed the importance of acknowledgment and validation. Clients must, above all, feel heard and understood throughout the process of therapy or change in other areas will not likely occur.

O'Hanlon's work has served to push the envelope in regard to ideas associated with solution-based approaches to therapy. He has drawn attention to the idea that people became stuck not only in doing of their problems but also in their viewing, and in regard to contextual propensities associated with their situations. This has expanded the barriers of solution-based approaches by helping clients to be heard and understood in the realm of experience and to change in three areas—views, actions, and context.

O'Hanlon has also emphasized the significance of language. The way we talk about problems and solutions makes a difference. The subtle ways that therapists use language can be of central importance in how problems are conceptualized. O'Hanlon has discussed how cocreating solvable problems is necessary because the therapist plays a role in defining and shaping, within the therapeutic context, what is possible. Thus, his focus is on what is realistic and attainable.

Not one to be confined by purist thinking, O'Hanlon has moved to include ideas from other perspectives and expand his efforts to specific types of problems facing mental health practitioners today. These include working with chronic mental illness, sexual abuse, and trauma (Bertolino & O'Hanlon, 1998; O'Hanlon & Bertolino, 1998; O'Hanlon & Bertolino, 1999; Rowan & O'Hanlon, 1998). Study of his methods finds ideas from Ericksonian, strategic, behavioral, solution-based, and narrative approaches, with no allegiance to any one model.

Solution-Focused Therapy: The Brief Family Therapy Center

The Brief Family Therapy Center (BFTC) in Milwaukee, Wisconsin, is considered the home of solution-focused brief therapy. This approach evolved out of the roots of the MRI (Mental Research Institute) brief therapy model (de Shazer, 1985, 1991). A major distinction between the two approaches is that the solution-focused model shifts the conversation from problems to solutions. Thus, therapists utilize solution talk with clients and work to highlight abilities, strengths, and resources. A main tenet of this approach is that the therapist does not need to know a lot about the problem in order to resolve it.

Steve de Shazer and Insoo Kim Berg are considered the originators of the solution-focused approach, although several notable clinicians including Peter De Jong, Larry Hopwood, Eve Lipchik, Scott Miller, Michele Weiner-Davis, Wally Gingerich, Alex Molnar, and Elam Nunnally have at one time or another worked on the development of the theory as members of the BFTC team. It is also important to acknowledge Don Norum, who was not associated with the BFTC, but wrote the first paper (in 1978) emphasizing a solution focus (Bertolino & O'Hanlon, 1998).

The solution-focused approach relies heavily on clients to educate therapists about how they can best help them. Therefore, the notion of resistance is not considered a helpful assumption. The belief is that there is only cooperation. A major contribution of the BFTC is the *miracle question* (de Shazer, 1988). In much the same way that Erickson would work with his patients to delve into the future with pseudo-orientation in time, de Shazer and colleagues developed a nonhypnotic approach to help people identify a time in the future when their problem was no longer a problem. The therapist could then work with them to make that vision a reality.

Another development was the advent of the first session task (de Shazer, 1985). Given at the end of the initial session, the therapist would orient the client(s) toward what was happening that they preferred as opposed to what was wrong. The BFTC group directs their interest toward exceptions and times when people aren't having their problems. The idea is that no one has a problem twenty-four hours a day.

The work at BFTC informs a collaborative, competency-based approach on several accounts. First, there is an emphasis on clients' abilities, strengths, and resources. Next, the focus is on exceptions—when people experience their problems to a lesser degree or when they're absent altogether. Finally, a future-orientation is employed. Together these ideas support the notion of emphasizing solutions with clients.

Narrative Therapy: Michael White and David Epston

Michael White of Australia and David Epston of New Zealand are credited as being the creators of the narrative approach to therapy (Epston, 1989; Epston & White, 1992; White, 1989; White & Epston, 1990). Instead of focusing on how people have problems, White and Epston became interested in how problems become oppressive in people's lives. Problems can be influenced by social, cultural, religious, political, and other dominant discourses. According to this perspective, when people's stories about themselves and their lives become problem saturated, problems arise.

A main focus of the narrative approach is the use of *externalizing conversations* whereby people and their problems are talked about as being separate entities. In essence, the person is never the problem—the problem is the problem. These types of conversations can help people to move outside of the stories that confine them. Focus is also on *unique outcomes,* which represent alternative stories or aspects of lived experience that run counter to problem-saturated stories. Although White and de Shazer have argued differently, unique outcomes for narrative therapists seem to share some similarity with that of exceptions in solution-focused and solution-oriented therapies (de Shazer, 1993; White, 1993).

Narrative therapy emphasizes the meanings that people construct through interaction. Words such as escape and overcome are common with this approach in that people are seen as heroes and heroines who have loosened the grips that problems have tried to maintain on them. At the end of therapy, certificates are often given to clients signifying their victories over previously oppressive problems. Narrative ideas offer alternative ways for therapists to talk with clients about their problems and potential solutions. This unique use of language is conducive to a competency-based approach.

The Collaborative Language Systems Approach: The Houston-Galveston Institute

The work of Harlene Anderson and the late Harry Goolishian at the Houston-Galveston Institute (HGI) is based on the concepts of language and conversation and is referred to as the collaborative language systems approach (Anderson, 1993, 1997; Anderson & Goolishian, 1988, 1992; Goolishian & Anderson, 1987). Rooted in social constructionism and hermeneutics, emphasis is on the creation of meaning through conversation. Anderson (1993) relates:

> Human action takes place in a reality of understanding that is created through social construction and dialogue... we live and understand our lives through socially constructed narrative realities, that is, that we give meaning and organization to our experiences and to our self-identity in the course of these transactions. (p. 324)

Therapy, then, is understood to be a process whereby therapists and clients engage in collaborative conversations leading to the cocreation of new narratives. It is through conversation that problems dissolve. The process of therapy involves dialoguing with not to. The therapist maintains a nonexpert, unknowing position by assuming no preconstructed knowledge about the client. The use of language in this approach contributes to the humanization of therapy and informs a possibility therapy perspective.

The Reflecting Team: Tom Andersen

For years, second-wave family therapists used the one-way mirror as a format for teaching and developing strategic interventions. This was based on the notion that family systems were essentially stable, with governing homeostatic mechanisms. However, in the late 1970s the Milan group of Selvini Palazzoli, Boscolo, Cecchin, and Prata (1978, 1980) began to understand families as evolving and changing. In line with these observations and with therapies that were becoming more focused on change and meaning-making systems, Norwegian psychiatrist Tom Andersen began to introduce ways of using teams in a collaborative effort—reflecting teams.

Lynn Hoffman (1995) explained:

> This method asked a team to share comments on the conversation between the therapist and family while the family watched and listened. The family would then comment on the team's ideas in turn. This innovation proved to be a great leveler, modifying the concealment that the use of the one-way mirror had so long imposed. (p. xi)

Reflecting teams have helped to further remove barriers between clinicians and clients previously dictated by theoretical assumptions. Over the past decade many innovative versions of this approach have followed as ways of helping individuals, couples, and families to become unstuck (Friedman, 1995).

Although some of the approaches just described have similar names, they also are different in many ways. Rather than highlight the differences, our intention over the course of this text is to bring together the ideas that bind these approaches and present a framework that honors and values many theoretical contributions while serving no single model—making it a collaborative, competency-based approach.

We've now provided an overview of the historical roots of psychotherapy and the evolution of third-wave approaches. In the next chapter we'll outline the foundations of a collaborative, competency-based approach to counseling and psychotherapy.

PART ONE

Creating a Context for Change through Collaboration

As a whole, the field of psychotherapy has undergone significant changes since the first talk therapies gained prominence. As discussed in the Introduction, we now find ourselves exploring new directions in clinical practice. In Part One of this book we'll investigate these new directions and demonstrate how therapists can become both client- and outcome-informed.

To do this, we discuss the foundations of a collaborative, competency-based approach to counseling and therapy. This includes an exploration of forty years of outcome research, ideas associated with this perspective, and four areas of creating change with clients. We also offer ways of creating collaborative relationships prior to and in opening sessions of formal therapy.

In the first part of this book we will also explore how therapists can attend to clients' stories and ways of using language and learn about clients' theories of change. Additionally, therapists will be introduced to multiple ways of attending to clients' internal experiences as well as their views, while opening up the possibilities for future change.

CHAPTER

1 Foundations of a Collaborative, Competency-Based Approach to Counseling and Therapy

This book represents a significant shift in the field of counseling and therapy because it brings together a multiplicity of collaborative, competency-based ideas into one volume. We offer an orientation that is respectful and creative, goal-oriented yet flexible, and one that values the contributions of other theoretical models. Most important, we propose a client-informed approach because we believe successful clinicians work collaboratively with their clients and utilize a variety of ideas in advocating positive change.

One of the major differences between a collaborative, competency-based approach and pure approaches is that we are not restricted to viewing problems from a single perspective. We do not try to fit clients into theoretical boxes that represent single, preferred realities. Instead, ideas are generated through our conversations and interactions with clients (Berger & Luckmann, 1966). In a sense, we are creating new realities and possibilities each time we interact with our clients. We accommodate treatment to clients' views of the therapeutic relationship and treatment processes, and we collaborate on goals and tasks to achieve those goals and what we refer to as *preferred outcomes*. Thus, a collaborative, competency-based approach is contingent on the unique voices of clients throughout the therapeutic process.

Foundations of a Collaborative, Competency-Based Approach

A collaborative, competency-based approach is based on a set of underlying ideas. We prefer the term *ideas* as opposed to *assumptions* because we are continually learning from our clients what works and thereby expanding our ways of working respectfully and effectively. The ideas posited here reflect two major influences:

1. The evolution and contributions of collaborative, competency-based approaches—what we call the *third wave* in therapy
2. An emphasis on psychotherapy outcome research with a focus on the question: "What works in therapy?"

In the introductory chapter we discussed the first of these influences. We'll now explore the findings, implications, and influence of outcome research on collaborative, competency-based therapy and psychotherapy.

Forty Years of Outcome Research: What Works in Therapy?

Since the mid-1960s, the number of therapy models has increased from 60 to more than 250 (Garfield, 1982; Henrink, 1980; Kazdin, 1986). This represents an increase of more than 400 percent. Each of these approaches offers a different explanation of how to approach the therapeutic relationship, conduct assessment, utilize interventions, and create change. Despite the fact that clinicians have many models from which to choose, forty years of psychotherapy outcome research has demonstrated that while most models effect change, no one approach is significantly more effective than another (Doherty & Simmons, 1995, 1996; Lambert & Bergin, 1994; Lambert, Shapiro, & Bergin, 1986; Luborksy, Singer, & Luborsky, 1975; Smith, Glass, & Miller, 1980).

These findings led researchers to shift their thinking. Instead of comparing models to determine what makes one approach more effective than another, researchers asked the question: "What works in therapy?" Such a question involved researching theories of therapy to find out what commonalities or similarities occur across all modalities when the end result is positive change. This led researchers to study how theories were more similar rather than different. As a result, Miller, Duncan, and Hubble (1997) found the following:

> The evidence makes it clear that *similarities* rather than *differences* between therapy models account for most of the change that clients experience in treatment. What emerges from examining these similarities is a group of common factors that can be brought together to form a more *unifying language for psychotherapy practice:* a language that contrasts sharply with the current emphasis on difference characterizing most professional discussion and activity. (p. 15)

Researchers learned that when positive change does occur in therapy, there are consistent, non-theory-based commonalities that account for that change. These commonalities are present regardless of the model being used. As early as 1936,

Saul Rosenzweig argued that the clinical effectiveness of different therapies depended on their common elements rather than their theoretical differences (Miller, Duncan, & Hubble, 1997). Jerome Frank (1973) later concurred that a core group of factors was responsible for similar outcomes with therapy models. Researcher Michael Lambert (1992) followed with the idea of commonalities among theories when he identified four therapeutic factors. Hubble, Duncan, and Miller (1999a) later referred to these as "common factors" (p. 8). These factors are extratherapeutic, relationship, placebo, and model and technique.

Extratherapeutic Factors: The Contribution of Clients and Chance Events

Extratherapeutic factors account for much of the improvement that occurs in any form of psychotherapy. Lambert (1992) estimated that these factors account for 40 percent of the variance in outcome.Extratherapeutic factors are the resources that clients bring to therapy, including their strengths, abilities, resources, and social support systems. The research clearly indicates that the client is the single, most potent contributor to outcome in therapy (Bohart & Tallman, 1999).

Extratherapeutic factors also include external influences, such as spontaneous or chance events that occur outside therapy. These are events that occur during the course of therapy but that typically have little or no correlation to the treatment itself. By identifying and amplifying positive, spontaneous changes, therapists can help clients see that change is constant in their lives. Further, therapists can explore with clients the significance of such changes and work with them to expand and build on them in the future.

Other essential extratherapeutic factors include focusing on change and being mindful of clients' contributions to change processes. Therapists who are change-focused emphasize pretreatment and between-session change, and potentiate change for the future by identifying and amplifying change. Recognizing clients' contributions to change includes honoring clients' worldviews and tapping into their worlds outside of therapy. Therapists who work in these ways make the most of client and extratherapeutic factors.

Relationship Factors: The Contribution of the Therapeutic Alliance

The therapeutic relationship is a central factor in successful therapy. Researchers estimate that as much as 30 percent of the variance in treatment outcome can be attributed to relationship factors (Lambert, 1992). Perhaps the two most significant factors in this realm are the quality of the client's participation and the degree to which the client is motivated, engaged, and joined in the therapeutic work (Orlinsky, Grawe, & Parks, 1994; Prochaska, 1995; Prochaska, DiClemente, & Norcross, 1992; Prochaska, Norcross, & DiClemente, 1994).

Researchers have expanded the therapeutic relationship to a broader concept known as the *therapeutic alliance*, a more encompassing term that emphasizes collaborative partnership between clients and therapists (Bordin, 1979; Duncan & Miller, 2000). Therapists can promote the therapeutic alliance by adjusting treatment to fit the client's motivational level or stage of change, goals and preferred outcomes for therapy, and view of the therapeutic relationship.

Clients who are engaged and connected with therapists may benefit most from therapy. In contrast, the strength of the therapeutic bond is not highly correlated with the length of treatment (Horvath & Luborsky, 1993). In other words, there can be an instant bond between the therapist and client. Essential here are clients' perceptions of the therapeutic relationship. In fact, client ratings of therapists as empathic, trustworthy, and nonjudgmental are better predictors of positive outcome than therapist ratings, diagnosis, approach, or any other variable (Duncan & Miller, 2000; Horvath & Symonds, 1991; Lambert & Bergin, 1994).

Overall, the therapeutic alliance can be most beneficial and an excellent predictor of outcome when:

- Therapists agree with clients on goals and preferred outcomes.
- Therapists collaborate with clients on tasks to accomplish those goals and preferred outcomes.
- Clients have a favorable view of the therapeutic relationship.

Placebo Factors: The Role of Hope and Expectancy

Research has demonstrated that the average person treated with therapy was better off than 80 percent of those who did not receive treatment (Asay & Lambert, 1999; Smith, Glass, & Miller, 1980). Other literature, ranging from clinical studies to *Consumer Reports* articles, has also supported the effectiveness of therapy (Barker, Funk, & Houston, 1988; Lambert & Bergin, 1994; Lambert, Shapiro, & Bergin, 1986; Lipsey & Wilson, 1993; Prioleau, Murdock, & Brody, 1983; Seligman, 1995; Shapiro & Shapiro, 1982; VandenBos & Pino, 1980). Further, research has indicated that brief trials of therapy can reduce medical utilization by as much as 60 percent (Cummings & Follette, 1976; Follette & Cummings, 1967).

Placebo factors relate to the role of hope and expectancy in therapy and contribute approximately 15 percent of the variance in therapeutic outcome (Asay & Lambert, 1999; Lambert, 1992). According to Duncan and Miller (2000), "This class of therapeutic factors refers to the portion of improvement deriving from clients' knowledge of being treated, the installation of hope, and how credible the client perceives therapy's rationale and techniques" (p. 58).

Therapists' attitudes in the opening moments of therapy can promote or dampen hope. For example, an attitude of pessimism or an emphasis on psychopathology or the long-term process of change can diminish hope. In contrast, therapists' attitudes that positive change can and does occur and an emphasis on possibilities and improvement can instill and promote hope. This does not mean downplaying the real-life difficulties that clients face but instead acknowledging the difficulties and simultaneously conveying that there are possibilities for an improved future.

Expectancy corresponds to the expectations that clients have when beginning therapy. It also relates to both the client's and therapist's believing in the restorative power of the treatment, including its procedures. A client's expectation that therapy will help can serve as a placebo and counteract demoralization, activate hope, and advance improvement (Frank & Frank, 1991; Miller, Duncan, & Hubble, 1997).

In accordance with the placebo factors, therapists can further enhance the therapy process by:

- Showing interest in the results of the therapeutic procedure or orientation
- Making sure the procedure or orientation is credible from the client's frame of reference
- Making sure the procedure or orientation is connected with or elicits previously successful experiences of the client
- Having a future focus in treatment
- Working in a way that enhances or highlights the client's feeling of personal control
- Being sure to depersonalize the client's problems, difficulties, or shortcomings

Model and Technique Factors: The Role of Structure and Novelty

Every theory makes use of techniques and procedures—behaviorists use methods associated with conditioning, Freudian analysts use analysis of transference, structural family therapists use enactment, solution-focused therapists ask the miracle question, and narrative therapists use externalization. Techniques and procedures include, but are not limited to, asking particular questions, using specific interventions, assigning tasks, making interpretations, and teaching skills. Most techniques or procedures are designed to get clients to do something different, such as experience emotions, face fears, change patterns of thinking or behavior, and develop new understandings or meanings.

Lambert (1992) suggested that model and technique account for about 15 percent of outcome variance. This is partly due to the fact that therapists are much more interested in techniques than clients. In fact, when asked what is helpful about therapy, clients rarely mention therapeutic interventions or techniques. Instead, clients typically respond with statements such as "My therapist listened to me" or "I felt as though the therapist understood me," which fall into the extratherapeutic and relational factors categories.

Therapists can work to improve the effectiveness of therapeutic techniques by considering whether the orientation, techniques, and strategies:

- Fit with, support, or complement the client's worldview
- Fit with or complement the client's expectations for treatment
- Capitalize on client strengths, abilities, and resources
- Utilize the client's environment and existing support network
- Capitalize on the spontaneous changes that a client experiences while in therapy
- Would be considered empathic, respectful, and genuine by the client
- Increase the client's sense of hope, expectancy, or personal control
- Contribute to the client's sense of self-esteem, self-efficacy, and self-mastery

In summary, outcome research informs collaborative, competency-based therapy and psychotherapy in the following ways:

- Treatment should be client-informed and accommodate clients' views of the therapeutic relationship, therapy processes, goals and preferred outcomes, and tasks to accomplish those outcomes.
- Treatment should focus on change as opposed to focusing on finding causes or explanations for problems, except when this focus does not fit with or invalidates the client.
- Emphasis should be put on the strengths, abilities, and resources of clients as opposed to deficit and pathology.
- Treatment should be future-oriented.
- The therapeutic relationship is paramount.
- Therapists' attitudes heavily influence therapeutic outcome. A focus on possibilities is essential.
- Clients should be treated as human beings, not depersonalized as labels or diagnostic categories.
- Successful therapy has less to do with technique (to which therapists often attribute positive change) and more to do with client factors and the therapeutic relationship.
- Techniques are enhanced when they fit with clients' belief systems and ideas about how change will occur.

As therapists, it is very important that we maintain an eye on what works for whom in treatment. This not only means being client-directed but also outcome-informed (Duncan & Miller, 2000). Such a focus requires that clinicians have conversations with their clients about what they experience in therapy. This allows more emphasis to be put on what clients view as important. The utilization of client feedback throughout the treatment process is an invitation to clients to be full and equal participants in virtually all aspects of therapy.

From Theoretical Assumptions to Guiding Ideas

Each approach to therapy has a set of underlying assumptions. As discussed earlier, our preference is to highlight ideas for respectful and effective therapy. Let's explore the ideas that reflect forty years of outcome research and are associated with a collaborative, competency-based approach to therapy and psychotherapy.

A Client-Informed, Collaborative Process

Recall that research overwhelmingly indicates that the client is the single most important contributor to therapeutic outcome. Negative outcome is often traced to clients who are left out of therapeutic processes. Models with theory-based explanations often take precedence over client voices, even when theories held by therapists run counter to those of clients. Clients are then fit into theoretical boxes, and a one-size-fits-all approach is implemented. This ignores the uniqueness of clients. Erickson once stated,

> Each person is an individual. Hence, psychotherapy should be formulated to meet the uniqueness of the individual's needs, rather than tailoring the person to fit the Procrustean bed of a hypothetical theory of human behavior. (as cited in Zeig & Gilligan, 1990, p. xix)

More recently, Duncan, Hubble, and Miller (1997) stated, "Impossibility, we decided, is at least partly a function of leaving clients out of the process, of not listening or of dismissing the importance of their perspective" (p. 30). Clients have ideas, which often go largely unheard by therapists, as to how problems have developed and what may help in resolving them. From a collaborative, competency-based perspective, clients are consulted about their preferences, goals and preferred outcomes, methods of accomplishing those goals and outcomes, and overall processes used in the context of therapy. In turn, therapists' ideas and questions are not imposed on clients but instead are offered in a nonauthoritarian way. This way clients have the space to agree or disagree, modify, or correct what has been said or done.

Clients determine what needs to be different in their lives. They are experts on their lives and generally know what is best. Erickson believed that at some level people have internal compasses and know where they want to go. His task was to steer them in the right direction and let them find their way. The following story illustrates this idea:

> When Erickson was a young man a horse wandered into his yard. Although the horse had no identifying marks he offered to return it to its owners. To accomplish this, he mounted the horse, led it to the road, and let the horse decide which way it wanted to go. He intervened only when the horse left the road to graze or wander into a field. When the horse finally arrived at the yard of a neighbor several miles

> down the road, the neighbor asked the young Erickson, "How did you know that horse came from here and was our horse?"
>
> Erickson replied, "I didn't know—but the horse knew. All I did was keep him on the road." (Rosen, 1982, pp. 46–47)

Collaboration means showing clients the road and letting them choose the direction. We also recognize that clients sometimes choose directions and goals that are not acceptable. An obvious one is the establishment of illegal goals such as child abuse, discrimination, committing crimes, and so on. Another is when unrealistic or unachievable outcomes are set. In such cases, the therapist must work with clients (and others who may be involved) to establish goals that are ethical, legal, realistic, and attainable. When realistic and attainable goals are established, therapists collaborate with clients on tasks to accomplish those goals, resulting in clearer, more focused interventions.

It's also important to extend a collaborative stance to outside helpers (family members, social service workers, parole officers, juvenile officers, teachers, etc.) who may be involved in the therapy. If discouraging ideas are offered from outside helpers, the therapist can gently and subtly challenge those unhelpful ideas by first acknowledging their possible validity and then introducing alternative perspectives. Our first loyalty remains with clients.

Promoting the Therapeutic Relationship

Research indicates that the therapeutic relationship is the second largest contributor to outcome. Studies have demonstrated that client perceptions of the relationship are the most consistent predictor of improvement (Duncan & Miller, 2000; Gurman, 1977; Lafferty, Beutler, & Crago, 1989). As discussed earlier, the therapeutic alliance is an extension of the therapeutic relationship and emphasizes a partnership between clients and therapists. Thus, therapists work with clients to establish goals and preferred outcomes and tasks to achieve those goals and outcomes.

To strengthen the client–therapist bond, it is important that clients feel they are heard and understood and that their theories of change are honored. Therefore, therapists listen and attend to clients, acknowledging and validating whatever they experience. These experiences include their feelings, sense of self, bodily sensations, sensory experience, and automatic thoughts and fantasies. It's important that therapists acknowledge and validate all internal experience. This can be done in a variety of ways. At a basic level, the use of empathy and respect conveys acknowledgment. Other ways include the use of verbal and nonverbal behaviors, questions, constructing clear outcomes, and therapeutic interventions.

Although all feelings are okay, the views held and the actions taken in response to those feelings are not always okay. Some of the ways that clients view the world are helpful and direct them toward goals—others do not. Further, some of the actions, interactions, and behaviors that people undertake are positive, legal, and move them toward goals—others are not. Examples of actions that are not acceptable are those that are illegal, unethical, or ones that cause danger to the client or others. In such cases, therapists must take appropriate action to ensure the safety of everyone involved.

Another significant way of promoting the therapeutic relationship and creating change is by listening closely to clients' use of language. Client satisfaction ratings are significantly related to similarity in the client–therapist linguistic style (Patton & Meara, 1982). Special attention is paid to matching clients' use of language. How (process) and what (content) clients communicate are pathways for learning their theories of change. Thus, therapists attend to how clients describe problems, their efforts to solve those problems, and potential solutions.

Change-Oriented Treatment with an Emphasis on Future Change

Each model or theory of therapy offers an explanation as to why people have problems and how to solve those problems. Conversely, research has consistently demonstrated that no one model is more effective than another. Therapists' theoretical explanations about why people have problems rarely lead to consistent resolution of problems. We've learned that the best explanations available regarding problems, possibilities for change, and potential solutions are the ones to which clients ascribe.

Milton Erickson's client-informed, change-oriented approach to therapy illustrates this point. Although Erickson was referred to as strategic, analytic, cognitive, and systemic, among other things, he was not interested in labeling his approach or patients. Instead, he was interested in helping his patients change. To do this, he focused less on explaining why his patients were having problems and more on how and what would help them change. The meta-analytic research of Miller, Duncan, and Hubble (1997) echoes Erickson's untraditional, change-oriented approach to problems. They report that a growing body of literature suggests:

> Therapeutic time is spent more productively when the therapist and client focus on and enhance the factors responsible for change-in-general rather than on identifying and then changing the factors a theory suggests are responsible or causing problems-in-particular.... Indoctrinating clients into a particular model of problem causation might actually... [undermine] the very factors responsible for the occurrence of change by drawing clients' attention to whatever a particular theory suggests is causing their suffering. (p. 127)

Erickson did not subscribe to any one model and developed his ideas on a case by case basis, with the uniqueness of each patient in mind. Like Erickson, we too have learned, through outcome research, that positive therapeutic outcome has little to do with the explanations that therapists give for the causes or roots of problems. In fact, we've found that an explanatory-only focus can be counterproductive, as it tends to stigmatize and blame people for their problems. The exception to this is when focusing only on change alienates people who insist on finding explanations before making a change. We have found few of these people in our practices. In our experience, previous or current explanation-oriented clinicians who insist on the necessity of explanations often influence such persons.

From a collaborative, competency-based perspective, it's important to consider what works for a particular client. This involves maintaining a collaborative relationship in which ideas are interchanged between clients and therapists, with clients having the ultimate say in what fits for them. For clinicians, the naming of an idea, technique, or intervention is only relevant in the teaching of it. Clients are uninterested in therapeutic techniques and are more interested in change. With this in mind, it's important that therapists keep an eye on procedures that are respectful, promote change, and evolve out of collaborative conversations with clients.

In order to facilitate change we need to find out about and honor clients' theories of change, as opposed to carrying alliances with models. Duncan and Miller (2000) stated:

> Honoring the client's theory occurs when a given therapeutic procedure fits or complements the client's preexisting beliefs about his or her problems and the change process. We, therefore, simply listen and then amplify stories, experiences, and interpretations that clients offer about their problems, as well as their thoughts, feelings, and ideas about how those problems might be best addressed. As the client's theory evolves, we implement the client's identified solutions or seek an approach that both fits the client's theory and provides possibilities for change. (p. 84)

In honoring clients' theories of change, we have conversations with them about how they feel their problems developed, what has been tried to resolve them, to what degree those efforts have or haven't worked, what they've considered but haven't tried, and what they might consider in the future to attain the change they desire. This orientation to change relies on the recognition that change happens and is inevitable. It is a constant in our lives and in the lives of our clients. Clients' problems will fluctuate in frequency, intensity, duration, and so on. They are not static. There will be better days, worse days, symptom-free, and symptom-laden times. By orienting toward change, therapists can enlist change-effecting propensities such as client competencies and support systems.

Emphasis also is on future change. Outcome research supports the notion that treatment should be oriented toward the future (Miller, Duncan, & Hubble, 1997). A focus on the present and an orientation toward the future does not dismiss the possible significance of past events. If a client is oriented toward the past, the therapist should be respectful and follow him or her. However, the clinician does not hold the assumption that this is what clients need to resolve their conflicts.

Therapists must contend with theoretical maps and constructions that can greatly alter the course of treatment (Efran & Lukens, 1985). Therapists who maintain the view that change is possible can convey this belief through their language and interaction. This, in turn, can engender hope, promote clients' expectancy for change, and facilitate future change. Conversely, as previously outlined with outcome research, therapists who are guided by pathology or unhelpful theoretical assumptions can extinguish hope and create a situation in which positive change seems impossible.

Clients Have Competencies

There has been, and continues to be, an overwhelming consensus among theorists that for therapy to be effective an emphasis on pathology and/or deficits is necessary. This contention has led therapists to focus heavily on problems and ask: "What's wrong with this individual/couple/family?" What typically follows are first- and second-wave jargon (or psychobabble as we sometimes refer to it) and explanations such as codependent, narcissistic, disengaged, and dysfunctional.

Although many theorists and clinicians continue to subscribe to pathology or problem-focused approaches, there exists no solid evidence to support the idea that clinicians must explain the roots of dysfunction, explore past events, or focus on pathology to help clients change (Beutler, 1989; Held, 1991, 1995; Prochaska & DiClemente, 1982, 1984, 1986). Put simply, we find it disrespectful to talk about people or view them as being irrevocably maimed or damaged in some way as pathological labeling suggests. Further, our contention is that it is equally disrespectful to suggest that people are to blame in some way for their conditions or the situations they are in. However, this is, in fact, what a pathology focus implies.

Clients have abilities, strengths, and resources that can be helpful in solving problems and resolving conflicts. We are not suggesting that all clients have all the competencies they will ever need. We do not subscribe to the *hidden gem theory*, which holds that clients have untapped reservoirs with all the answers they need. Instead, we believe that clients have competencies and internal and external resources that have been helpful in the past and can be used in the present and future. However, therapists and clients are often unaware of such competencies and resources because therapists' theories don't allow for them. Therefore therapists don't ask about them.

Competencies can go unnoticed when therapists who have been trained to discover problems, pathology, and underlying conflicts continue to search and find inabilities, liabilities, and deficiencies. In our experience, what is often referred to as pathological is simply the result of unhelpful views on the part of therapists or other professionals involved. Subsequently, these unhelpful views are then situated in language and magnified, then communicated to others as problem areas.

To identify competencies, therapists shift from a focus of "what's wrong?" to one of "what's right?" Such a shift in attention does not mean downplaying the real-life difficulties, pain, and suffering that clients face in everyday life. As discussed earlier, it means acknowledging and attending to the hardships that people face, while simultaneously focusing on the possibilities for change that exist.

A collaborative, competency-based approach relies heavily on language as a vehicle for creating possibilities and change. This requires a shift from pathological language. Instead of focusing on pathology and deficit, therapists can use language that is more respectful and validating, builds on expectancy, and promotes hope. To further illustrate this shift, see Table 1.1.

We also rely on clients' expertise. They know what they've experienced in their lives, what their concerns are, and what hasn't worked, as well as what feels right and wrong, respectful, and disrespectful. It is both respectful and collabora-

TABLE 1.1 Competency-Based Vocabulary

Pathology-Based	Competency-Based
Fix	Empower
Weakness	Strength
Limitation	Possibility
Pathology	Health
Problem	Solution
Insist	Invite
Closed	Open
Shrink	Expand
Defense	Access
Expert	Partner
Control	Nurture
Backward	Forward
Manipulate	Collaborate
Fear	Hope
Cure	Growth
Stuck	Change
Missing	Latent
Resist	Utilize
Past	Future
Hierarchical	Horizontal
Diagnose	Appreciate
Treat	Facilitate
End	Beginning
Judge	Respect
Never	Not yet
Limit	Expand
Defect	Asset
Rule	Exception

Note. Adapted from Hoyt, M. F. (1994). Introduction: Competency-based future-oriented therapy. In M. F. Hoyt (Ed.), *Constructive therapies.* New York: Guilford; and, Metcalf, L. (1995). *Therapy toward solutions: A practical solution-focused program for working with students, teachers, and parents.* New York: Center for Applied Research in Education.

tive to allow the expertise of clients to emerge in therapy. By allowing each person's story to evolve, clients can teach therapists what they need to know.

The therapist's expertise is in creating a context that facilitates positive change. This includes establishing a safe atmosphere where clients' stories can evolve and helping them access new pathways with possibilities through conversation and action. This can involve the use of metaphors, stories, ideas, thoughts, tasks, and other change-facilitating processes that are offered or suggested, not imposed, as part of an ongoing client–therapist dialogue.

Change Is Predictable

Research indicates that regardless of the model employed, the average length of time a client attends therapy is six to ten sessions (Doherty & Simmons, 1996; Garfield, 1989; Koss & Butcher, 1986; Levitt, 1966; Miller, 1994). Further, Miller and others (1997) wrote that "all large-scale meta-analytic studies of client change indicate that the most frequent improvement occurs early in treatment" (p. 194). Studies have shown that change is predictable, and that the most positive impact in therapy happens during the first six to eight sessions (Smith, Glass, & Miller, 1980). Further studies have demonstrated that 60–65 percent of clients experience significant symptomatic relief in the first one to seven sessions, 70–75 percent after six months, and 80–85 percent after one year (Brown, Dreis, & Nace, 1999; Howard, Kopte, Krause, & Orlinsky, 1986; Howard, Moras, Brill, Martinovich, & Lutz, 1996; Lambert, Okiishi, Finch, & Johnson, 1998; Smith, Glass, & Miller, 1980; Steenbarger, 1992; Talmon, 1990; Talmon, Hoyt, & Rosenbaum, 1990).

Clients can benefit from therapy that extends beyond eight sessions. However, as treatment progresses there is a course of diminishing returns with more and more effort required to obtain just noticeable differences in client improvement (Howard et al., 1986). Even though the amount of change decreases over time, as long as progress is being made and clients are interested, then therapy can remain beneficial. Further, if the client experiences meaningful change in the first handful of sessions, the probability of positive outcome significantly increases (Garfield, 1994). In contrast, when clients show little or no improvement or experience a worsening of symptoms early on in treatment, they are at significant risk for negative outcome (Lebow, 1997).

Another important contribution is that in many mental health settings, regardless of the theoretical model employed by the therapist, the majority of clients will attend just a single session of therapy (Talmon, 1990). Though people end therapy after one session for a variety of reasons, often the reason is they got what they wanted in a single session. This research suggests that therapists ought to attend to what clients want from the start of therapy, as opposed to their own ideas about what needs to happen during the initial session.

This idea is representative of the model practiced by medical physicians. Medical doctors do not spend multiple appointments forming a therapeutic relationship with their patients. Nonetheless, most people trust their doctors. Further, physicians seldom search for pathology in areas that are not of concern to patients.

For example, if a patient were complaining about a sore throat, the doctor wouldn't ask about the big toe on his or her left foot. Focus would be placed on the patient's concern. Yet therapists have been and continue to be trained to ask questions about the past, and to uncover and discover pathology, regardless of clients' concerns. We liken this search for "what's wrong" to the following story:

> A man flies into St. Louis, Missouri. After deplaning, he spots a concierge and approaches him. He says, "Excuse me, can you tell me how to get to the Holiday Inn?"
>
> The concierge replies, "Where did you come from?"
>
> "Well, I came from Santa Fe, New Mexico. Can you tell me how to get to the Holiday Inn?"
>
> "Do you live in Santa Fe?"
>
> "Well, yes I do. Listen, I'm really tired, if you could just tell me how to get to the Holiday Inn, I'd be much obliged."
>
> "Do you have family in Santa Fe?"
>
> He was becoming irritated. "Yes I do."
>
> "Then you must work there as well."
>
> "Yes, I work in Santa Fe too. I really need to get to the Holiday Inn. Please give me directions!"
>
> "You sound angry."
>
> "Well, yes, I am getting angry. I'm tired and want to get to the hotel!"
>
> "Is anger something that runs in your family?"

Unlike the story, when a person visits a medical doctor, he or she is treated for the current problem. If a patient needs to return for a follow-up visit, it is not simply because the physician thinks there's more pathology to explore and uncover. We reiterate that therapists can learn from medical doctors that attention ought to be on what the patient or client is concerned about. In therapy, to work efficiently in searching for openings with possibilities for solutions and change is the respectful, practical, and ethical position.

Research shows that clients only attend a handful of sessions regardless of the therapist's orientation. Therefore, therapists must learn to be efficient. Similar to general medical practitioners, it is essential that therapists work to maximize the effectiveness of each session. With that said, some clients will need one, three, or eleven sessions, and others will need thirty sessions. From a collaborative, competency-based perspective it is not the number of sessions that is most important, but collaborating with clients to determine where they want to go, when things are better, and when goals and preferred outcomes have been achieved. This, by nature, makes for therapy that is generally briefer and client-informed.

The ideas discussed serve as a guide for therapists and will be expanded on throughout the course of this book. As supported by outcome research, it is our belief that these ideas facilitate and enhance change processes. We find it imperative that therapists be respectful and genuine, change-oriented, collaborative, and competency-focused. This will allow change to occur in clients' views, actions, and in regard to the contextual propensities that are associated with their problems. These domains will be discussed next.

Four Areas to Create Change: Experience, Views, Action, and Context

Each and every model of psychotherapy posits an explanation about how problems develop and how change will come about. Emphasis is either on the affective (internal experience), cognitive (patterns of attention, thinking), or behavioral (actions or interactions) realm. Although some theories (i.e., cognitive-behavioral, conjoint family therapy) cross two domains, few suggest that change can occur in any domain. In contrast, research clearly shows that change has more to do with clients' theories than therapists' theories. Clients have taught us that change occurs in all of the aforementioned realms. Therefore, from a collaborative, competency-based perspective, therapy encompasses four realms for creating change: experience, views, action, and context. Table 1.2 offers an outline of these areas.

Experience relates to that which happens internally. This can include feelings, sensations, fantasies, and anything that contributes to the person's sense of self. Experience is a subjective and personalized thing. Throughout this book it will be emphasized that all internal experiences are acceptable. The main way of attending to clients' internal experience is through the use of acknowledgment and validation.

Views come in several varieties. First, clients have explanations, interpretations, evaluations, assumptions, and beliefs about their problems and possible solutions. Second, people pay more attention to certain aspects of their lives than others. That is, what they notice and do not notice can make a significant difference in the construction of their concerns and potential areas for creating change.

TABLE 1.2 Four Realms for Creating Change

Experience	Views	Actions	Context
Feelings	Points of view	Action patterns	Time patterns
Sense of self	Attentional patterns	Interactional patterns	Spatial patterns
Bodily sensations	Interpretations	Language patterns	Cultural background and propensities
Sensory experience	Explanations	Nonverbal patterns	Familial and historical background and propensities
Automatic fantasies and thoughts	Evaluations		Sociorelational propensities
	Assumptions		Biochemical and genetic background and propensities
	Beliefs		Gender training and propensities
	Identity stories		Spiritual and religious ideologies

People's views are not truths but instead reflect how they see the world. There are multiple ways of viewing the world, and thus these views are changeable.

Last, there are identity stories, which relate to how people describe themselves and others. Identity stories are subject to continual renegotiation. As with the other views discussed, they do not symbolize truth but instead represent a person's perception of the world, created through experience and interaction. Some stories are supportive and spawn hope. Others are problematic or problem-saturated, in which the possibility of change seems virtually nonexistent. Attending to views is a helpful way of learning about clients' theories of change. We'll discuss this at length in Chapter 5.

Action is what a person actually does. As mentioned, some actions are acceptable and others are not. Actions that help clients achieve their goals and are healthy, legal, and ethical are acceptable. Actions or behaviors that move clients away from their goals, or are unhealthy, harmful, illegal, or unethical are unacceptable. Chapter 6 will focus on action.

Context can be understood in two ways. The first relates to spatial and time patterns that are often associated with problems. That is, when and where the problem occurs, how frequently it occurs, how long it lasts, and who's around when it occurs. We'll focus on these aspects of context in Chapter 6 when we discuss action. A second way to discuss context is in relation to a person's history and background, including cultural, genetic and biochemical, familial, sociorelational, and gender propensities, and spiritual and religious ideologies. These contextual aspects can be problematic in a client's creation or support of a problem, but helpful aspects are sometimes buried and unnoticed. We'll discuss this in Chapter 7.

We've now discussed the basic ideas of collaborative, competency-based therapy and psychotherapy. In the next chapter we'll begin to put these ideas to work through the formation of collaborative relationships.

Summary Points for Chapter One

♦ A collaborative, competency-based approach values the contributions of other theoretical models.

♦ The most important contribution to the therapy process is the client. Treatment is accommodated to clients' views of the therapeutic relationship and therapy processes.

♦ Forty years of therapy outcome research has demonstrated that no one theoretical model is more effective than another. What works in therapy is related more to four common factors than to any one model. The four common factors are extratherapeutic factors, relationship factors, placebo factors, and model and technique factors.

♦ A collaborative, competency-based approach is based on a set of ideas as opposed to assumptions. Ideas reflect our willingness to learn from clients and therefore expand our ways of working respectfully and effectively.

♦ A collaborative, competency-based approach helps clients change in all domains: experience, views, action, and context.

CHAPTER

2 Creating Collaborative Relationships through Attending, Listening, and Language

We believe that successful therapy begins with collaboration. This means including clients' experiences and views throughout the process of therapy. But why is collaboration so important? First, as we've learned from outcome research, what therapists often see as resistance or lack of motivation is largely a product of clients being left out of therapeutic processes (e.g., being consulted on outcomes and interventions). Next, therapists are not the only experts in the therapeutic milieu. While therapists carry expertise in facilitating and creating a context for change, clients are experts on their own lives and experiences. They know what does and does not feel right, what has or hasn't worked, what might work in the future, and they oftentimes have ideas about how to accomplish the change they desire. In our experience, leaving clients out of therapeutic processes translates into lack of respect for clients and their experiences and can be a recipe for negative outcomes. In turn, we see collaboration as respectful and essential in opening up possibilities for change.

To further illustrate the significance of collaboration, we'd like to share a story about Walt Disney:

> Walt Disney's vision of Disneyland was based on his very strong ideas, beliefs, and convictions. He imagined that the rides would operate in certain ways, the buildings would be built to specific scales, and that certain materials would be used in the construction of various aspects of the park. The problem with Disney's vision was that much of what he dreamed seemed unachievable or impossible in the eyes of the park engineers. They would often say, "Walt we can't do that. It's impossible."
>
> What Disney realized was that the word *impossible* was used by people who did not understand the needs, visions, and preferences of one another. Thus, he needed to change his relationship with the park engineers. To do this, Disney learned how to read architectural drawings

and speak the language of the park engineers. This way, he could communicate with them in a common language. The result was a collaborative relationship between Walt and the park engineers that allowed each person's vision to be acknowledged. The word *impossible* was dropped from their conversations. Sometimes Walt or the engineers would have to slightly shift their views for the park, but through collaboration they were always able to reach an achievable and realistic end.

More than thirty years later, Disneyland is considered an architectural masterpiece by many master architects. Further, Walt Disney's ability to work collaboratively with numerous others led to developments in animation, filming, audio recording, animatronics, theme park attractions, and many more significant innovations.

When there are changes that we feel others should make in their lives we often have strong views. However, our positions on such matters reflect only one point of view. If therapists leave out the perspectives of clients and others involved we risk not only alienating them, but not learning about their theories of change and missing opportunities to tap into a multitude of possibilities. We can learn from Walt Disney that impossibility is often the result of attending only to our own perspectives and leaving out the views of others. Collaboration, in our view, is an important key to unlocking possibilities because it calls for therapists to work with clients in conversational, change-oriented processes.

Collaboration takes on many forms within the context of counseling and psychotherapy. In this chapter we'll explore a variety of ways that therapists can invite clients into collaborative relationships from the start of and throughout therapy. First, we'll detail ways of collaborating with clients prior to the start of formal therapy. Next, we'll offer ways of beginning therapy that are client-informed. That is, they are respectful of clients' theories, worldviews, and ideas about the process of change. Last, we'll outline ways of acknowledging and validating clients by making subtle language changes to open up possibilities for present and future change.

Deconstructing Therapeutic Practices: Consulting and Collaborating with Clients, not Theories

Each approach to psychotherapy comes equipped with a set of preestablished guidelines that set forth the dos and don'ts of a given model. The premises associated with various theories value the therapist as the only expert in the therapeutic milieu. Thus, the clinician and his or her theory of choice determine what happens throughout the therapeutic encounter. Whether deliberately or inadvertently, the experiences and views of clients become obsolete.

Psychotherapy research has indicated that the single best predictor of therapeutic outcome is the quality of the client's participation in therapy (Orlinsky, Grawe, & Parks, 1994). This implies that a client should be involved in the therapeutic process from beginning to end. In addition to the empirical evidence supporting client involvement in therapy, we view this as the respectful position. Therefore, we must challenge theoretical assumptions that tend to leave clients out of therapy processes. To challenge long-held assumptions we consult with our clients (instead of our theories) in a variety of ways, thereby acknowledging and honoring their perspectives and promoting collaborative relationships.

Now let's explore three specific ways that a therapist, prior to the start of therapy, can challenge unhelpful theoretical assumptions and begin to create a context for change by inviting clients into collaborative relationships. We'll refer to these as *collaboration keys.*

Collaboration Key 1: Who Should Attend Sessions?

Since the late 1950s there have been two rivaling paradigms in the field of therapy. These are the psychological and systemic-relational paradigms (Cottone, 1992). The psychological paradigm, which represents the first wave, holds that the root cause of problems is intrapsychic and lies within the mind or psyche of the individual. It is believed that people are essentially held captive by internal cognitive processes or are shaped or conditioned by external factors. Therefore, the target of the treatment is the individual. Even when family therapy is the course of treatment, the focus remains on helping individuals change internal processes, which in turn benefits interpersonal relationships. In contrast, the systemic-relational paradigm, which represents the second wave, holds that problems are interpersonal in nature and originate from dysfunctional patterns of interaction. Relationships are targeted in therapy with as many family members as possible present for treatment. First- and second-wave approaches differ with regard to the target of treatment and who should attend therapy. The first wave focuses on individuals, the second wave on relationships.

Although many first- and second-wave theorists argue otherwise, there are no right or correct ways regarding who should be seen in therapy. In fact, one of the factors that can inhibit positive change is when therapists' rules about therapy (e.g., who should attend sessions) run counter to those of clients (Miller, Duncan, & Hubble, 1997). That is, even though clients may have preferences and theories, therapists bypass them and favor their own theories on how change will come about.

Research indicates that attending to clients' views about how change will occur facilitates change and is important from the start of therapy (Hubble, Duncan, & Miller, 1999b). Thus, it is our contention that clients, whether coming for individual, couples, or family therapy, should be consulted about their preferred ways of meeting with the therapist. To do this, the therapist invites the person making the appointment to bring whomever he or she thinks will be helpful in resolving the concern. The person initiating contact can also choose to consult with others (e.g., family members) to decide how to proceed. This way, clients' ideas about how therapy should proceed and how positive change might occur are acknowledged and respected before formal treatment has even started.

To further illustrate this idea, here is an example of how a therapist might talk with a person setting an appointment for family therapy:

CALLER: I was wondering, who should come to the appointment?

THERAPIST: That's a terrific question. Since I can never know you or your family the way you do, I'd like to ask, what are your ideas about who should attend?

CALLER: I'm not sure.

THERAPIST: Well, one way to think about it is to invite the people who you think can help with the concern that you or your family is having. Another possibility is to ask each person involved if he or she would like to come.

CALLER: Okay, that makes sense. But I have another question. Can therapy still work even if everyone doesn't come? I mean, I don't think there's any way my husband will come in. He doesn't think there's a problem.

THERAPIST: Therapy can work without every family member present. Although you may choose to invite several people to come, some might not be able to make it because of work or a scheduling conflict and others just flat-out won't want to. It's your call as to whether you make someone come. Again, there aren't any right or wrong ways of going about this, so whatever you decide is okay with me. I'm confident that we can move toward the change you want with those who come in.

Clients have ideas about who should attend therapy. When we listen to their ideas we increase the likelihood of positive outcome. We sometimes do family therapy with only a couple of family members or couples therapy with only one member of a couple. We've learned that positive change can occur whether the therapist is working with an individual, one member of a couple, three members of a five-person family, or some other nontraditional configuration.

We believe that both clients and therapists have expertise, and we often share our opinions with clients. There may be times, for example, when a therapist believes that bringing in another family member could help the therapy move along. The difference here is that a collaborative therapist would not hold or present the idea that this must occur or that this is the only way that positive change will take place. Instead, the therapist might suggest that bringing in another voice might offer a different perspective or lead to the generation of some new ideas. Ultimately, clients decide whether such ideas are acceptable to them and whether they are within their personal theories about how change will come about. This allows therapists to remain collaborative by introducing ideas without imposing them on clients. In addition, because clients' preferences about who should attend can change over time, we continue to consult with them in future sessions and throughout the course of therapy.

Collaboration Key 2: How Should We Meet?

Clients are also consulted on how they would like to meet for therapy. If a family is seeking therapy, some members may prefer that the entire family be seen together. Other family members may express the desire to spend some time individually with the therapist. The same holds true for couples therapy. Once again, how clients are seen can vary from session to session, so it's important that the therapist remain flexible and ask clients about their preferences throughout the course of therapy.

When asked about their preferences, clients will often respond with, "What do you think?" or "What do you usually do?" Again, we believe that it can be helpful for therapists to share their preferences as long as they are not imposed on clients. The following is an illustration of how a therapist might talk with a family during an initial session:

THERAPIST: There aren't any rules about how we should meet. Some families prefer to have everyone meet together. With others, each person may want to spend a few minutes with the therapist and spend the rest of the time together as a family. Does anyone here have a preference about how you'd like us to meet?

MOTHER: I'm not sure. We haven't done this before.

THERAPIST: Okay, that's fine. Does anyone else have an opinion?

(No response from the other family members)

THERAPIST: Okay. Well, would it be okay with all of you if we continued meeting together, just as we are now?

(Heads nod around the room)

THERAPIST: Great. We can make changes from session to session if one or all of you decide that you would like to have different meeting arrangements in the future.

In working with couples and families, there are circumstances in which it can be helpful for therapists to take a more directive approach. One is when there are multiple clients with multiple goals. In these cases it is important to learn from each person what he or she wants. Oftentimes therapists will be able to keep everyone together and obtain descriptions from each person regarding what he or she is concerned about and wants to see change. At other times, in order to hear each person's perspective and help him or her to feel heard and understood, it will be helpful to meet with each person individually for a few minutes. We'll discuss this further at the end of Chapter 4.

Another circumstance can require therapists to be much more directive. This is when clients' preferred styles of meeting might negatively affect change processes. Due to volatility, hostility, or other mitigating circumstances between clients, therapists may have to directly intervene. Therapists may need to separate people due to one or more persons behaving in ways that may be self-destructive or harmful to others. For example, if a therapist's efforts to curb a couple's verbally abusive statements toward each other prove ineffective, he or she might decide to separate the two until things are calmer. In such cases, the therapist can communicate to the couple that they can be brought together again at a later time, but that another meeting arrangement is necessary until each is willing to be respectful of the other.

The issue of where to meet can also be a consideration with some clients. Although some therapists may be limited to a specific setting, oftentimes there are opportunities to be flexible in terms of the context in which therapy takes place. Case Example 2.1 illustrates this point.

Case Example 2.1 ***Can We Do That?***

Brian, a fifteen-year-old, was placed in the emergency shelter where Bob was a therapist. Prior to meeting with Brian, his mother informed Bob, "Therapy won't work with Brian. We've already tried it." When asked to elaborate, the mother would only say, "He hates to sit and talk. And even if he does sit down with you, he won't say anything more than 'yes' or 'no' to your questions."

Before his first meeting with Brian for therapy, Bob asked him if he preferred to talk inside the house in an office, outside in the yard, or on a walk around the neighborhood. With a surprised look, Brian responded, "Can we really go outside and talk?" "Sure," Bob said.

Bob and Brian ended up talking outside on the stairs of the emergency shelter. During that time, Brian, perhaps for the first time, expressed himself and talked about what he had been experiencing.

We've done therapy sessions in offices, homes, restaurants, cars, on playgrounds, basketball courts, indoors, and outdoors. This can be particularly important for those who work with children and adolescents. We have no preconceived ideas about what context therapy should occur in. Therapy can occur anywhere at anytime. Although it may not always be possible to change the meeting place, consulting with clients about their comfort level with regard to different contexts can let them know that you are sensitive to their needs. Again, a collaborative approach hinges on the voices of clients as opposed to the preconceived ideas of therapists.

Collaboration Key 3: Becoming Outcome-Informed from the Beginning

Therapists are increasingly being expected to demonstrate the effectiveness of their approaches. We applaud this trend. In fact, we believe that being outcome-informed starts prior to formal therapy. For example, studies have demonstrated that explaining the therapy process to clients and explaining the rationale for treatment prior to formal therapy decreases dropout (Garfield, 1994). We believe that therapists should inform clients during the initial contact what therapy will entail, and that ways of monitoring progress and change will be involved (Duncan & Miller, 2000). Here's one way therapists can attend to outcome prior to formal therapy and introduce clients to therapeutic processes:

> I'd like to tell you about how we like to work at our (agency, clinic, practice). We are dedicated to helping our clients achieve the results that they want in therapy. So from the start we're going to be talking with you about what's been helpful to you, what's not, what's working, and what's not. We may also ask you to do a brief questionnaire between sessions or at the end of therapy to see how things are going or have gone from your perspective. Essentially, your ongoing feedback will let us know if and how we're being effective, if anything needs to change, if therapy with us is helping you with the concerns you came in for, or whether a referral to another service would help you to get what you want.

Some years ago, Bill incorporated this idea into his week-long and weekend trainings with mental health professionals (Bertolino, 1998; Bertolino & Caldwell, 2000; Bertolino & O'Hanlon, 1998). He informed the participants that he would be checking in with them periodically to see what was coming across, what was working, what was not, and what they wanted more or less of as the training progressed. The participants' preferences were influential in determining the direction of training. By being outcome-informed, Bill was able to make adjustments based on the needs of the group. This was also a way to show the therapists in the group the continual checking-in and assessment process.

Throughout the remainder of this book, we will continue to introduce ways that therapists can be outcome-informed. It's important to invite clients into collaborative relationships in which they can share their ideas, theories, and worldviews. This creates a context that is conducive to positive change. Now that we've discussed some ways of being collaborative prior to discussing concerns and problems with clients, let's get started with the process of therapy itself.

Getting Started with the First Session in Therapy

It is our belief that respectful and effective therapy begins with careful attention to clients and their concerns. This means that collaborative, competency-based therapists allow clients to tell their stories from the opening moments of the therapeutic encounter. They do not immediately delve into a search for problems or solutions. Instead, therapists let clients know that they can speak freely about whatever they feel comfortable with, but that they do not have to speak about anything they are not comfortable with. We believe that the value of such an invitation cannot be measured because it allows clients to choose where to begin and brings forth their personal expertise.

We find it best to start from a position that allows clients to tell their stories, devoid of therapists' theoretical interruptions. Although all questions request certain information and are directive to some degree, we believe that the ones listed here invite clients to begin where they feel most comfortable:

What has brought you in?
Where would you like to begin?
What would you like to talk about today?

Aside from being respectful, there are other reasons that clients should begin where they feel comfortable. First, when a therapist initiates his or her own agenda without allowing clients to relate their experiences and stories, it's as if the therapist is applying his or her theory regardless of the person or the circumstances. In such instances, a "one-model-fits-all" approach takes precedence, leaving out the uniqueness of each client. Milton Erickson taught us that therapy ought to be client-driven, not theory-driven.

Second, research indicates that for many clients the most important part of the therapeutic milieu is the opportunity to tell their stories and be heard (Lawson, McElheran, & Slive, 1997). Carl Rogers (1951, 1961) taught us the importance of attending and listening to clients. At a basic level, we can do this by not attempting to fit clients into theoretical boxes. In a previous publication, Bob (Bertolino, 1999) discussed this point:

> When a therapist attends mainly to his or her theory, and attempts to fit the client into its confines, the person may go unheard. If we did this in our everyday conversations, people would walk out on us or stop talking. After all, when you talk with others, do you ordinarily start to intervene with problem or solution-loaded questions right from the start? Probably not. Do you let the person say what he or she needs to say? Probably. The idea here is that... [clients] and others ought to have space for their stories to be told and heard. (p. 37)

There is a third reason that clients should be given the space and permission to tell their stories. If we do not invite clients into this sort of collaborative relationship—if we cut them off during conversations or attempt to intervene too quickly—we risk not learning about their perceptions and experiences regarding problems, possibilities, and solutions. That is, how clients understand their difficulties, what they have done to try to solve them, including how those attempts have fared, and their ideas about what may lead or contribute to the change they are seeking.

Not learning about clients' experiences can negatively influence the therapeutic relationship and desired outcomes. For example, clients can become disheartened when therapists suggest remedies that have already been tried but were unsuccessful. In addition, therapists can lose credibility when attempts at problem solving or solution building are misguided or premature. We believe that these things can be avoided when clients are given the space to share their stories, and when therapists lend more attention to learning and honoring clients' theories of change.

Language as a Vehicle for Creating Possibilities and Change

We've learned about the importance of allowing clients to tell their stories. This gives therapists a chance to learn about clients' internal experiences, preexisting beliefs, interpretations of problems, and ideas about how concerns might best be addressed. This relative matrix of information represents the client's theory.

But a question quickly arises. Do clients need to talk for hours or multiple sessions to feel heard and understood and for their personal theories to be acknowledged? Because each person is different, there is not a set answer to this question. As we discussed in the previous chapter, there is little correlation between the strength of the therapeutic alliance and the length of therapy. Therefore, it is not only possible to achieve an immediate bond with clients, in our experience it's commonplace. Although with some clients it will take longer, it is our contention that through careful attending and listening, most clients can feel heard and understood rather quickly.

With regard to attending and listening skills, we again refer to Carl Rogers's (1951, 1961) ideas of unconditional positive regard, empathy, trustworthiness, and genuineness. Research has identified these, and corresponding relational elements, as important factors in achieving positive outcomes. We agree with Rogers that clients' internal experience must be acknowledged and validated.

Acknowledgment means attending to what clients have communicated both verbally and nonverbally. This involves letting them know that their experience, points of view, and actions have been heard and noted. A basic way of acknowledging is to say, "uh huh" or "I see." Another way is to reflect back to clients, without interpretation, what they said. For example, a therapist might say, "You're sad" or "I heard you say that you're angry." This can also be done when acknowledging nonverbal behaviors. For example, a therapist could say, "You shuddered as you spoke" or "I can see the tears."

Validation means giving clients permission to experience whatever difficulties they are having and letting them know that these experiences are valid. Clients should not feel that they are bad, crazy, sick, or weird for being who they are and experiencing what they may. Validation also lets clients know that others have experienced the same or similar things. To validate we add words such as "It's okay," or "That's all right," to our acknowledgments and reflections.

In summary, a therapist using acknowledgment and validation might say, "It's okay to be angry," or "It's all right if you're mad," or "I heard you say that you're sad, and it's okay for you to be sad." It's important to remember that as therapists we must continue to attend to clients' internal experience throughout the therapeutic process. However, as discussed in Chapter 1, we do not validate all client actions and behaviors because some may be harmful to the client or others.

By carefully attending and listening to clients' stories we are not encouraging ongoing, aimless conversation. If clients go on aimlessly with their stories, two things are likely to occur. First, as our colleague Steve Gilligan would say, "Clients will put you into a trance. They will [seem to] say, 'I'm depression. When you look at me all you will see is depression. All I've ever been is depression. All I'll ever be is depression.'" When this happens, therapists can fall prey to clients' stories. At that point it becomes difficult for therapists to help because they have become engrossed in their own problematic narrative.

A second concern is that if clients speak aimlessly about themselves and their situations they will likely use what we refer to as *language of impossibility.* That is, they will use words that convey hopelessness and impossibility. Ultimately, some clients will paint themselves into corners with the words they use. In turn, therapists run the risk of becoming intertwined in stories of impossibility.

To avoid the pull of impossibility and to go beyond basic attending and listening skills, we offer some ways of acknowledging and validating clients while subtly changing language of impossibility to that of possibility. We refer to these methods as *dissolving impossibility talk* and *future talk* (Bertolino, 1999; Bertolino & Thompson, 1999; O'Hanlon & Beadle, 1994, 1999; O'Hanlon & Bertolino, 1998). Both of these methods offer ways of using language as a vehicle for creating change.

The ideas that we will introduce for working with clients' language reflect what Frank and Frank (1991) identified as therapeutic rituals. All approaches make use of rituals—methods and procedures—to facilitate change processes and promote hope. Although rituals are not necessarily causal agents of change, they can mobilize placebo factors and enhance the therapeutic relationship, highlight client competency, promote change, and orient treatment toward future possibilities.

Dissolving Impossibility Talk: Acknowledgment and Possibility

Bob's first job in the field was as a residential counselor at an emergency shelter for runaway and homeless youth. The shelter also operated a 24-hour crisis hotline. One of Bill's first jobs was as a suicide hotline crisis worker. By spending many hours doing crisis therapy, we learned the importance of establishing a connection with callers in crisis and working toward problem resolution quickly. If this did not happen, they might hang up and hurt themselves or someone else.

To remedy this, we learned to acknowledge callers and their experiences by asking them direct questions about their situations, what they needed, and what they wanted to change. This seemed to provide the internal validation that clients were seeking, while allowing us to intervene in some way to alleviate the crisis.

Although we had learned an effective way of working with people in crisis over the phone, we found something very disconcerting happening with our outpatient clients. In our individual therapy sessions, we listened and reflected. We acknowledged but did not direct. Although clients seemed to respond well to this process, few experienced the change they desired. We realized that our clients needed more to facilitate positive change, so we turned to Milton Erickson.

During Bill's studies with Erickson, he learned that this psychiatrist was very effective at developing rapport with his patients while also being directive. Contrary to the traditional idea of listening, reflecting, then stepping back, Erickson would move into his patients' experience and initiate a search for possibilities. In this way he combined acknowledgment with possibility to facilitate change. This is precisely what we needed in our work as outpatient therapists—a combination of Carl Rogers and Milton Erickson.

Carl Rogers taught us the importance of acknowledging and validating the internal experience of clients. However, if we only reflect experiences and views, many will continue to describe their views of themselves and their situations in ways that close down possibilities for change. It can be very difficult for therapists to find possibilities within problem-saturated descriptions. Thus, it is clear that most clients will need more intervention on the part of the therapist or they will continue to find themselves in impossibility land. To do this, we add a twist to the idea of pure reflection. The following are three ways of doing this.

1. *Using the Past Tense.* Reflect clients' problems in the past tense.

CLIENT: I'm depressed.

THERAPIST: So you've been depressed.

CLIENT: I feel like a failure.

THERAPIST: You've felt like a failure.

CLIENT: My life's a mess.

THERAPIST: Your life's been a mess.

As illustrated, when a client gives a present tense statement of a problem, acknowledge and reflect the problem using the past tense. By doing this, we introduce the possibility of a change in the present or future. This is a very subtle linguistic shift that involves both acknowledgment and validation and simultaneously introduces possibility into the conversation.

If we only acknowledge and validate, most clients will not move on. They will continue to describe situations of impossibility. Further, if we simply stress that they should move on, it may be seen as invalidation. We've found that this hybrid of Carl Rogers's use of acknowledgment and validation through reflection and Milton Erickson's emphasis on possibilities through subtle changes in language provides therapists with a way of introducing possibilities into otherwise closed statements and conversations.

2. *Translating General Statements into Partial Statements.* Take clients' general statements, such as *everything, everybody, nobody, always,* and *never,* and translate them into partial statements. This can be done by using qualifiers related to time (e.g., recently, in the past month or so, much of the time), intensity (e.g., a lot, a bit less, somewhat more), or partiality (e.g., a lot, some, most, many). We do not want to minimize or invalidate clients' experiences. Instead, we want to gently introduce the idea of possibilities.

CLIENT: I'm always depressed.

THERAPIST: You've been depressed a lot of the time.

CLIENT: Nothing ever goes right in my life.

THERAPIST: Sometimes things haven't gone right in your life.

CLIENT: I'm so frustrated.

THERAPIST: Recently, you've felt frustrated.

By acknowledging and validating clients and using qualifiers to change global statements, we can introduce the element of possibility into impossibility-laced statements. This can create little openings where change is possible.

3. *Translating Absolute Statements into Perceptual Statements.*Translate what clients see as statements of truth or reality into perceptual statements or subjective realities.

CLIENT: Things will never change.

THERAPIST: Your sense is that things will never change.

CLIENT: I'm a terrible parent.

THERAPIST: You've gotten the idea that you've been a terrible parent.

CLIENT: I can't make good decisions.

THERAPIST: Your sense is that you haven't made good decisions.

Statements such as these are not the way things are, but are clients' perceptions of events, situations, or themselves. By reflecting these statements as perceptions, the element of possibility can be introduced.

Notice that it's possible to combine different methods of changing language. Examples we used earlier include, "You've been depressed a lot of the time" (past tense/partial statement), and "Your sense is that you haven't made good decisions" (perceptual statement/past tense). In our experience, the more therapists practice with such changes in language, the more comfortable and consistent they become in identifying and attending to words, phrases, and statements that suggest impossibility.

It's important that therapists capture the essence of clients' experiences when introducing possibilities. We do not want to echo the voices of society that say they must move on or get over it. Clients have heard enough of such talk, which generally translates into invalidation and blame for them. If clients feel their experiences are being minimized or they are being pushed to move on, they will likely respond with a statement such as:

CLIENT: Not most of the time! All the time!

If the clients react this way, then we are not getting it right. We must then validate further to make sure clients feel heard and understood. We can still do this while keeping an eye on possibilities. For example, a therapist might respond to the previous client statement by saying:

THERAPIST: Okay. Your sense is that things have been bad all the time.

This way we are continuing to acknowledge and validate while injecting the idea of possibility into a statement of impossibility. Thus, we are not coercing clients, but are inviting them into different perspectives. We want to let clients know that we have heard and understood their problems, concerns, experiences, and points of view—without closing down the possibility of change. To do this, we offer the idea that even though things have been difficult, painful, overwhelming, and so on, positive change is possible. We stated in an earlier publication (O'Hanlon & Bertolino, 1998) that as a result of changing clients' basic language, we hope for the following:

> When acknowledgement and validation are combined with language of change and possibility in ongoing therapist reflections, clients begin to shift their self-perceptions. This process continues throughout the therapy. In time, clients can develop a more possibility-oriented sense of themselves. (p. 49)

Now let's look at a second way of using subtle changes in language. We refer to this as *future talk.*

Future Talk: Acknowledgment and a Vision for the Future

Consistent with outcome research, a collaborative, competency-based approach focuses on the future. Yet some clients use language that seems to hold them as prisoners of the present or past, with little or no sense of a future without problems, pain, or suffering. Just as with dissolving impossibility talk, acknowledgement is the necessary building block from which we work. This time, however, we'll begin to offer small changes in language that open up the possibilities for future change.

We liken this idea to the moving walkways in airports. Both of us travel quite a bit and find it helpful to climb aboard these moving conveyor belts that take us to our destinations with little or no effort. We can use language to move clients along, in the direction of possibilities, without them actually having to take steps toward those goals and preferred outcomes. Here are three ways of doing this:

1. *Assuming Future Solutions through Future Talk.* Assume that clients, and others involved, will find solutions. Using words such as *yet* and *so far* presupposes that even though things feel stuck or unchangeable now, things will change sometime in the future. This simple shift in language can help to create a light at the end of the tunnel.

CLIENT: Things will never go right for me.

THERAPIST: So far things haven't gone right for you.

CLIENT: I'm always in some kind of trouble.

THERAPIST: You haven't found a way to stay out of trouble yet.

CLIENT: My life is going downhill.

THERAPIST: Your life hasn't gone in the direction you'd like yet.

Although we are only making small changes in language, we are introducing the possibility that change may occur in the future. This seemingly simple shift gently challenges closed views and can open doorways to further, more significant changes.

2. *Turning Problem Statements into Goals.* Take client problem statements and change them into statements about a preferred future or goal.

CLIENT: I'll never have the kind of life that I want.

THERAPIST: So you'd like to be able to find a way to have the kind of life you want?

CLIENT: I'm worthless.

THERAPIST: So one of the things we could do is help you find some self-worth?

CLIENT: I'm always in trouble.

THERAPIST: So one of the things we could focus on here is finding a way to change your relationship with trouble?

This way of changing language serves several purposes. First, as with the previous methods outlined, it offers a way of acknowledging clients. A second purpose relates to a situation that therapists often find themselves in. In the course of listening to a client's story it can become difficult to discern which problem concerns the client most. Therapists must routinely make decisions regarding which client words, phrases, comments, and remarks should gain more or less attention. By turning problem statements into goals, therapists can acknowledge clients' statements and clarify which problems are most important to them. Here's an example of how this works:

CLIENT: I don't have any friends. I'm not doing very well in school. Everything is going downhill.

THERAPIST: It sounds as if you've got a lot going on. And if I'm hearing you right, some of the things we could focus on here are developing friendships, doing better in school, and just getting things going in a better direction for you.

CLIENT: Kind of... I mean, I do want friends but I really want to get my grades up first. That's the most important thing. Then I think I'll feel better about the way my life is going.

By utilizing a collaborative posture and recasting the problem statement into a statement about a preferred future or goal, both clients and therapists can begin to gain some clarity about what clients want different in their lives. In this way, therapists can set aside their ideas about what should or should not be focused on and for clients' to indicate their preferences. We find this to be particularly helpful to those just learning to become therapists because it is a very specific way of gaining clarity with regard to clients' concerns.

3. *Presupposing Changes and Progress.* Assume changes and progress toward goals by using words such as *when* and *will.*

CLIENT: All I do is get into trouble.

THERAPIST: So when you've put trouble behind you, you'll feel as though things are heading in a better direction.

CLIENT: No one wants to be in a relationship with me.

THERAPIST: So when you get the sense that you have found people who might be interested in having a relationship with you, we'll know that we've made some progress.

CLIENT: I'm always getting angry and then saying things I shouldn't say.

THERAPIST: So when you are able to experience anger without saying things that you might later regret, then you'll feel better about things.

Erickson used presupposition in his hypnotic work to link the specific movements of his patients with the suggestion of internal, automatic changes. For example, he might say, "When your hand begins to lift, I wonder what changes you'll make within yourself." In a nonhypnotic manner, we can use the same concept to presuppose future changes and progress toward goals and preferred outcomes.

To do this, use the word *when* in restating what the client said, followed by either *how* or *what* combined with *will* to form a question for the client. Here's how to do this:

CLIENT: No one wants to be in a relationship with me.

THERAPIST: So when you get the sense that you have found people who might be interested in having a relationship with you, what will be different for you?

It can also be helpful to add the use of conjecture, wonderment, or speculation (Andersen, 1991; Hoffman, 1990; Penn & Sheinberg, 1991). The use of conjecture allows the therapist to respond with a statement or a question. In other words, the question can be framed as speculation or as an inquiry as to how future changes will make a difference for the client. To use conjecture, simply add "I wonder" or "I'm curious." Here are two illustrations of this:

CLIENT: I'm always getting angry and then I say things I shouldn't say.

THERAPIST: So when you are able to experience anger without saying things that you might later regret, I wonder what will be different in your life.

Here's how to combine conjecture with the use of a question.

CLIENT: All I do is get into trouble.

THERAPIST: So when you've put trouble behind you, I'm curious, how will your life be different?

We have learned from our work with clients that intense emotional reactions (e.g., hopelessness, pain, fear) are often exacerbated by a lack of a vision for the future. That is, they don't have a sense that the pain or suffering they are experiencing now will be alleviated in the future. There is a growing body of literature in the field of medicine indicating that people who have a sense that things will improve in the future have a higher incidence of recovery from chronic illness. We have found the same to be true in our work. Presuppositional language implies that things can change, without minimizing the problems and suffering which clients are currently experiencing.

Beyond the Basics: Advanced Competency-Based Attending and Listening

In our initial interactions with clients and throughout therapy we are inviting clients to tell their stories. Such invitations let them know that we are interested in their experiences and views, and that we want to form collaborative relationships and learn about their theories of change. We facilitate this process through attending, listening, acknowledging, and validating. We also listen for words, phrases, statements, and stories that suggest impossibility and may inhibit change. When we hear suggestions of impossibility, we make subtle changes in language to create openings for possible future changes.

So far we've discussed two ways of using acknowledgment to promote the therapeutic relationship while introducing possibilities through language. In this section we'll offer further ways of working with clients' language and personal theories to create change. Ultimately, different clients will need different things from different therapists. We've found the methods offered here to be helpful in attending to clients' experiences, without imposing our theories of change on clients. These methods include *giving permission, utilization, inclusion, reading reflections,* and *matching language.* Let's explore each of these.

Giving Permission

People have internal experiences such as feelings, sensations, involuntary thoughts, and images. While we can control actions, internal experience is another matter. We want to let clients know that whatever they are experiencing is acceptable, and that they can move on. One way we do this is by giving permission. There are two kinds of permission:

1. *Permission to:* "You can."
2. *Permission not to have to:* "You don't have to."

Some clients feel there is something wrong with having certain thoughts or experiences. In these instances, clients need to be given permission to think or experience whatever is going on internally. Perhaps the best way of doing this is to normalize, which provides validation and permission. This lets clients know they're not bad, crazy, or weird—and that others have felt similarly. Here are some ways to give permission to:

CLIENT: I know I shouldn't think about ending the marriage. I just can't help it. I must be a bad person.

THERAPIST: It's okay to think about ending the marriage, and that doesn't make you a bad person.

CLIENT: I can feel the anxiety building.

THERAPIST: You can go with it and just let it be there. I'm right here.

Other clients will feel that they are being dominated by internal experiences or that they should be having some internal experience that they are not. They might need permission not to have the experience. Here are some ways of giving permission not to have to:

CLIENT: People keep telling me that I need to remember the abuse, but that's the problem!

THERAPIST: You don't have to remember the abuse if it's not right for you.

CLIENT: In the support group I attend for parents who've lost their spouses, everyone keeps saying that I need to express my anger because that's a stage of grieving. But I've never felt anger. Is something wrong with me?

THERAPIST: Each person goes through grief in his or her own way. Some people will experience anger and some won't. It's okay if you don't feel angry. You can take your own path to healing.

We also have found it useful, in some situations, to give both permissions at the same time. Here are some ways of doing this:

CLIENT: Should I be angry or not? I don't know.

THERAPIST: You can be angry and you don't have to be angry.

CLIENT: That was a really bad situation. I can't believe I'm not more upset about it.

THERAPIST: It's okay to feel upset about it and you don't have to feel upset about it.

If we give only one type of permission, some clients may feel pressured to experience only one part of the equation or may find the other side emerging in a more compelling or disturbing way (O'Hanlon & Bertolino, 1998). For example, if we only say, "It's okay to remember," the client might say, "But I don't want to remember!" We can counter this bounce-back response by giving permission to and not to have to, "It's okay to remember and you don't have to remember."

It's important to note that giving permission for an internal thought does not mean you are giving permission for action. While all internal experiences are okay, be careful regarding which actions you extend permission for. For example, a therapist might say, "It's okay to feel like hurting yourself and you don't have to feel like hurting yourself." However, a therapist would not say, "It's okay to cut yourself and you don't have to cut yourself." Never give permission for harmful or destructive behavior.

Utilization

Erickson was interested in how he could use what his patients brought to therapy as resources to initiate change. No matter how small, strange, or negative the behavior or idea may seem, it can be used to open up the possibilities for change. This is in direct contrast with more traditional approaches, which often view such things as symptoms or liabilities. Here are some ways of using client behaviors and ideas as vehicles for change.

CLIENT (Referring to child): He wastes his time playing those stupid computer games.

THERAPIST (To the child): So you've learned to play computer games? How did you do that?

CLIENT: My family is extremely dysfunctional and chaotic.

THERAPIST: So you've had some experience dealing with dysfunction and chaos.

CLIENT: I'm terrible at sports.

THERAPIST: Now that you've ruled out sports, how can it be helpful to you to know that your efforts may be better spent on other things?

Utilization allows therapists to take behaviors and ideas that are typically seen as deficits, inabilities, symptoms, or negative things in general, and turn them into assets. This can be helpful to get clients moving in the direction of the change they are seeking, if they aren't already doing so.

Inclusion

At times people feel they are in a bind, experiencing opposite or contradictory feelings that seem to present conflict. In this case we want to include any parts, objections, feelings, aspects of self, or clients' concerns that might have been left out or seen as barriers to the therapy or goals and preferred outcomes. As with utilization, we use what the client has brought to therapy. In addition, we include anything that may have been left out, devalued, or seen as irreconcilable opposites. To do this we use "and" to link client experiences together. Here are some ways of doing this:

CLIENT: I need to tell you something but I just can't.

THERAPIST: It's okay to feel like you can't tell me and maybe there is a way you can tell me.

CLIENT: I hate my life. Nothing will ever change for the better.

THERAPIST: You can hate your life and things can still change for the better.

CLIENT: My husband makes me so angry. I can't be around him.

THERAPIST: You can be angry with your husband and find a way to be around him.

If clients are feeling stuck, it's often because they are leaving out some part of their experience or don't feel as if they have room for it. The use of inclusion allows therapists to pull together ideas and feelings that seem to be in opposition and may be hindering the change process. This allows clients to experience all aspects of a situation and move on.

Reading Reflections

One premise we hold is that there is no such thing as resistance, only communication, client reflections, or feedback. In fact, client reflections are a rich source of information, as they tell us whether we're working in ways that are helpful to clients. To read reflections we must attend to clients' verbal and nonverbal communication. This reminds us of a story about Ernest Rossi, a Jungian analyst who studied with Erickson.

During their time together, Erickson would often look over at Rossi and see him staring at the ceiling, having theoretical conversations with himself about what was happening with Erickson and his patients. Erickson would reorient Rossi and remind him that the patients were not on the ceiling, but were sitting in front of him. It's important for therapists to remember that active listening and feedback reading involve paying attention to clients, not having conversations with theories.

Although we are continually attending to what clients are communicating, reading reflections can be particularly important at times when clients appear to be resistant, disagreeable, uncooperative, overly quiet, or tuning us out (O'Hanlon & Beadle, 1994, 1999). Again, we do not interpret such communication as resistance or lack of cooperation; instead, we consider it to be information indicating that what we have been doing as therapists is not working. In many instances it's because we are pushing for change too quickly and are not doing enough acknowledging. Thus, we need to change what we are doing and try to communicate better with clients so that they will feel heard and understood. Here are some ways of reading reflections.

CLIENT: I don't think you're following me.

THERAPIST: Okay. I'll try harder to follow you. Can you tell me what I said or did to give you the sense that I wasn't following along?

CLIENT: Are you suggesting that I try and face him? Because that just flat out wouldn't work for me.

THERAPIST: Okay. Please tell me a little more about how you see it and your ideas about what you think needs to happen.

CLIENT: **(Silence)**

THERAPIST: It has become a little quiet in here, and I'm not sure what that means. If it's okay with you, I'd just like to check out a few possibilities. (**Watching client closely**) I wonder if you're feeling a bit discouraged, or perhaps misunderstood. Maybe you're feeling that I'm moving too quickly or not quick enough. Or maybe this is just really difficult for you. (**Client nods**) Okay, that's fine. We can approach this in whatever way feels most comfortable for you.

Therapists' sensitivity to verbal and nonverbal messages can help alleviate tension and discomfort that clients may be experiencing. It can also help therapists clarify the needs of clients. Oftentimes situations that appear bogged down require therapists to pay closer attention to the reflections being given by clients.

Matching Language

People often speak in verbal patterns. Outcome research indicates that higher ratings of client satisfaction are significantly related to similarity in client–therapist linguistic style (Duncan & Miller, 2000; Patton & Meara, 1982). Thus, another way of attending and listening to clients is to match their language by using similar words and phrases, speed, intonation, and patterns. This can help therapists join with clients and contribute to a foundation for future change. To illustrate this idea, we offer a case of Erickson's:

> A man named George was picked up by the police for irrational behavior and was committed to the state mental hospital. His only rational utterances were "My name is George," "Good morning," and "Goodnight." All of his other verbal offerings were a continuous word salad—a mixture of made-up sounds, syllables, words, and incomplete phrases. On any given day George might be heard saying, "Bucket of lard," "Didn't pay up," "Sand on the beach," or irrelevant, mixed-up words that didn't make sense.
>
> For a few years, George sat by himself and mumbled his word salad. Psychiatrists, psychologists, social service workers, nurses, other personnel, and even other patients had tried to engage him in intelligible conversation to no avail. George would simply continue his word salad. Over time, George began to greet people who entered the ward with an outburst of word salad. In between, he sat by himself, seeming to be mildly depressed. When approached, he would typically spit out a few minutes of angry word salad.

Erickson joined the hospital staff during the sixth year of George's stay. He quickly learned about George. Erickson tried on occasion to learn his name, but all he got was an outpouring of garbled language. So, Erickson enlisted his secretary to transcribe George's words in shorthand. Although no meaning could be discovered from the transcriptions, Erickson found that he could make use of them.

Erickson carefully studied and learned George's word-salad patterns. He then paraphrased the word salads but used words that were not likely to be found in George's rants. Erickson then improvised a word-salad pattern that was similar to George's, but with a completely different vocabulary.

Erickson began to sit alongside George on a hospital bench that the patient frequented. He did this in increasing amounts, until he was able to sit with George for an hour. At that point, Erickson addressed the empty air and identified himself but gained no response from George. The next day, he again identified himself, but this time directly to George. To this, George responded with an angry offering of word salad. In reply, Erickson voiced out an equal amount of carefully contrived word salad. George seemed puzzled and uttered a small amount of word salad back with an inquiring intonation. Erickson responded, in word salad, as if to answer the inquiry. After a few more interchanges, George lapsed into silence.

At their next meeting they exchanged greetings, and then George launched into a long word-salad speech. Erickson replied. He continued to visit with George on a regular basis and had word-salad conversations each time. Some of the conversations were very long and taxing on Erickson.

One morning, after their usual greetings and a few sentences of nonsense, George said to Erickson, "Talk sense, Doctor." "Certainly, I'd be glad to. What's your name?" asked Erickson. "O'Donovan, and it's about time somebody who knows how to talk asked. Over five years in this lousy joint..." (to which a couple of sentences of word salad were added) replied George. Erickson responded, "I'm glad to get your name, George. Five years is too long a time..." (adding an equal amount of word-salad at the end).

The conversation continued, and Erickson gained a complete history from George, which was sprinkled with word salad. Each time Erickson responded, he interspersed the same amount of word salad that George had. Although George's speech was never perfect, he spoke clearly with only an occasional offering of unintelligible mumbles. This led him to be discharged from the hospital within a year and become gainfully employed. George eventually moved to a distant city, and he informed Erickson of his satisfactory adjustments. He ended his last correspondence with Erickson by signing his name properly and adding a few jumbled syllables. (Erickson, 1980; Gordon & Meyers-Anderson, 1981)

This case example of Erickson's illustrates the importance of speaking the same language your client speaks. Move away from psychological jargon that often accompanies conversations with clients. The only jargon we are interested in is clients' jargon. We are using clients' words and adjusting to them, as opposed to making clients adjust to our words. Here are some respectful ways of joining with clients through matching language.

CLIENT: I, just, don't . . . I mean, I kind of, but I, ah, don't know.

THERAPIST: You, just, don't know . . . I wonder if it's, a bit confusing.

CLIENT: The way I see it, I'm a fool for believing he would change.

THERAPIST: The vision you've had of yourself is that you've been a fool for believing that he could change for the better.

CLIENT: Life just keeps . . . **(Silence)** . . . well, it just keeps on dealing me bad cards.

THERAPIST: Life just keeps on . . . **(Silence)** . . . I wonder what cards you'd like to be dealt?

So far we've learned about how to create a context for change through attending and listening. We've discussed the importance of listening to clients' stories, the role of acknowledgment and validation, and how to use language in subtle ways to create small openings for change. All of the methods offered here represent ways of introducing possibility into otherwise closed situations. We're not talking about drastic movements or major turns in conversation, just ways of attending to clients' use of language and opening up pathways for change. Now let's look at the opening of an initial session to see how these ideas come together.

Constructing Conversations for Change: The Opening Moments

The following is a case illustration of how a therapist might use some of the ideas offered in this chapter during an initial session. See if you can identify which methods of changing language are employed, and where. At the end we'll show you which ones were used.

THERAPIST 1: Hi. I'd like to welcome you to the therapy center.

CLIENT 1: Thanks.

THERAPIST 2: So, what's brought you in today?

CLIENT 2: Well, my life is just a complete mess. Nothing's going right. I feel like the world is just collapsing around me and there's no way out.

THERAPIST 3: Sounds like you've been experiencing a lot of things. You feel like your life has been a complete mess, things haven't been going right, and your sense is that there's no way out.

CLIENT 3: That's right.

THERAPIST 4: Can you tell me a little more about what's been happening?

CLIENT 4: It's kind of hard... but I guess what I've noticed lately is that I can't get my work done. My school work that is. I don't feel very motivated at all. And worst, I'm failing out of college.

THERAPIST 5: It's been a bit hard... you haven't been getting your work done and that has shown up in your grades. Is that right?

CLIENT 5: Yeah, and I don't want to fail out of school. Plus, if I fail out I'll have to go back home and live with my folks again. I definitely don't want to do that!

THERAPIST 6: I see. So there's not doing well in school lately, and not wanting to return to your folks. Are there other things that have happened with you that you think I should know about?

CLIENT 6: The only other thing is my girlfriend. She's really smart and I'm not doing as well as her and that's really hard. And she doesn't know how bad I'm doing. If she found out she might think that I'm stupid.

THERAPIST 7: It sounds like you really value your girlfriend and her views. And your sense is that she might think you're stupid if she knew about your grades.

CLIENT 7: Exactly.

THERAPIST 8: Anything else?

CLIENT 8: No, that's it.

THERAPIST 9: So there's a few things that we could focus on in here—getting your work done and doing better in school...

CLIENT 9: That's really the key for me. I need to get my grades up but it seems like such a long haul. I mean, I don't really feel like I can turn the corner with this.

THERAPIST 10: Yeah, it can seem that way. You can feel like you can't turn the corner with this, and you can still turn the corner.

CLIENT 10: Yeah. It's not impossible, but it sure seems like it.

THERAPIST 11: Right. It just feels that way sometimes, and so far you haven't seen any signs of the change that you're looking for.

CLIENT 11: You got it.

THERAPIST 12: So when you do begin to turn the corner, what will be different for you?

CLIENT 12: Well, my grades will be better and I'll feel better about myself, for starters.

What did you notice about the conversation between the client and the therapist? In our experience with attending to and introducing possibilities through language, clients, colleagues, students, and aliens from other planets don't notice anything out of the ordinary. It just seems like a conversation between people. Now, which of the ways of working with clients' language did you identify? Here are the therapist responses and respective methods used:

THERAPIST 3: Sounds like you've been experiencing a lot of things. You feel like your life has been a complete mess, things haven't been going right, and your sense is that there's no way out. [using the past tense, translating into perceptual statement]

THERAPIST 4: Can you tell me a little more about what's been happening? [using the past tense]

THERAPIST 5: It's been a bit hard... you haven't been getting your work done and that has shown up in your grades. Is that right? [matching language, using the past tense]

THERAPIST 6: I see. So there's not doing well in school lately, and not wanting to return to your folks. Are there other things that have happened with you that you think I should know about? [using the past tense]

THERAPIST 7: It sounds like you really value your girlfriend and her views. And your sense is that she might think you're stupid if she knew about your grades. [translating into perceptual statement]

THERAPIST 9: So there's a few things that we could focus on in here—getting your work done and doing better in school... [turning problem statements into goals]

THERAPIST 10: Yeah, it can seem that way. You can feel like you can't turn the corner with this, and you can still turn the corner. [translating into perceptual statement; inclusion]

THERAPIST 11: Right. It just feels that way sometimes, and so far you haven't seen any signs of the change that you're looking for. [assuming the possibility of future solutions]

THERAPIST 12: So when you do begin to turn the corner, what will be different for you? [presupposing changes and progress]

As we listen to client narratives we're taking care to acknowledge and validate experiences and views and learn about clients' theories of change. At the same time, we're listening for statements that reflect stories of impossibility and working to introduce possibilities into these otherwise closed views.

From a collaborative, competency-based perspective we've learned how to begin therapy in a way that allows clients to tell their stories. We've also learned how to use language as a vehicle for creating change. This is the foundation from which we will continue to work. We will also continue to focus on language throughout the book. In Part Two we'll discuss ways of clarifying client concerns and complaints, including their goals and preferred outcomes.

Summary Points for Chapter Two

- Collaboration relationships are formed prior to beginning formal therapy and used in determining who should attend therapy and how to meet.
- It's important to begin therapy with a question that allows clients to tell their stories, devoid of therapists' theoretical interruptions.
- Clients must feel heard, understood, acknowledged, and validated. It is possible for therapists to help clients to feel heard and understood quickly.
- As clients tell their stories, therapists listen for statements that reflect stories of impossibility.
- When impossibility statements are identified, therapists can use a variety of methods to acknowledge and validate clients, while introducing possibilities for change. These include:
  - Dissolving impossibility talk
  - Future talk
  - Giving permission
  - Utilization
  - Inclusion
  - Reading reflections
  - Matching language

PART TWO

Clarifying Concerns, Complaints, Goals, and Preferred Outcomes

In the second part of this book we continue to explore ways in which therapists can use language that promotes hope and possibilities. Language is the primary vehicle for facilitating change. Therefore, the conversations that counselors engage in with clients can enhance or dampen positive change. The two chapters in this section also delve into two forms of assessment—formal and ongoing. Formal assessment procedures typically only occur at the start of treatment. Ongoing assessment, however, begins with the first session of therapy and continues until termination. This part of the book also offers therapists ways of establishing directions through goals and preferred outcomes and finding out from clients how therapy needs to happen for treatment to be deemed successful.

CHAPTER

3 Creating Change through Collaborative, Competency-Based Conversations

As therapists it is important that we attend and listen to clients' stories. Through acknowledgment and validation we can help them feel that they are heard and understood. Consistent with psychotherapy outcome research, we strive to be change-oriented even in our initial interactions with clients. We do this by learning how a client uses language, and by working to create small openings in a client's otherwise closed description of his or her life or situation. In the previous chapter we offered several subtle ways to acknowledge and validate clients while simultaneously opening up the possibilities for change. In this chapter we will discuss further ways of using language to invite clients into conversations.

We will begin by discussing the role of psychiatric diagnosis. Second, we'll offer ways of moving from pathology-focused language to language that promotes client competencies (e.g. their strengths, abilities, and resources). Next we show the contrast between the use of traditional therapeutic conversations and collaborative therapeutic conversations. We will illustrate how the latter can help therapists become more change-oriented in the therapeutic milieu. Last, we'll discuss the multiple roles that assessment serves, and how therapists can work with clients in collaborative, competency-based ways when utilizing formal instruments. The ideas offered in this chapter can help therapists (1) continue to create small openings and possibilities through the use of language, (2) learn more about clients' concerns and complaints, and (3) begin to gain a focus in therapy.

The Role of Diagnosis in Collaborative, Competency-Based Therapy

Since it's inception, the number of categories in the DSM has leaped from 66 in the first edition to 286 in the fourth. In fact, we often say that it's easy to tell when a new psychiatric diagnosis or label has gained popularity because it usually has an acronym (e.g., ADD—Attention Deficit Disorder; DID—Dissociative Identity Disorder; ODD—Oppositional Defiant Disorder). Psychiatrist Jerome Frank (1973) once observed that therapy might be the only treatment that creates the illness it treats.

Many argue that diagnosis can help mental health professionals further understand the psychiatric and psychological problems that people experience. The classification of symptoms into diagnoses has led to further research in an attempt to determine more effective therapeutic approaches and techniques. However, this philosophy runs counter to outcome research, which has clearly demonstrated that there are no best approaches and techniques. What are most important are clients', not therapists', theories about the etiology of problems as well as what it will take to bring about change.

Despite the compounding evidence of outcome research, funding for research studies on DSM diagnoses has remained consistent. From the late 1980s to 1990 there was a decrease of nearly 200 percent for non-DSM-related research studies (Wolfe, 1993). Although there is no evidence of a significant increase in the incidence of mental illness in the general population, such a focus suggests that people are getting sicker (Garfield & Bergin, 1994).

The advent of the DSM has brought along with it staunch proponents and opponents. There are many arguments both in favor of and against diagnostic labeling in therapy. The problem with adopting a single point of view is that clients' voices are passed over in favor of mental health professionals' perspectives. Whether clinicians view diagnosis as necessary or not, clients' ideas, thoughts, and theories are left out.

When we set aside our theoretical conceptualizations and include the views of clients, we often see things very differently. For example, many people have experienced validation by virtue of a diagnosis. Bill once ran an advertisement in a local newspaper looking for people to attend a therapy group he was offering. The group was to consist of people who would eat too much, then make themselves vomit. To his astonishment, he was inundated with phone calls. Some of the people who called were even tearful—they couldn't believe that others did the same thing.

At that time the label *bulimia* did not exist in the DSM. Once a diagnostic category was constructed and added to the DSM, many people no longer felt they were alone. Similarly, parents of children with ADD, and other disorders, found support groups very helpful. Meeting others with similar problems can help counter frustration and self-blame and provide relief and support.

Some people will experience relief by the assignment of a diagnosis. Many more will report that the stigmatizing effects are overwhelming. Some will feel as though they did something wrong, or that they are to blame for passing along genetic traits. Others will blame themselves for poor parenting skills, and so on. Perhaps more devastating is when outsiders, including mental health professionals, either directly or indirectly impart blame. The implication is that the affected individual's parents or family members (or others involved) caused the condition.

Further concern arises when clients begin to identify themselves as the assigned label. To illustrate this point, we refer to the Rodgers and Hammerstein musical *The Sound of Music.* Early on in the musical, Maria is introduced to the Von Trapp children. After the captain leaves, she asks the children to introduce themselves a second time. Notice the way the two boys refer to themselves:

FRIEDRICH: I'm Friedrich. I'm fourteen. I'm impossible!

MARIA: Really? Who told you that?

FRIEDRICH: Fräulein Josephine, four governesses ago.

(After Louisa and Brigitta speak, Kurt introduces himself to Maria)

KURT: I'm Kurt. I'm eleven. I'm incorrigible.

MARIA: Congratulations.

In essence, the person develops an identity consistent with the label. The person essentially becomes the disorder and a sense of self seems absent. In some instances clients will say things such as, "I'm bipolar" or "Didn't you know that I'm ODD?" In addition, people may be referred to in terms of their label or diagnosis. For example, one might say, "He's as ADD as they come" or "She's borderline." Now others begin to look through diagnostic lenses at people who have been labeled, seeing only the symptoms associated with the label. We liken this phenomenon to a Zen tale:

> Once a man found that his axe was missing, and suspected his neighbor's son of having taken it. Observing the youth walking around, the man was convinced that his was the walk of a thief. The youth looked like a thief and talked like a thief; everything he did pointed to his having stole the axe. Then one day, the man happened to find his missing axe. After that, he noticed his neighbor's son wasn't looking like a thief anymore. (Cleary, 1993, p. 66)

As depicted in the story, one of the dangers in labeling is that the expectation becomes the person. Once a label has been attached, it can be extremely difficult for individuals to change their views of themselves, and for others to see such persons as being separate from the diagnoses assigned to them.

Another concern is that some people will attempt to deny personal accountability because of their condition. They assume a position of powerlessness, in regard to the assigned label, and say things such as, "I can't help it, I'm OCD," or "I don't think about it. It just happens because I'm impulsive." They will let the label determine their actions and consider themselves unaccountable.

Adding to the dilemma, we must consider that even mental health professionals with so-called expertise in diagnostic procedures are subject to disagreement, inconsistency, and misdiagnosis. Studies have shown that nearly half the time different clinicians come up with completely different diagnoses for the same individual (Williams et al., 1992). When we combine misdiagnosis with a lack of consensus among so-called experts, we learn that diagnostic labeling is often unreliable.

Diagnoses also change with the times (Beutler & Clarkin, 1990). For example, homosexuality was once considered a mental disease. Ironically, when gay activists protested being identified as sick, homosexuality was "cured" by a vote of the American Psychiatric Association. It's very clear that diagnoses are related more to economic, political, and social factors than to scientific or empirical factors (Duncan & Miller, 2000).

Diagnoses are socially constructed explanations that are unhelpful in understanding the unique experiences of each person. They do not capture the essence of a person, and they tend to impart blame and promote hopelessness and helplessness. Because diagnoses primarily place focus on the individual, little or no emphasis is placed on relational, environmental, and cultural influences. Therefore, as previously stated, we therapists must learn a client's theory regarding his or her diagnosis.

In addition, most employee insurance plans now include mental health benefits. When third-party reimbursement is sought to pay for mental health services, the assignment of a diagnosis is almost always required. Thus, we must contend with diagnoses, as they may be necessary for some clients to receive the services they need.

In our experience, what's important is that clients are informed. That is, do they understand that diagnosis is necessary to obtain services and for third-party reimbursement? Are they invited into conversations about the diagnosis that will be assigned? Do clients understand the potential implications of a label, positive or negative? Are they informed that there is the option of paying out of pocket to eliminate third-party reimbursement, hence the need for diagnosis?

These and other questions allow clients the space to make decisions that are right for them. Therapists should make the issue of diagnosis a collaborative one with clients' perspectives guiding the way. Given options, some will choose to stay with the process of developing a diagnosis while others will choose to pay for mental health services. To further assist therapists in working with clients in collaborative, competency-based ways when diagnosis is a necessary part of treatment, we've included Table 3.1.

From a collaborative, competency-based perspective, whether diagnosis is given or not, we work with clients and their concerns, not diagnoses, labels, or conditions that have been attributed to them. We want to learn about and honor clients' concerns and complaints as well as their theories about potential possibilities and solutions. Learning about a person's unique circumstances, goals, and preferred outcomes for therapy are better indicators of what treatment to apply than diagnosis (Beutler & Clarkin, 1990).

When working with clients we pay close attention to our language and what it communicates. What therapists communicate through their theories, attitudes, and beliefs, particularly in the opening moments of therapy, can greatly influence

TABLE 3.1 Considerations with Psychiatric Labeling and Diagnosis

1. Use labels that empower and validate, not ones that invalidate, discourage, or blame.
2. Labels that describe behavior that people complain about are more relevant for change than therapists' ideas about people's inner motivations and personality traits. All labels and diagnoses are constructed but not all are equally speculative or as easily changed.
3. Be careful not to use diagnosis to suggest that people aren't accountable for what they do or that their diagnosis determines their choices.
4. Diagnosis can be done in a collaborative, transparent manner.

clients' expectations for change (Miller et al., 1997). Therapists who emphasize possibilities and a belief that positive change can occur can help build hope for clients. Conversely, pessimism, or an emphasis on psychopathology or on the long-term nature of change, can adversely affect clients. Unfortunately, the DSM and the language associated with it focus almost exclusively on what's wrong with people, emphasizing their deviancies from what experts have established as normal.

We consider a pathology-only focus, as represented by the DSM, to be detrimental and a potential contributor to what Erickson once referred to as *iatrogenic injury*. In 1961, while giving a lecture, Erickson stated:

> While I have read a number of articles on this subject of iatrogenic disease and have heard many discussions about it, there is one topic on which I haven't seen much written about and that is iatrogenic health. Iatrogenic health is a most important consideration—much more important than iatrogenic disease. (as cited in Rossi & Ryan, 1983b, p. 140)

Iatrogenic injury refers to methods, techniques, assessment procedures, explanations, or interventions that harm, discourage, invalidate, show disrespect, or close down the possibilities for change. We view the use of pathology-oriented language as one way of contributing to iatrogenic injury. In contrast, iatrogenic healing refers to those methods, techniques, assessment procedures, explanations, or interventions that encourage, are respectful, and open up the possibilities for change (O'Hanlon, 1993, 1999). We view language as the primary iatrogenic healing agent in therapy. Language is the vehicle through which assessment, intervention, and other procedures to promote change are filtered. An emphasis on iatrogenic healing allows us to move from emphasizing pathology and impossibility to emphasizing competency and possibility.

In the next section we'll discuss how to begin to change our language to promote iatrogenic healing in therapeutic conversations.

From Iatrogenic Injury and Pathology to Iatrogenic Healing and Competency: Language That Promotes Hope and Possibilities

As discussed, DSM and traditional first- and second-wave approaches emphasize pathology with regard to clients. In fact, both of us were trained as "pathology detectors." This included becoming adept at discovering, uncovering, and explaining what was wrong with clients. Such training required us to focus on deficits, inabilities, liabilities, and weaknesses. Needless to say, we had a hard time with such a negative orientation to human beings and therapy processes.

"What's wrong with this (person, couple, family, situation)?" is the inherent question to an orientation to pathology in therapy. It is assumed that therapists are able to answer this question, and they are expected to use pathology-laced language to explain their findings. Such language can unnecessarily stigmatize clients and inhibit positive change.

We know that clients face difficult problems and limitations. We want to acknowledge those aspects and be sure that clients feel heard and understood. At the same time, we want to make it clear that oftentimes problems are socially constructed through language. Clients' and mental health professionals' use of language can create unhelpful problem descriptions and labels that contribute to stigmatizing the clients and closing down possibilities for change. Thus, we advocate a shift in how therapists use language.

We've found two specific ways that therapists can move from pathology-based conversations to more competency-based conversations with clients. One way is by eliciting and evoking competency from clients, and the other is by using collaborative conversations. Let's explore each of these ideas to see how therapists can further develop a collaborative, competency-based orientation to counseling and psychotherapy.

Elicitation and Evocation: Searching for the Presence of Competency

Most theoretical approaches focus on pathology, deficits, and the absence of something. For example, a person may be seen as lacking social skills, self-control, self-esteem, the ability to focus, and so on. In promoting iatrogenic healing, we learned from Erickson how to search for the presence of something—to elicit and evoke abilities, strengths, and resources from within people or their social systems. This focus requires a shift in how we describe what people are experiencing, hence, a shift in language. To better understand this, let's refer back to the scene from *The Sound of Music* discussed earlier. In particular, let's view the rest of the interchange between Maria and Kurt:

KURT: I'm Kurt. I'm eleven. I'm incorrigible.

MARIA: Congratulations.

KURT: What's incorrigible?

MARIA: I think it means you want to be treated like a boy.

If seen as incorrigible, Kurt would be deemed as an unruly, out-of-line boy. One might speculate that he can't control himself, is unable to pay attention, and doesn't follow rules. But Maria doesn't see it that way. She sees him as one who is expressing his desire to be treated like a boy. While one view holds Kurt as being incorrigible and lacking ability, the other assumes the opposite and represents a shift away from pathology. The implications of therapists' views are great because what they focus on significantly influences virtually every aspect of therapy.

To further illustrate this shift in focus and language, we've enclosed Table 3.2. The left side of the table offers some pathology-based terms. The right column offers a translation of these terms into competency-based language.

In changing our basic language, we begin to consider what is present in terms of the presence of competency. But changing our basic language extends beyond words or sentences. Our overall conversations with clients emphasize collaboration and an exploration for competency. In this way clients can construct new meanings through our interactions with them. Meaning and perception are embedded in language and language becomes the vehicle for change as reflected in the vocabulary used; the worldview is mirrored in the language (Becvar & Becvar, 2000).

Collaborative Conversations as a Vehicle for Creating Change

The language we use with clients can be extremely influential. For example, we have both encountered numerous clients that have learned to speak the language

TABLE 3.2 Pathology versus Competency-Based Descriptions

Pathology Based	Competency Based
Hyperactive	Very energetic at times
Attention Deficit Disorder	Multiple interests
Anger problem	Often expresses intense emotion
Low self-esteem	Searching for self-value
Oppositional	Stands up for self/beliefs
Rebellious	Developing his/her own way
Codependent	People are important to him/her
Depressed	Introspective
Family problems	Concerned about his or her home life
Shy	Takes a little time to know people
Isolating	Likes being by himself or herself
Out of control	Still learning the rules

of the DSM (e.g., Attention Deficit, Oppositional Defiant, Borderline) better than us. How did they learn such language? We suspect that it's mostly from their interactions with mental health professionals.

As discussed in the introductory chapter with regard to social constructionism, therapists use language in very specific ways to create change with clients. We've learned that how we use language and what we focus on is directly related to our theories about why people have problems and how they change. For example, if you're a cognitive therapist you'll ask many questions that will help you to learn about your clients' patterns of thinking. You will study thought processes searching for cognitive distortions and systematic biases and ways of correcting them. If you're a behaviorist, you'll ask questions about the behaviors (operants) that your clients partake in and how they may have been conditioned to respond in particular ways. You'll then help your clients change their maladaptive behavior. Further, if you're a therapist thinking in family systems terms, you'll ask questions about relationships and search for ways of changing patterns of interaction between people.

The questions we ask and the conversations we engage in with clients reflect our theories and can either close or open up the possibilities for change. Our main tool of intervention is language. Therefore, we would like to make a distinction between what we refer to as traditional and collaborative conversations.

Traditional Therapeutic Conversations. Most traditional approaches to therapy rely on conversations that are designed to explain or interpret verbal and nonverbal communication, to promote insight, understanding, or awareness, to invite the expression of emotion, or to uncover mental illness and pathology. Therapists are considered the only experts in this therapeutic milieu. In our experience, these kinds of ideas are disrespectful of clients and tend to close down avenues of change. To illustrate this we've included Table 3.3.

Collaborative Therapeutic Conversations. A collaborative, competency-based approach moves away from traditional types of conversations to dialogues that value people in the therapeutic process. All involved in the therapeutic encounter bring in expertise. Clients have expertise in their own experiences, and therapists, through conversation and interaction, are experts in creating a climate that is conducive to change. Therapy is considered a collaborative partnership and this is represented by a shift in language.

This shift in language moves therapists away from traditional types of conversations that search for underlying pathology, suggest cathartic rituals, or are based on insight and understanding. Instead the medium becomes one of collaborative conversations whereby therapists use language in a respectful way to value and support clients, to open up possibilities for the present and future, to evoke strengths, abilities, and resources, and to create an overall context that is conducive to change. Table 3.4 illustrates how collaborative conversations can be used.

TABLE 3.3 Traditional Conversations

Conversations for Explanations

Searching for evidence of functions for problems

Searching for or encouraging searches for causes and giving or supporting messages about determinism (biological, developmental, psychological)

Focusing or allowing a focus on history as the most relevant part of the client's life

Engaging in conversations for determining diagnosis, categorization, and characterization

Supporting or encouraging conversations for identifying pathology

Conversations for Inability

Conversations for Insight or Understanding

Conversations for Expressions of Emotion

Eliciting adolescent's expressions of feelings and focusing on feelings

Conversations for Blame and Recrimination

Attributions of bad personality or bad intentions

Adversarial Conversations

The therapist believes that clients have hidden agendas that keep them from cooperating with treatment goals and methods

Using trickery or deceit to get the client to change

The therapist is the expert and clients are nonexperts

Collaborative conversations offer clinicians a respectful way of using language to open up possibilities and create change in many areas of clients' lives. It's important to note that although we have emphasized the importance of being collaborative and competency-based in therapy, a person observing such conversations with clients would not notice anything out of the ordinary. As Bill stated in an earlier publication (O'Hanlon & Wilk, 1987):

> A "fly on the wall" who did not know we were doing psychotherapy would not necessarily suspect what we were doing; he would see and hear only an ordinary conversation. What defines the conversation as psychotherapy is simply our goal in conducting the conversation. (p. 177)

Collaborative, competency-based conversations are the threads that weave new client stories. Thus we'll continue to refer to ways of using these conversations in all aspects of therapy. Next we'll discuss how to be collaborative and competency-based in the realm of assessment.

TABLE 3.4 Collaborative Conversations

Conversations for Change
Highlighting changes that have occurred in clients' problem situations
Presuming change will and is happening
Searching for descriptions of differences in the problem situation
Introducing new distinctions or highlighting distinctions with clients
Conversations for Competence
Presuming clients' competence
Searching for contexts of competence away from the problem situation
Eliciting descriptions of exceptions to the problem or times when clients dealt with the problem situation in a way they liked
Conversations for Possibilities
Focusing the conversation on the possibilities for the future
Introducing new possibilities for doing and viewing the problem situation
Conversations for Goals or Results
Focusing on how clients and others will know that they have achieved their therapeutic goals
Conversations for Accountability
Holding clients or others accountable for their actions
Presuming actions derive from clients' intentions
Conversations for Action Descriptions
Channeling the conversation about the problem situation into action descriptions
Changing characterizational or theoretical talk into descriptive words
Focusing on actions clients or others can take that make a difference in the problem situation

Expectation, Influence, and Language: Considerations in Assessment

Throughout the opening chapters of this book we have stressed the importance of language used in therapy. We believe that the role of language in assessment is especially crucial. This is because therapists must contend with their personal and professional biases, expectations, preconceived ideas, and methods. All of these elements will carry influence in therapeutic conversations and interactions. But what are the implications? In this section we will discuss several areas that therapists should consider when conducting assessments of any form. These include the

Pygmalion principle, hardening of the categories, language is a virus, and theory countertransference. Following a discussion of each of these points, we'll describe ways that assessment procedures can be used from a collaborative, competency-based perspective.

The Pygmalion Principle

Through our assessment procedures and therapeutic conversations we influence our clients unconsciously or inadvertently with our expectations. A series of experiments by Robert Rosenthal (1966) and colleagues showed that when experimenters had an idea of what to expect from the experiment, they could influence the results of the experiment without even knowing they were doing so.

Some years ago, one of Rosenthal's students, J. R. Burnham (1966), performed an interesting study of the effects of experimenter expectancy. He had psychology students teach rats how to navigate a maze. Half the rats had portions of their brains surgically removed. The remaining half received identical incisions, but no brain tissue was removed. To outside observers, the rats looked the same.

The experimenters were told that the purpose of the experiment was to learn the effects of brain lesions on learning. Some of the experimenters were told that they had brain-lesioned rats, but were actually given rats with no brain damage at all. Some of the experimenters were told that they had rats with no brain damage, but were actually given rats with brain lesions. Some were told the truth about the actual condition of their rats. These were the results:

1. Rats that were brain damaged did not perform as well as rats that were not damaged.
2. Rats that were *thought* to be lesioned, but that were intact, did not perform as well as rats *thought* to be unlesioned.
3. The lesioned rats that were *thought* to be unlesioned performed somewhat better than the unlesioned rats that were thought to be lesioned.

The second and third findings are of particular interest to us. The actual brain state of the rat had less to do with the outcome than the experimenter's bias about the probable outcome. One can imagine the subtle difference in the ways the experimenters handled the rats and observed the data that might account for the varied performance of the rats in the maze. We are not talking about dishonesty, but about the inevitable influence of expectations on the actions and perceptions of the experimenter on the data. To further illustrate this, we'd like to share a story Bill heard when he was teaching a seminar for the Memphis public schools:

> A particular class of students had become unmanageable. Their teacher, who was nearing retirement, decided she had had enough and took an early retirement rather than spend her last year in a constant battle with the class. Another teacher from the school was brought in and was also quickly defeated by the class. In desperation, the school called a teacher

who had recently finished her student teaching, was just fresh from university, and had applied for a job but hadn't received one. The principal feared that if this new teacher were told the true nature of the class she was getting, she wouldn't accept the job, so he said nothing about the previous problems with the class.

After about a month, his guilt finally got to him and he decided to do a class visit. To his amazement, the class was very well behaved. He stayed after the students left and told the teacher that he was very impressed with the results she had shown with the class. She thanked him for making it so easy by giving her such a great group of kids for her first real teaching job. He asked her what had given her the idea that they were a great group. She smiled and told him that she had discovered his secret on her first day with the class, upon which she opened the desk drawer and pointed to a list for the students in the class followed by numbers from 135 to 170. "I found this list of their IQ scores the first day. I realized that these were gifted children who really needed to be engaged in a challenging way or else they would be bored and troublesome, so I completely changed my teaching plan with them. They responded very well after a few days of rambunctiousness." The principal looked at the list and responded with incredulity, "But those are their locker numbers, not their IQ scores!" No matter. The teacher had already acted on her perceptions and changed the classroom situation for the better.

In social situations, what we expect often influences what we get. Rosenthal (1966) called this the Pygmalion principle, after the Greek myth in which a sculptor made a statue so beautiful that he fell in love with his creation. The gods were so impressed with his art and with his love, they brought his statue to life. In a similar way, we can fall in love with our expectations and bring them to life in front of our eyes.

Suppose you have just received a new referral along with background information such as, "John is resistant to therapy," or "This client is a borderline personality," or, "This is a multiproblem, court-referred family." In what ways do you think that this information might influence your expectation of what is possible (or not possible) in therapy? We suggest that therapists' expectancy biases, whether positive or negative, will influence the course and outcome of therapy.

Hardening of the Categories: Delusions of Certainty

A physicist named Werner Heisenberg pointed out some years ago that it is impossible for physicists to make precise observations on the subatomic level without disturbing the data they wish to study. It is like having a very large-handed man try to move the furniture around in a tiny dollhouse. Things that are not intended to be affected are. The very act of observation changes the thing that is observed. This has come to be called the Heisenberg Uncertainty Principle in physics. Although there are different observational tools and assessment procedures used in therapy, therapists cannot help but influence the data being observed.

Unfortunately, many therapists have what we call *delusions of certainty* or *hardening of the categories*. They believe that the observations they make during the assessment process are real and objective. They are certain they have discovered real problems.

There was a time not too long ago when there were no bulimics and no borderline personalities. These are relatively recent discoveries. Yet therapists who have been in the field a relatively short time find this hard to believe. To them, the diagnoses are real and seem to have always existed. Such diagnoses are linguistic constructions and are subject to change as our language and ideas change. Therapists now and therapists of the future will probably be using an entirely different set of distinctions and diagnoses.

Language Is a Virus: Linguistic Epidemics

There are certain to be other psychiatric disorders that are discovered or invented in the future. Why aren't we noticing them now? It's because we haven't yet distinguished them in language. We notice things as *things* by distinguishing them in language. Did the pioneers crossing the plains of America suffer from stress? They may have, but they never felt the need to see a therapist about it. They didn't really know what they were experiencing because stress hadn't been invented yet. The same holds for low self-esteem. Cavemen probably didn't work on their self-esteem because it hadn't been thought of yet.

Problems do not exist in a vacuum. They exist only in a context—a linguistic, social, cultural context. In therapy, we must acknowledge the therapist as part of the problem context. Therapists help create problems by the way they carry out therapeutic conversations and endeavors, by the language they use, and the assumptions they make (O'Hanlon & Wilk, 1987).

Why can't we diagnose problems without influencing them in some way? Because we live in an atmosphere of language, which steers our thinking, experience, and behavior in certain directions.

Seeing Is Believing: Pygmalion on the Couch

We maintain that there are no such things as therapy problems. We think therapists, for the most part, give their clients problems. That is, therapists negotiate problem definitions out of the raw material of clients' concerns by conversing with clients. They either come up with a problem definition that is agreeable to both client and therapist or they try to convince the client that he or she has a certain type of problem.

It seems to be more than a coincidence that when clients have seen a Gestalt therapist for more than a few sessions they usually have Gestalt-type problems and start to use Gestalt jargon. Likewise, psychodynamic therapies engender psychodynamic-type problems. Behavior therapists always seem to identify and treat behavioral problems, neurologists usually find neurological problems, and biological psychiatrists almost always discover biochemical imbalances and disorders.

Clients do not usually determine which theory will work best for them and then seek out a practitioner who subscribes to that theory. They come in to the therapy situation complaining about or concerned about something, and the therapist helps shape those complaints and concerns into a therapy problem. They find a problem that therapy can solve. Further, some problem is found that this particular therapist with this particular approach knows how to solve.

Therapists advertently or inadvertently influence the problem descriptions clients give them. Therapists usually only allow descriptions of problems that fit their theories, that they know how to cope with, make sense of, or solve. They subsequently filter out other potentially useful ways of construing the situation.

Psychiatrist Jerome Kroll (1988) discussed the political and rather arbitrary nature of psychiatric diagnosis, especially the diagnosis of borderline personality. He wrote:

> If we want to describe a horse or a tree, it might be easiest to walk to a field and point to a horse or a tree. If you want to describe a borderline person, we first have to decide what one is; then, based upon what we have already decided to look for, we could then go out and find one.... We tend to reify our concepts, to think we have discovered real entities in nature and real discontinuities between normal and abnormal. (p. xi, p. 3)

So, by combining the Heisenberg Uncertainty Principle with the Pygmalion effect, we come to the idea that there is no way to discover what the real problem is in any therapeutic situation. The therapist influences the data and the description in directions that are biased toward his or her theoretical models. We refer to this as *theory countertransference* (Hubble & O'Hanlon, 1992). Let's explore this further.

Theory Countertransference

Inherent to assessment procedures and therapeutic methods are ideas that can close down pathways to possibilities. Although traditions are important in all human pursuits, they can also inhibit change and even have damaging consequences (Duncan, Hubble, & Miller, 1997). Theory countertransference represents clinicians' loyalties to theoretical constructs. In an earlier publication, Bill and a colleague (Hubble & O'Hanlon, 1992) wrote:

> Lacking from the discussion of countertransference in the psychoanalytic literature has been much examination of the ways in which the therapist's "theory" influences the work. While it was widely accepted that the person of the psychoanalyst ...could be facilitative or disruptive, less attention was paid to how the clinician's overall conception of the human condition and therapy would affect treatment outcomes. (pp. 25–27)

Countertranference is a largely unconscious emotional process that takes place in the therapist and is triggered in relationship to the client and intrudes into the treatment. We suggest that a similar process of projection takes place in the theoretical realm, with the therapist unconsciously intruding on the client with his or her theoretical biases and unrecognized assumptions.

It's important that therapists are aware of how their theoretical constructs influence the content, process, and direction of therapy. Truly, therapists will have ideas, thoughts, and theories. The same is true with clients, outside helpers, and so on. Clients' points of view must be acknowledged from the start of therapy and throughout the process or the situation can close down quickly. The premise here is to remain in a collaborative relationship where clients' theories are honored.

Exploring Possibilities: Assessment as Intervention

Most approaches to therapy make use of assessment procedures in one form or another. Some of the more common uses of assessment are as a way of assessing mental status, identifying intrapsychic pathology and interpersonal problems including patterns of familial dysfunction, determining diagnosis, establishing goals, and treatment planning. All of the aforementioned procedures and methods of gaining and assessing information are communicated to clients through therapists' comments and questions. As discussed, language is of central importance.

It is important to note that whether we are attending and listening to clients' stories, utilizing assessment procedures, setting goals, or exploring potential areas of change, we prefer to use the term *conversation* versus *interviewing*. The term interviewing implies a one-sided relationship with the therapist doing something to the client. The term conversation, however, suggests a collaborative relationship. Even though we will be discussing assessment procedures, we remain collaborative in all phases of assessment and adjoining processes.

From a collaborative, competency-based perspective, assessment takes on two forms:

1. Formal assessment involves attention to both the difficulties that people experience, as well as their competencies. Most assessment instruments maintain a problem or pathology focus. Collaborative, competency-based clinicians attend to the difficulties that people face and also explore competencies such as abilities, strengths, and resources that may be of assistance is resolving concerns and complaints. In recent years, therapists have created innovative ways of using assessment in more competency-based ways (Berg, 1994; Bertolino, 1999; Bertolino & Thompson, 1999; Durrant, 1993, 1995; O'Hanlon, 1996, Selekman, 1997)
2. Ongoing assessment begins with the first session and ends with the termination of therapy. From the opening moments of treatment, therapists attend to the therapeutic relationship, listen to clients' stories, and begin to learn clients' theories of change. They also begin to use language in a way that opens up possibilities. In addition, therapists begin to work with clients to learn their conversational and relational preferences, concerns, and problems, and

ways of establishing and determining progress toward goals and preferred outcomes. In this way, assessment is ongoing and continues throughout therapy, as goals are met, modified, and changed. People and their concerns are not static. Assessment should be flexible in meeting the needs of clients at all points of therapy.

First we'll discuss formal assessment. In the next chapter, we'll discuss ongoing assessment.

Formal Assessment: Identifying Pathways with Possibilities

Most formal assessment procedures are designed to discover or uncover clients' problems. The emphasis is on identifying deficits and pathologies that are defined by the clinician and assessment tool being utilized. We believe differently. We view formal assessment as a way of:

- Facilitating the therapeutic relationship and alliance
- Building on or creating hope for the future
- Allowing clients to tell their stories
- Learning clients' ways of using language
- Making small changes in clients' statements that reflect impossibility
- Learning about clients' concerns and complaints
- Eliciting and evoking clients' strengths, abilities, and resources
- Learning clients' theories of change

All of these ways of utilizing assessment do two things. They enhance the client–therapist relationship and provide a way of intervening and facilitating change from the beginning of treatment. In our estimation, assessments that are predominately problem-focused or pathology-oriented are typically only attending to what's wrong and are not attending to possibilities and potential solutions. We concur with Vaughn, Cox, Young, Webster, and Thomas (1996) who stated:

> We believe that an exclusive focus on pathology, deficits, and risk factors without evaluation and documentation of strengths, resources, and mitigating factors can put both the client and institution at risk for unnecessary hospitalizations, increased length of stay, and ineffective treatment. We therefore gather assessment data concerning the problem, but we maintain a balance between history, strengths, exceptions, and the *client's* goals. (p. 107)

In our experience, assessment procedures that focus primarily on pathology and problems tend to promote two things. First, clients can feel further invalidated and blamed. Next, problems can become reified in the eyes of clients and therapists. The more clients talk about their problems, and the more therapists emphasize what's wrong through questions, both become subject to the idea that things are actually worse than they first imagined. To counter this, we recommend more of a balance between problem- or pathology-based questions and possibility-oriented questions. In addition, should a particular setting require the use of formal or standardized assessment tools or procedures, we recommend that the therapist let the client know that every client goes through the same or similar procedure. This can normalize the process.

We also find it important to talk with clients about the purpose of the assessment. Here are two ways of doing this:

> If it's okay with you, I'd like to ask you some questions that we ask of all people who come to see us. The information you give will help us understand what you're concerned about and how that has affected you, what you'd like to see change, what has worked and hasn't worked for you in trying to manage your concerns, and how we can be of help to you. And as we proceed, if you feel like or think we've missed something please be sure to let us know. We want to make sure that we fully understand your needs. How does that sound?

> There are some questions that I'd like to ask you that we ask of everyone who comes here. These questions will help me to understand what's happening with you or in your life that's of concern. Once we get finished with those questions, we'll move on to some others that will tell me more about what you do well and what has or might work for you in the future regarding your concerns. How does that sound? (Bertolino, 1999)

Even though traditional assessment procedures tend to focus almost exclusively on problems and pathology, we've found that such tools are amenable to competency-based questions. They allow room for therapists to ask questions that elicit client strengths, abilities, and resources, therefore introducing some balance to the assessment.

For example, a therapist working this way might focus on the complaint and say, "Tell me more about the trouble that you've experienced with your coworker." The therapist might then explore another aspect of the dynamic and say, "Tell me a little bit about a relationship that you have or had with another employee that went a little better" or "What kinds of people do you tend to relate to better?" Rather than focusing solely on trouble in the work environment or problems with relating to others we are able to learn the differences in work and other relationships for the client. This way, we learn that the client has experienced both difficulty and success in work (and perhaps other) relationships.

As discussed earlier in this book, people's problems tend to be in a state of flux. They vacillate on a continuum between things not working and working. We want to know both sides and consider the gray area in between. We can then learn about both the influence the problem has had over the person and the influence the person has had over the problem. We're drawn to the possibilities that formal assessments can bring to light as opposed to the sense of impossibility that often accompanies traditional instruments, tools, and procedures.

To further illustrate this idea of focusing on competency and possibilities, we'd like to share a story that Bill was told by Milton Erickson when he studied with the psychiatrist in the 1970s (see also Gordon & Meyers-Anderson, 1981; Zeig, 1980):

> An aunt of one of Dr. Erickson's clients was living in Milwaukee and had become seriously depressed. The colleague was worried that his aunt might even be suicidal. He asked Dr. Erickson if he would stop in and see her, as he would be in the area doing a lecture. Dr. Erickson agreed.
>
> The woman was secure financially because she had inherited a fortune from her family. She lived alone in a mansion, had never married, and had lost most of her close friends and relatives. Now in her sixties, she had developed some medical problems that required her to use a wheelchair. This had significantly altered her social activities.
>
> Dr. Erickson arrived at the woman's home following his lecture. She was expecting him because her nephew had told her that he was coming. On his arrival, the two met and she began to give him a tour of her home. Although the woman had had some changes made to her home to make it more wheelchair accessible, it appeared to be largely unchanged from its original 1890s structure and décor. The house showed faded glory and the scent of must. Dr. Erickson was struck by the fact that the curtains were drawn, contributing to an overall feeling of darkness. It was as if the majestic old home was a place of depression instead of happiness.
>
> The woman saved the best part of the tour for last. She finished by showing Dr. Erickson her pride and joy—a greenhouse nursery that was attached to the house. It was in this greenhouse that the woman had spent many tireless, happy hours working with her plants. As the two admired the flowers and plants, she showed Dr. Erickson her most recent project, which was to take clippings of African violet plants and grow new plants from them.
>
> Following the tour, the two continued to speak with one another. Dr. Erickson learned from the woman that although she was very isolated, at one time she was quite active in her local church. But since being confined to a wheelchair she only attended Sunday services. The woman described how she had hired her handyman to take her to and from church and because the church was not wheelchair accessible, he would lift her in and out of the building. Worried about blocking foot traffic, the woman told Dr. Erickson that she would arrive late and leave early.
>
> After hearing the woman's story, Dr. Erickson told her that her nephew was worried about how depressed she had become. She admitted that the situation had become quite serious. Dr. Erickson told the woman that he did not think that depression was the problem. Instead, what had become clear to him was that she had not been being a very good Christian. The woman was immediately taken aback by this comment, aghast that he would say such a thing.

> Dr. Erickson continued, "Here you are with all this money, time on your hands, and a green thumb. And it's all going to waste. What I recommend is that you get a copy of the church directory and look in the latest church bulletin. You'll find announcements of births, deaths, graduations, engagements, and marriages in there—all the happy and sad events in the lives of people in your congregation. Make a number of African violet cuttings and get them well established. Then repot them into gift pots and have your handyman drive you to the homes of people who are affected by these happy or sad events. Bring them a plant and your congratulations or condolences and comfort, whichever is appropriate to the situation. After hearing Dr. Erickson's recommendation, she agreed that perhaps she had fallen down on her Christian duty and agreed to do more.
>
> About ten years later an article appeared in a local Milwaukee newspaper. It was a feature story with a headline that read, "African Violet Queen of Milwaukee Dies, Mourned by Thousands." The article detailed the life of this incredibly caring woman who had become famous for her trademark flowers and her charitable work with people in the community.
>
> When Bill asked Dr. Erickson why he had chosen to focus on the African violet plants as opposed to the depression, he replied, "As I walked through the house the only sign of life I saw was the African violet plants and the nursery. I thought it would be much easier to grow the African violet part of her life than to weed out the depression."

In every therapeutic encounter there are multiple ways of looking at things. We want to recognize the limitations that people may face and simultaneously search for openings with possibilities. Even when the information being obtained from assessment seems very problematic, we search for exceptions or times when things went differently in regard to the problem (de Shazer, 1988, 1991; O'Hanlon & Weiner-Davis, 1989). Exception-oriented questions ask for information about times when the concern or problem is less dominating, occurs less frequently, or is absent altogether. We also ask about what the person did differently in such instances. Not only can information about exceptions and differences serve as a way of intervening in the present, but it can also serve as building blocks for future change.

In the midst of learning about the influence of the problem in the person's life, there are many general questions and inquiries that therapists can make at the start of assessment to begin to understand the influence of the person over the problem. Here are some examples:

- It seems that when the concern that brought you in is happening, things are pretty difficult. When does the concern seem a little less noticeable to you?
- Tell me about a time recently when things went a little bit better for you in regard to the concern that brought you in.
- How did that happen?

- What did you do differently?
- What's different about those times?
- What's different about the times when you're able to get more of an upper hand with the problem?
- What persons, places, or things were helpful to you?
- How will you know when things are better? What will be different in your life?

Notice that the questions offered do not inquire about extremes. We're not asking, "When don't you have the problem?" That's too big a leap for most clients. It's important that we let clients know that we understand their pain and suffering and give ample time to their concerns. In turn, we use questions that elicit small differences. This can be enough to get things moving in the direction of positive change.

With formal assessments, there are often distinct areas that garner attention. These tend to include, but are not limited to, employment, school, family and social relationships, hobbies and interests, and previous treatment experiences. In addition to gathering information about concerns, each of these areas hold opportunities to inquire about strengths, abilities, and resources as well as exceptions and differences. Here are some questions that can assist therapists in each of these areas:

Employment

- How did you come to work at your current place of employment?
- How did you get yourself into position to get the job?
- What do you think your employer saw in you that might have contributed to your being hired?
- What have you found to be most challenging or difficult about your job?
- How have you met or worked toward meeting those challenges and difficulties?
- What keeps you there?
- What skills or qualities do you think your employer sees in you?
- What qualities do you think you possess that are assets on the job?
- (If self-employed) How did you have the means to start your own business?
- (If unemployed) What kind of employment would you like to see yourself involved with in the future?
- What would be a first step for you in making that happen?

School

- How did you manage to make it through ______ (9th grade, high school, trade school, junior college, a four-year university, two years of college, graduate school, etc.)?
- What qualities do you possess that made that happen?
- What did you like best about school?
- What did you find most challenging about school?
- How did you manage any difficulties that you many have encountered while in school? (e.g., completing homework assignments, tests, getting to school

on time, moving from one grade to another, teacher/classmate relationships, sports)

- In what ways did school prepare you for future challenges?

Family and Social Relationships

- Who are you closest to in your ______ (life, family, etc.)?
- What do you appreciate most about your relationship with ______?
- What would (he, she, they) say are your best qualities as a ______ (friend, spouse, parent, child, grandparent, colleague, etc.?
- How is that helpful for you to know that?
- What does it feel like to know that?
- Which relationships have been more challenging for you?
- How have you dealt with those challenges?
- Whom can you go to for help?
- Who has made a positive difference in your life?
- How so?
- What difference has that made for you?
- When are others most helpful to you?

Hobbies and Interests

- What do you do for fun?
- What hobbies or interests do you have or have you had in the past?
- What kinds of activities are you drawn to?
- What kinds of activities would you rather not be involved with?
- What would you rather do instead?

Previous Treatment Experiences

- What did you find helpful about previous therapy ______ (individual, couples, family, group, etc.)?
- What did the therapist do that was helpful?
- How did that make a difference for you?
- What wasn't so helpful?
- (If currently or previously on psychotropic medication) How was the medication helpful to you?
- What, if anything, did the medication allow you to do that you wouldn't have otherwise been able to do?
- What qualities do you possess such that you were able to work with the medication to improve things for yourself?

Formal assessment can help therapists to learn from clients what's worked in the past (to any degree) and what might work in the future. We then look to apply or replicate what's worked in the past in the present and the future. We also find it particularly important to find out what hasn't worked. For example, if a client has been in therapy before but did not find it helpful, we want to know what was unhelpful so that we do not replicate that aspect of therapy in our work with the client. Case Example 3.1 illustrates this point.

Case Example 3.1 *Is That in a Book?*

A father, mother, and stepmother came to see Bob because their sixteen-year-old daughter had been staying out after curfew, drinking, smoking marijuana, and failing two classes in school. The daughter did not accompany the parents during the initial session as they said she refused to attend. Curious, Bob inquired as to why the daughter had refused. The father replied, "She won't really say. But I think it's because we were in therapy before with another guy and it didn't go too well." At the end of the session, all three parents expressed their desire to have the daughter attend. Bob suggested that they ask her once more, letting her know that her views were very important.

At the next session, to Bob's surprise, the daughter was in attendance. Over the next three months, Bob met with the daughter and her parents six more times. The situation had improved considerably, and during the last session Bob said to the teenager, "I had heard that you wouldn't come to see another therapist because you had a bad experience. I don't know if that's accurate or not, but I wanted to thank you for coming in and sticking it out." To this, the young woman replied, "This was much different than I expected. You acted like a real person. I think that other guy only knew two questions. He kept asking me about things 'on a scale of one to ten' and the other one was,'If a miracle happened what would your life be like?' I was, like, is that a question in a book or something? Everything was about miracles or on a scale of one to ten. I hated that."

Fortunately, Bob did not ask any scaling questions or the miracle question. Had he, it's likely that the client would have felt invalidated, as if she were treated the same by all therapists, or a host of other things. This could have negatively impacted the therapy in a variety of ways. It's important to ask about both sides when using assessment procedures, what worked and what did not.

Another area to explore that can be especially helpful during assessment is pretreatment change (Weiner-Davis, de Shazer, & Gingerich, 1987). To inquire about pretreatment change, the therapist asks: "Many times, people notice in between the time they make the appointment for therapy and the first session that things already seem different. What have you noticed about your situation?" (p. 360). Studies have indicated that 60–65 percent of clients experience some form of positive pretreatment change (Lawson, 1994; McKeel & Weiner-Davis, 1995; Weiner-Davis, de Shazer, & Gingerich, 1987). Case Example 3.2 illustrates this idea.

Case Example 3.2 *Change Happens*

Phillip had been in trouble at school on a regular basis. With the school year in its final quarter, he had not gone for an entire week without having to be sent to the principal's office for disrupting the class. The school recommended that he see a therapist. Phillip was informed that he would be seeing a therapist a week later. During the week leading up to the appointment he did not get into trouble at school. His mother called the therapist and said, "I'm not sure if I should bring him or not. I mean, Phillip hasn't been in any trouble all week and he hasn't done that all year."

For some people, just scheduling an appointment will set positive change in motion. By inquiring about pretreatment change, therapists can elicit, evoke, and amplify what clients have already done in the direction of positive change. We'll revisit this idea again in Chapter 6.

Formal assessment procedures are often viewed solely as a means of uncovering and discovering deficiencies and deviancies with clients and their lives. However, as we've learned, they can assist with learning about clients' abilities, strengths, and resources, and in searching for exceptions and differences. Although not everyone will use formal assessment, it can be a way to facilitate the therapeutic relationship and move toward clarifying what clients want from therapy. In the next chapter we'll discuss ongoing assessment, to help further clarify clients' preferences, goals, and preferred outcomes.

Summary Points for Chapter Three

- ♦ The effects of psychiatric diagnosis can be positive or negative for clients. What is most important is that clients are invited into conversations where they can understand the implications of diagnoses and determine what is best for them.
- ♦ While traditional therapeutic conversations emphasize what's wrong, including clients' inabilities and deficits, collaborative conversations invite clients into conversations for change, competence, goals, accountability, and action descriptions.
- ♦ Inherent to assessment procedures are therapists' biases and expectations that are communicated through language and can influence therapy processes.
- ♦ Collaborative, competency-based therapy incorporates two forms of assessment:
  1. Ongoing assessment that coincides with the start of therapy and continues throughout as established goals and preferences are met, modified, and changed. (This will be discussed in Chapter 4.)
  2. Formal assessment is an opportunity to learn both about clients' concerns as well as exceptions and differences in regard to the problem concern. This includes an exploration of abilities, strengths, and resources.
- ♦ Formal assessment procedures provide therapists with ways of:
  - Facilitating the therapeutic relationship and alliance
  - Building on or creating hope for the future
  - Allowing clients to tell their stories
  - Learning clients' ways of using language
  - Making small changes in clients' statements that reflect impossibility
  - Learning about clients' concerns and complaints
  - Eliciting and evoking clients' strengths, abilities, and resources
  - Learning clients' theories of change

CHAPTER

4 Creating and Clarifying Preferences, Goals, and Preferred Outcomes

As discussed in the previous chapter, from a collaborative, competency-based perspective, there are two ways of conceptualizing assessment. The first involves formal procedures, typically conducted during initial sessions. Yet while the use of traditional assessment instruments is commonplace in mental health settings, not every therapist will be interested in or required to make use of formalized procedures. Further, although formal assessment is a pathway to learning about clients, including their concerns and competencies, it tends to be a one-time affair. In our view, if formal assessment procedures are used at the start of treatment they should be extended throughout therapy. Therefore, in this chapter we'll discuss how ongoing assessment is used as an intervention, and how it can be used with or without formal assessment procedures.

Before we explore ongoing assessment, let's briefly review what we've covered to this point. In previous chapters we discussed the following processes that accompany the start of therapy:

- *Invite clients into collaborative relationships prior to the start of therapy.* We learn from clients what their ideas and beliefs are about who should attend therapy and how they should meet. These can be early indicators of clients' theories of change. In addition, we strive to be outcome-informed. We check in on clients periodically to see what is working for them and what is not. Based on this information, we can make changes to help clients to achieve the outcomes they desire.
- *Listen and attend to clients' stories.* We invite clients to tell their stories, which reflect their points of view, including ideas, beliefs, assumptions, explanations, evaluations, and interpretations. We also acknowledge and validate clients' views. Recall what Carl Rogers taught us about unconditional positive regard—we don't have to agree with clients or share their ways of seeing the world, we merely acknowledge and validate their internal experiences and views. It is important that we don't intervene or claim to understand before they get a chance to tell the story in their own way.

- *Begin to create small, subtle changes in clients' language to open up possibilities for change.* As we listen to clients' stories, we adapt to their style of using language. We also listen for words, phrases, and statements that suggest impossibility. By making subtle language changes we can help clients feel heard and understood, and suggest that positive change is possible.
- *Formal assessment involves attention to both the difficulties that people experience, as well as their competencies.* Formal assessment procedures help therapists learn about clients' strengths, abilities, and resources. In addition, assessment allows therapists to further build the therapeutic alliance, and learn clients' theories of change.

The first three processes help therapists work with clients to establish collaborative relationships. The fourth process allows therapists to gather more information about clients' concerns and competencies. Let's now explore the role of ongoing assessment.

Ongoing Assessment: Becoming Client and Outcome-Informed

Formal assessment procedures tend to have distinct beginnings and endings. Ongoing assessment, however, occurs from moment to moment, from the first session and through the last. Ongoing assessment is a collaborative process between therapists and clients. This way the process of therapy remains flexible, with modifications and changes being made based on clients': (1) conversational and relational preferences, (2) concerns and complaints, (3) goals and preferred outcomes, and (4) progress toward goals and preferred outcomes.

Conversational and relational preferences refer to clients' preferences about what is discussed in therapy, as well as their expectations regarding the role of therapists in the therapeutic relationship. Concerns and complaints relate to what brought clients to therapy and what is posing difficulty for them. Goals and preferred outcomes refer to what clients want to change about their lives and the expectations they have for the future as a result of attaining their goals. Last, progress toward preferred outcomes relates to learning from clients how they will know that progress is being made in the direction of established goals.

While we will refer to these aspects of ongoing assessment in a somewhat sequential manner, we do not view therapy as a step-by-step process. It's generally easier to teach ideas in a sequential fashion, but that's not how we conceptualize treatment. Instead, we consider ongoing assessment as a process that is consistent with the flow that occurs in therapy sessions. In other words, therapists need to be flexible with their procedures and accommodate clients' conversational preferences and views of therapy processes. Also, therapy is often more messy and richly complex than sequential descriptions of it.

Each therapist will use ongoing assessment in a way that is respectful of individual clients' theories and conversational processes. This allows space for clients to speak about what they are comfortable with and introduce some sense of structure or direction. This is essential because research has indicated that one of the best predictors of negative outcome is a lack of focus and structure (Mohl, 1995; Sachs, 1983). Being goal- and outcome-oriented enables us to learn whether treatment is helpful from the perspective of the client. The ideas outlined here serve as a guide for learning from clients what they want to see different in their lives and for knowing when they've achieved those changes, with clients' and their theories being the compasses that guide therapy.

Orienting to Client Conversational and Relational Preferences

For therapists, treatment involves a series of choices. What should we attend to? What should we focus on? What questions should we ask? At any moment during the twists and turns of therapy sessions clinicians must make decisions. Yet as stated throughout, what we are most interested in are clients' preferred directions and ideas about change. Further, clients have preferences about the therapeutic relationship that are reflected in conversation. They have expectations about the positions that therapists take. Even though we have our own preferences and biases, we want to be sure that we are working in ways that clients see as helpful and effective. This means checking with clients about their conversational preferences to find if we are having the kinds of conversations that they feel are important and helpful.

By asking clients about their views of therapeutic conversations and relationships, we can learn and do more of what is working for them, change what is not, and make any other necessary adjustments. This way we are being client- and outcome-informed. Here are some questions to consider asking clients that can assist learning about their conversational and relational preferences:

- What ideas do you have about how I can help you?
- In what ways do you see me helping you reach your goals?
- Are there certain things that you want to be sure that we talk about?
- Do you feel we're talking about what you want to talk about?
- Are we moving in a direction that seems right for you?
- How has this conversation been helpful?
- What have I been doing that has been helpful or unhelpful to you?
- Are there other things that you think we should discuss instead?
- Is there anything I should be doing differently?

If clients indicate that they need something different from our conversations and relational postures, then we adjust to meet their needs. We want to make sure we are having the types of conversations that clients prefer. We also want to be sure we are relating to them in ways that they deem helpful. While we are focusing on learning and adapting to clients' conversational preferences early on, we should note that questions such as the ones above can be used at any point during the process of therapy.

Orienting toward Client Concerns and Complaints through Action-Talk and Videotalk

As stated earlier, therapy involves a series of choices and decision-making efforts on the part of therapists. Clients will say many enticing things during our conversations with them, but therapists must not jump to any conclusions. It is easy for therapists to presume that they know what clients' real problems are. Therapists can avoid this by focusing on clients' perspectives as opposed to their own. Clients are the single most important factor in the therapeutic milieu. They define problems, and they ultimately decide what will change in their lives. To get an idea of what clients are most concerned with and what they want to change, we can ask questions such as:

- What is most concerning you at this point?
- What would you like to change in your life?
- What would you like to be different in your life?
- What goals do you have for yourself?
- What did you (hope/wish/think) would be different as a result of coming to treatment?
- What would have to be minimally different in your life to consider our work together a success?

Ironically, some therapists who claim to be working in collaborative competency-based ways do not leave space for or ask about clients' concerns and problems. Instead of learning about clients' pain and suffering, some therapists will direct clients toward immediate positive change and solutions. We find it important to let clients share what they feel comfortable sharing—including their concerns and complaints. We warn therapists about being afraid of engaging in problem talk. We see this as disrespectful of clients and their experiences. When therapists' views are privileged and their approaches are inflexible and too directive, clients' voices and preferences are left out. We invite clients to respond to our questions in whatever way feels right for them.

In our experience, clients generally respond to the questions listed in one of two ways. First, they will begin to describe what they want or what they don't want. What they don't want represents their concerns and problems. What they do want represents their goals. When asked questions such as the ones previously listed, clients often respond with statements such as, "I want to be happy," "I just want some peace," "I have anxiety," "I don't want to be depressed," or "I don't want him to be so impulsive." The concern with such statements is that they are vague. They do not clearly depict what clients want or are concerned about.

When therapists are presented with vague words they are at risk for projecting their beliefs, biases, and theoretical opinions onto the client, assuming they know what the client means. Additionally, vague descriptions can lead to the use of misguided interventions.

For example, imagine a client tells you that he or she is suffering from stress. If you do not take time to find out what the client means by that word, you are in danger of checking in with your own experience of stress and working on that definition. That might be good treatment for you, but may or may not be helpful to this particular client. If therapists base their interventions on vague descriptions, the solutions and possibilities they employ may not fit with clients' views on how to resolve the problem. To avoid this we try to establish clear descriptions of clients' goals and concerns. Let's explore how to do this.

Gaining Clarity through Action-Talk

The clearer therapists are on clients' specific complaints, concerns, and goals, the clearer their attempts at problem resolution will be. Therefore, we strive to move clients from nondescriptive concerns toward clear preferences and outcomes. To do this we use *action-talk* (Bertolino, 1999; O'Hanlon & Bertolino, 1998). Although we'll refer to a variety of ways that therapists can use action-talk, here it involves determining how clients act on their problem concerns, and what they will be doing when they have reached their goals.

To use action-talk, therapists ask clients to describe their concerns by using behavioral, action-based language. This way therapists can get clear views of what exactly clients are *doing* when their problems are interfering with their lives. Case Example 4.1 is a brief illustration of this.

Case Example 4.1 *My Daughter Is Out of Control!*

CLIENT: My daughter is out of control.

THERAPIST: Okay. What has your daughter done that has indicated to you that she's out of control?

CLIENT: She throws tantrums.

THERAPIST: So if I were to see her throwing a tantrum, what would I see her doing?

CLIENT: She'd be kicking and hitting and throwing things.

THERAPIST: I see. Would she be kicking and hitting anyone who was around?

CLIENT: No, just me.

THERAPIST: Mm hmm. So if I were around she wouldn't kick or hit me?

CLIENT: Nope. She only takes it out on me.

THERAPIST: So does she mostly have tantrums around you?

CLIENT: She only has tantrums around me. I mean, someone else might be around, but she wouldn't do it if I weren't there. It's like she saves them up just for me!

THERAPIST: I can see why it would seem that way. And you mentioned that she throws things? What does she throw when she's having a tantrum?

CLIENT: Anything she can get her hands on.

THERAPIST: Mm hmm. Got it. So she'd be kicking and hitting you, and throwing just about anything she could get her hands on. Is there anything else she might be doing if I were to see her throwing a tantrum?

CLIENT: I think that's it.

The mother's description of her daughter as "out of control" is vague and can lead to misunderstanding between the client and therapist, misguided interventions, unclear outcomes, and so on. The therapist uses action-talk to learn from the mother what her daughter has done to indicate that she's out of control. What happens? The mother responds with another vague description—that her daughter throws tantrums. So the therapist continues with action-talk to find out what the daughter does when she has tantrums.

Through further inquiry, the mother teaches the therapist that there are very specific behaviors that indicate to her that her daughter is throwing a tantrum. In turn, the problem becomes one of hitting, kicking, and throwing things, as opposed to being out of control or throwing tantrums. In our experience, therapists are much more effective when they work with clients to change a clearly defined problem, as opposed to working with clients to change a vague label.

These conversations can also offer information that may be helpful with future intervention. For example, the mother related that her daughter only has tantrums when she is around. She also said that even if others are around, she only hits her mother. So after just a few moments of conversation, we learn that there are times and situations when the unwanted behaviors do and do not occur. Therefore, there are at least two possible areas for creating positive change.

When clients describe what they do not want, it's important to respect and follow their conversational processes. In turn, we view such conversations as an invitation to learn about their perspectives and problem descriptions, as well as their patterns of action and interaction associated with those problems or concerns. This can provide possible future areas of intervention, and help therapists learn more about clients' personal theories.

Case Example 4.2 also illustrates how to use action-talk to learn about clients' concerns.

Case Example 4.2 *I Need to Get Over My Divorce*

THERAPIST: It seems that you've got a lot on your mind. I'd like to ask, what concerns you most at this point?

CLIENT: I really want to get over my divorce.

THERAPIST: Okay. What do you mean by "get over your divorce"?

CLIENT: Well, I'm not really sure. I guess things just aren't going well for me.

THERAPIST: I see. You say that things haven't been going well for you. What specifically has been happening?

CLIENT: Well, I'm always feeling anxious. I mean ... I used to go out a lot, now I don't. My friend says I need to just move on.

THERAPIST: Uh huh. So you haven't been going out like you used to. That's part of it. And when you're feeling anxious, what else happens?

CLIENT: Well, I ruminate a lot. I think about everything I've done wrong—my past decisions. I just dwell on things.

THERAPIST: So when you ruminate you tend to think a lot about your past decisions and dwell on what you think you've done wrong ...

CLIENT: Yeah, and I also have trouble sleeping.

THERAPIST: Mm hmm, trouble sleeping. Tell me more about that.

CLIENT: I can't get to sleep because I keep dwelling on things.

THERAPIST: So it's trouble getting to sleep. And when you finally do get to sleep do you stay asleep?

CLIENT: Yeah. Once I fall asleep I stay asleep, but it takes three or four hours to get there. Then it's two or three in the morning and I have to get up at 5:30. I feel hungover at work and can't concentrate on what I need to do.

THERAPIST: I see. So not getting to sleep early enough really affects your work and how you feel the next day.

CLIENT: Right.

THERAPIST: Are there other things that you do, or don't do, when you feel anxious?

CLIENT: It's really just those things.

THERAPIST: Okay. So if I were to see you being anxious I'd see you staying at home and not going out, thinking about decisions you've made in the past, and not getting to sleep on time. Is that right?

CLIENT: Exactly.

In this case example, the client used many vague words and statements such as, "I want to get over my divorce," and "I guess things just aren't going well for me," "I'm always feeling anxious," and "I ruminate a lot." The problem with these statements is that they are vague. It remains unknown what exactly the client is doing that is a problem. Therefore it is important that the therapist get a clear description from the client. By attending to problem descriptions, therapists can begin to learn what it is that clients want instead.

Vague statements also tend to activate therapists' personal and theoretical views and guide treatment in ways that may be unhelpful to clients. For example, just by hearing the word *anxious*, some will immediately begin to ask questions about anxiety-provoking situations and consider an anxiety disorder. Others will hear *ruminate* and orient toward cognitions and a possible thought disorder. Still others will be drawn to the term *divorce* and begin to explore relational difficulties. The problem is, these are therapists' ideas about what to focus on and ask questions about, not clients'. As discussed earlier, it is important to check with clients to see if the conversations that are taking place are helpful to them and are in line with what they want.

Using Videotalk

Another method for gaining a clear action-based description is to use *videotalk* (Bertolino, 1999; Hudson & O'Hanlon, 1991; O'Hanlon & Bertolino, 1998; O'Hanlon & Wilk, 1987). Videotalk involves getting clients (and others who may be involved) to describe the problem or goal as if it can be seen or heard on videotape. This again involves the use of action-talk. To use videotalk we ask, "If I were to videotape you being ______, what would I see you doing on the videotape that would indicate to me that you were ______?" Case Example 4.3 shows one way to do this.

Case Example 4.3 *I Have a Fear of Failure*

CLIENT: The main thing for me is to get over my fear of failure, but that's easier said than done. I don't want to be scared of not doing things well.

THERAPIST: Mm hmm. Tell me more about your fear of failure.

CLIENT: Well, I keep finding myself going into situations and thinking the worst. Like everything is going to go bad.

THERAPIST: So you've found yourself in situations where you've thought that the worst was going to happen.

CLIENT: Right.

THERAPIST: So, if we were to catch you, on videotape, going into a situation where you were thinking the worst and fearing failure, what would I see happening on that tape?

CLIENT: I'd be pacing around a lot... and probably not doing my work, because I'd be obsessing about what might happen.

THERAPIST: Mm hmm, you would be pacing. And one of the ways that an outsider like myself would know that you were obsessing would be because you wouldn't be doing your work. Is that right?

CLIENT: Yes.

THERAPIST: Is there anything else that you would be doing that might indicate to myself or others that you were obsessing?

CLIENT: I would go home and think about it more.

THERAPIST: I see. What would you be doing at home while you were thinking about it?

CLIENT: Just sitting. Not eating or doing anything else that's important. Just obsessing.

THERAPIST: Okay, just sitting and not doing other things that you feel are important. And if I was able to see inside your mind and videotape you obsessing, what might I see happening?

CLIENT: That's easy. You'd see me thinking about the same thing over and over and thinking the worst. My only thoughts would be about failing.

THERAPIST: So let me see if I understand you. When you've experienced a fear of failure and have been scared of not doing well, you've paced and sat around obsessing. And the way you typically obsess is to think about the same thing over and over again—usually about failing.

CLIENT: That's right.

THERAPIST: And from what you've said, this has affected you because you haven't done the amount of work you'd like at work or at home.

CLIENT: Exactly.

THERAPIST: Are there other ways that this has affected your life?

CLIENT: I don't want to be so lazy and unproductive at home, but the main thing is not getting my work done at my job. I don't want to get fired. I can't afford to. I've got to stop obsessing and get things done.

THERAPIST: Okay.

In this case example, the client used many nondescriptive words and statements that could have led the therapist in any number of directions. The aim was for the therapist to learn from the client what he does when he's experiencing a fear of failure. We focus on actions and how they affect the person negatively. Thus, it is not the client's fear of failure that is of concern, but his actions (such as not doing his work). These actions are a result of the way he views himself and his situations. It is ultimately what people do or don't do, as a result of their perspectives, that affect their lives adversely.

In these case examples both clients described processes that were associated with their views and actions. Therefore, there are at least two different realms of possible intervention. Although we will come back to these case examples in later chapters, we want to reiterate that even early on in therapy sessions therapists can learn clients' ways of constructing problems and their actions regarding them.

By obtaining clear problem descriptions and listening to how clients describe their concerns, therapists can learn more about clients' theories and potential areas to intervene. For example, if a client spoke about feeling a certain way, we would acknowledge and validate more, focusing on internal experience and affect. If a client talked about seeing or doing things a certain way, we would focus more on views and behaviors. Therefore problem descriptions are one pathway for learning about clients' theories of problem formation and resolution. We'll discuss this at length in Part Three of the book.

Now we'll look at ways of using action-talk, videotalk, and other methods of helping clients move from what they don't want to what they do want—their goals and preferred outcomes for therapy.

Cocreating Client Goals and Preferred Outcomes

Regardless of the question asked, some clients will tell the therapist what they don't want. Others will describe what they do want, which can lead straight to the cocreation of goals. If clients begin treatment by orienting toward what they don't want and how their lives have become problematic, we follow their processes. We then work to learn from them what they would like to see happen *instead* of the problem. This represents the goals and preferred outcomes that clients are seeking.

When the Future Causes the Past: Viktor Frankl and a Vision of the Future

Viktor Frankl was a Viennese psychiatrist who created an existential approach to therapy called logotherapy (see Frankl, 1963, 1969). In 1990, he delivered the keynote address at the second Evolution of Psychotherapy conference held in Anaheim, California. As 7,000 people listened, Dr. Frankl told the compelling story of his life. He described the terrible things that happened to him while he was imprisoned in a Nazi concentration camp, and described how he nearly died many times. He was physically and psychologically abused and tortured. During his plenary, Dr. Frankl described one day in particular that seemed to be etched deeply within him:

> On a wintry day in Poland he was being marched through a field with a bunch of other prisoners. He was dressed in thin clothing, with no socks on and holes in his shoes. Still very ill from malnutrition and mistreatment, he began to cough. The cough was so severe that he fell to his knees. A guard came over and told him to get moving. He could not even answer because his cough was so intense and debilitating. The guard began to beat him with a club, and told him that he would be left to die if he did not get up. Dr. Frankl knew this was true, as he had witnessed it before. Sick, in pain, and being hit, he thought, "This is it for me." He didn't have the strength to get up.
>
> He lay on the ground in no condition to move on. Suddenly, he was no longer there. Instead, he found himself standing at a lectern in post-war Vienna giving a lecture on "The Psychology of Death Camps."

> He had an audience of 200 rapt with attention. The lecture was one that he had worked on the whole time he was in the death camp. He talked about the psychological factors behind dehumanization. He then described why, in his view, some people seem to survive the experience psychologically and emotionally better than others.
>
> It's a brilliant lecture, all in his mind's eye and ear. He no longer seems to be in the field but instead is vividly involved in the lecture. During the lecture, he told the imaginary audience about the day Viktor Frankl was in that field being beaten and was certain he didn't have the strength to get up and keep walking. At exactly that moment his body stood up in the field. The guard stopped beating him and he began to walk, haltingly at first, then with more strength. He continued to imagine this lecture all the while he was doing the work detail and through the cold march back to the death camp. He collapsed into his bunk, imagining this brilliantly clear speech ending and him getting a standing ovation.

Many years later and thousands of miles away, in 1990 in Anaheim, California, he received a standing ovation from 7,000 after his speech.

What did Viktor Frankl do differently than most people who are experiencing pain, suffering, and difficulty? He created a vision and a sense of a future with possibilities and meaning. He imagined a future that was different from the past; a future in which things worked out. That future vision became so compelling to him that he had to get up and walk. If he hadn't, he never would have given that brilliant speech. He had connected with the future. He had to take the actions that would get him to the future he knew was waiting for him. In order to get there, the first order of business was getting up off the ground and starting to walk.

That is what's missing from many clients—a well articulated and good connection to a future with possibilities. Our mission is to help clients to do what Viktor Frankl did, by rehabilitating and creating a sense of a future where things are different and possible. Some people will have some sense of that possibility-filled future, and we can help them to rehabilitate it and begin to move powerfully toward it. Others have no sense of it and may need to begin to imagine that it is possible to have a future that is different from or better than the past.

Many first- and second-wave theorists contend that people are held hostage by the past, and that the past causes the present and the future. Unless a client believes this, we've found this to be an unhelpful idea for therapists to hold. Waters and Lawrence (1993) stated, "One of the great deficits of most therapy is the lack of a proactive vision of what people need to move towards instead of a sense of what they need to move away from" (p. 9). Research has taught us that therapy should be future-oriented, and clients have taught us that by helping them to gain a vision for the future, the future can affect the present and the past.

Consider the following scenarios for a moment: If you knew that you were going to win a seven-figure lottery tomorrow would you go to work? Would you finish this book? (We hope you would!) If you knew that something terrible was going to happen to someone you care about would you take action to prevent it? By knowing the future, the ways that you perceive the past and present, as well as your actions in the present, can be influenced. Therefore, consistent with outcome research, we work with clients to create visions of what differences they want to see in their lives. We then work with them to take steps to achieve those outcomes. We also learn what difference it will make for clients when they've achieved the preferred outcomes and futures they desire.

In learning what clients' future visions entail, we've found the following questions to be useful:

- How will you know when things are better?
- How will you know when the problem is no longer a problem?
- What will indicate to you that therapy has been successful?
- How will you know when you no longer need to come to therapy?
- What will be happening that will indicate to you that you can manage things on your own?

Goals and preferred outcomes represent clients' visions of the future—when their lives are more manageable and the concerns, complaints, or problems that brought them to therapy are less intrusive or absent altogether. Oftentimes clients' goals are simply the opposite of their problem descriptions. Once again, both action-talk and videotalk can be extremely helpful in moving clients from vague descriptions to clearly delineated goals.

For example, if a client says, "I'm having relationship problems," we first ask her to describe how she *does* her relationship problems. We learn through action-talk that she yells at her partner when he's late, calls him a liar, and then refuses to talk with him for at least a day. Through further discussion we learn that she wants to be in a relationship with her partner where she is able to talk with him when she's angry. In turn, she will know that things are better when she is able to do this more times than not. This becomes the goal of treatment, not relationship problems or anger or any other therapist-derived conceptualization.

In learning what it is that clients want, we sometimes find that what clients are initially complaining about is not their primary concern. For example, a client will mention numerous concerns and the therapist will be unclear as to which ones take precedence. In such cases, many clients will just want their experience and views to be acknowledged and heard. They will then move on to concerns that are more significant for them. For this reason, we always check with clients to be sure that we clearly understand what it is that they want to see change. When clients have a number of complaints, we summarize and acknowledge them all, and then learn which ones are most pressing.

Sometimes a client indicates that all complaints or concerns are of equal weight. In this case, we work with clients to determine which one or two concerns should be addressed first. We assure clients that all of their concerns are important and will be addressed, but that we are just learning which ones are most troublesome and should be focused on initially.

To illustrate how to move from what clients don't want to what they do want we'll review the case examples presented earlier in this chapter. Let's start with Case Example 4.1. In this vignette, the therapist learned that the mother did not want her daughter to kick and hit her and throw things. To the mother, these actions were indicative of a tantrum. Let's see how the therapist collaborates with the mother using action-talk to get an idea of what she wants instead of the problematic behaviors.

Case Example 4.1 ***My Daughter Is Out of Control!*** **(continued)**

THERAPIST: Okay. So am I right in thinking that you want your daughter to stop kicking, hitting, and throwing things when she doesn't get her way?

CLIENT: Yeah.

THERAPIST: So what would you like to see your daughter do instead when she doesn't get her way?

CLIENT: I want her to behave and tell me what she wants instead of going into a flying fit.

THERAPIST: Given your experience raising your daughter, what might behaving and not flying into a fit look like?

CLIENT: Well, I don't expect her not to be upset, but she would probably say, "Mommy I don't want that" and then we could talk about it. She just wouldn't have the tantrum.

THERAPIST: Mm hmm. So she might get upset, and that would be okay with you, but then she would talk with you instead of hitting, kicking, and throwing things. Is that right?

CLIENT: Exactly.

THERAPIST: Uh huh. And if she didn't want to talk but also didn't have a tantrum, what else might be acceptable for her to do?

CLIENT: She could just sit down or go in another room. I'd prefer that we talk, but you're right, she might not sometimes. So she could do something else until she's calm and then we could talk later.

THERAPIST: I see. So there are several options.

CLIENT: Yes.

THERAPIST: And just so I'm clear, is that what you would like to work on here—finding ways of helping your daughter to respond by talking to you, sitting down, leaving the room, or other acceptable ways that we haven't yet explored, when she doesn't get her way?

CLIENT: Yes. That's what I want.

THERAPIST: Great. And when she does this on a regular basis, what will be different?

CLIENT: Things will be calmer for sure!

THERAPIST: Okay, calmer. How so?

CLIENT: She'll just go on playing or doing something else. Then I'll actually be able to get some things done.

What we learned from the mother is that the outcome she desires is for her daughter to talk with her, sit down, or leave the room instead of throwing a tantrum. Through action-talk we learned what she wants instead of he problematic behavior. This becomes the goal of therapy. We also learned from the mother what will be different when her daughter is behaving more the way she'd like. Let's now revisit Case Example 4.2.

Case Example 4.2 *I Need to Get Over My Divorce* (continued)

THERAPIST: Now I think I follow you, but for sake of clarity, I'd like to ask you another question if it's okay with you.

CLIENT: Sure.

THERAPIST: You've mentioned three things that seem to be troublesome for you. Which of the three—not going out, ruminating and thinking about your past decisions, or not getting to sleep is most concerning for you right now?

CLIENT: Definitely not getting to sleep.

THERAPIST: Okay... and as you said, when you don't get enough sleep it really affects you the next day at work.

CLIENT: That's right.

THERAPIST: So am I right in thinking that you'd like to find a way to get to sleep quicker, so you feel more rested in the morning?

CLIENT: No doubt.

THERAPIST: What's a reasonable amount of time for you to lie in bed before falling asleep?

CLIENT: If I could get to sleep within a half hour of lying down I'd be thrilled!

THERAPIST: Getting to sleep within a half hour would allow you to get a full night's sleep and perhaps be better rested for work?

CLIENT: Uh huh... that's what I need.

THERAPIST: What will be different when you're getting to sleep earlier and getting a full-night's sleep?

CLIENT: My head will be clearer.

THERAPIST: How so?

CLIENT: I'll be better rested and won't be ruminating so much.

THERAPIST: What difference will that make for you?

CLIENT: If I'm not ruminating then I'll be getting things done and going out more.

Although this particular client mentioned many concerns, he ultimately wanted to find a way of getting to sleep quicker. We must focus on clients' goals to be sure we are working in ways that are consistent with their preferences. In turn, when we learn about clients' goals and preferred outcomes we also learn what will be different for them as a result of achieving those outcomes. Now let's revisit Case Example 4.3 to see how we can use videotalk to gain clarity regarding client goals and preferred outcomes.

Case Example 4.3 *I Have a Fear of Failure* (continued)

THERAPIST: Okay. So the main thing is not getting your work done on the job. You can't afford to lose your job.

CLIENT: Right.

THERAPIST: So if we were to videotape you in the future, with things going the way you prefer, and you were getting your work done on the job, what would be happening that would indicate that you were getting your work done?

CLIENT: I would be completing my paperwork documentation and billing on time. Also, I wouldn't be late for meetings and appointments.

THERAPIST: When that's happening what difference will that make for you?

CLIENT: A ton! If I'm getting my work done then my boss will be off my case and I can keep my job.

We've already offered two ways of learning what clients want to see different in their lives and helping them to gain a sense of the future—action-talk and videotalk. Next we'll explore further creative possibilities including the crystal ball technique, the question, the miracle question, and the time machine.

The Crystal Ball

Milton Erickson (1954b) often used what he referred to as *pseudo-orientation in time.* This technique involved inviting his patients into a trance and having them imagine three crystal balls. One represented the past, one the present, and one the future. He would then have his patients peer into the crystal ball that represented the future and suggest that they would be able to achieve their preferred outcomes—when their problems were no longer problems. Erickson would then elicit detailed descriptions of how their problems were resolved including what they had done and how he (Erickson) had helped them.

Next, Erickson would suggest amnesia, and his patients would forget about the imagined future in which things worked out. After his patients finished their hypnotic experiences, he would suggest the actions they had described to him during their hypnosis as a way of resolving their problems and moving toward their preferred futures. Erickson's work with his clients in helping them gain a sense of the future seemed to have an effect on the present.

To use this in a nonhypnotic way, have the client peer through an imaginary window or imagine a crystal ball that represents the future. Then suggest to the client that he or she can envision a time in the future when the problem is gone. Follow this with questions such as "How was your problem resolved?" "What did you do?" "What did others do?" and "How is your life different as a result?"

The Question

In the 1920s, Alfred Adler (1956), the creator of individual psychology, developed *the question,* a strategy that oriented clients toward future goals and problem resolution. Later popularized by Rudolf Dreikurs (1954), therapists would ask, "Let us imagine I gave you a pill and you would be completely well as soon as you left this office. What would be different in your life, what would you do differently than before?" (p. 132). Decades later, this question can be helpful to therapists in learning how clients want their lives to be different in the future.

The Miracle Question

Steve de Shazer (1988) and his colleagues at the Brief Family Therapy Center (BFTC) in Milwaukee, Wisconsin, developed the miracle question as a way of helping clients envision their lives after their problem has been solved. Prior to being asked the miracle question, clients usually are informed by therapists that such a question will require them to use their imagination. They are then asked: "Suppose you were to go home tonight, and while you were asleep, a miracle happened and this problem was solved. How will you know the miracle happened? What will be different?" (p. 5).

The miracle question is another possibility for orienting clients toward their preferred outcomes and the changes they desire in the future.

The Time Machine

With younger clients it can be helpful to use a more age-sensitive approach in determining what they want in the future. In a previous publication, Bob (Bertolino, 1999) discussed how to use an imaginary time machine as a way of helping children and youth envision a future where things work out. Here's how he used the time machine:

> Let's say there is a time machine sitting here in the office. This time machine can take you wherever you want to go. Now let's say that you climb in and it propels you into the future, to a time when things are going the way you want them to go. After arriving at your future destination, the first thing you notice is that the problems that brought you to therapy have disappeared.
>
> This pitch is then followed by questions such as:
>
> Where are you?
> Who is with you?
> What is happening?
> What are you doing?
> How is your life different than before?
> Where did your problems go?
> How did they go away?

With all of the methods offered, therapists help clients gain clear, observable descriptions of the futures they are seeking. In essence, these methods answer the question, "How will you know when things are better?" Action-talk and videotalk can also be helpful in this process. Once therapists are clear on what clients want, they can begin to collaborate with clients on steps to make those preferred futures happen.

Realistic, Attainable, Ethical, and Legal Goals

Along with being clear and observable, we find it important to make sure that clients' goals and preferred outcomes are realistic, attainable, ethical, and legal. For example, it is not unreasonable for a client who has lost someone close to him or her to want that person to return. Even though this is not possible, it may be possible for the person to experience a caring relationship with another person. By acknowledging clients' internal experiences and views we can cut through many unrealistic expectations and cocreate solvable problems. Case Example 4.4 shows how to do this.

Case Example 4.4 ***I Miss My Dad***

CLIENT: My dad died last year. I wish he were still here. I really miss him. That's really what I want... him to be back.

THERAPIST: I'm sorry for your loss. What do you miss most about him?

CLIENT: He used to listen to me... really listen to me.

THERAPIST: How did you know when he was really listening to you?

CLIENT: He would look me in the eyes and not judge me.

THERAPIST: What did he do to let you know that he wasn't judging you?

CLIENT: Well, he didn't make comments like, "You should have . . ." or "That was stupid to do that."

THERAPIST: I see. And how did that help you?

CLIENT: I knew he valued me, and I haven't had that feeling since he died.

THERAPIST: Is that something you would like to experience again in a relationship with someone—that sense of being listened to, not judged, and valued?

CLIENT: I would love to have that again.

THERAPIST: What would be different for you as a result of having that again?

CLIENT: I'd feel great. I'd feel better about going through each day knowing that I could talk with somebody who understood me.

While it is not possible to bring back a deceased person, it is possible to be in a relationship where you feel listened to, not judged, and valued. So even when presented with goals that are not possible, oftentimes achieving what goals symbolize is possible.

From Resistance and Lack of Motivation to Stages of Change

Working with challenging clients can lead many therapists to deem them as resistant, unmotivated, unwilling, unable to change, and goal-less. In response, some theorists have advocated for a method of assessing the willingness to cooperate among clients. One popular method is the customer/visitor/complainant framework associated with solution-focused therapy (de Shazer, 1988). From this perspective, clients are labeled as *customers* when they demonstrate that they are willing and want to do something to resolve a complaint. *Visitors* are those clients who have come to therapy without a complaint or unwillingly. Last, *complainants* are clients who are concerned or worried about someone else's behavior, but aren't willing to do anything about it. The goal within this framework is to turn visitors and complainants into customers.

Although we characterize solution-focused therapy as a third-wave approach, we find theoretical frameworks such as the one just described to be counterproductive for at least two reasons. First, such a framework continues to unnecessarily label clients. Second, by labeling clients as visitors and complainants the issue becomes one of selling the client in some way such that he or she becomes a customer. This implies a lack of motivation on the part of the client. Fish (1997) stated:

> A central issue becomes how well [solution-focused therapy] does at converting complainants—who lack that motivation—to customers. As a clinical issue, the question becomes what to do with complainants who remain complainants after reasonable solution-focused efforts. One solution-focused response is to terminate and wish them well. (p. 269)

We do not hold the idea that clients must be converted into customers or that they lack motivation. In contrast, we agree with Duncan, Hubble, and Miller (1997) who stated:

> There is no such thing as an unmotivated client. Clients may not, as we have found all too often, share ours, but they certainly hold strong motivations of their own. An unproductive and futile therapy can come about by mistaking or overlooking what the client wants to accomplish, misapprehending the client's readiness for change, or pursuing a personal motivation. (p. 11)

This view is consistent with the work of Prochaska and colleagues who have studied people who are self-changers and those who have attended psychotherapy (Prochaska, 1995, 1999; Prochaska et al., 1992, 1994). These researchers have identified six stages of change. Their research has found that people tend to move through stages of change in one of two ways. Some will advance in a linear fashion, passing through one stage after another. More often though, people will go the second route. They will progress, relapse, progress, relapse, and cycle through the stages in a three steps forward, two steps back process.

Precontemplation. Clients in the initial stage of precontemplation typically don't know that a problem exists. The ones that acknowledge that there is a problem don't usually see their role in contributing to it. These clients often come to therapy against their will, and readily pass blame and shun accountability. For therapists working with clients in the precontemplation stage, it's important to acknowledge their points of view and not try to force them to do anything. The therapist works to create an environment where the client can feel heard and understood and consider the benefits of changing.

Contemplation. In the second stage of change, contemplation, clients may recognize that change is necessary. They may have an idea about a goal and even know how to reach that goal, but they aren't sure the change is worth the time, effort, and energy (Miller, Duncan, & Hubble, 1997). It's important that therapists are patient with clients in this stage and do not push them to change. Some have even suggested that in order to counter clients' ambivalence about change it can be helpful to suggest that they go slow, or discuss the dangers of change (Fisch, Weakland, & Segal, 1982). Although viewed as paradoxical, the intent is to match clients' teeter-tottering, ambivalent positions about change. Through a supportive context, therapists can help clients at this stage to go at their own pace and accommodate their state of readiness to change. Further, it can be helpful to encourage clients to think and observe as opposed to taking action.

Preparation. Clients in the third stage of change, preparation, are less delicate and ambivalent, and are more open to formalized assessment and collaboration with mental health professionals. The consideration for therapists working with clients in this stage is to help them to identify the change they desire and consider strategies for attaining that change. Clients in the preparation stage are more likely to identify the changes they want to make and the steps needed to accomplish those changes. Some clients will even have experimented with different methods of attaining change. Therapists can be more active in helping these clients identify past successes and problem-solving strategies, and begin exploring treatment options. In preparing clients for change, it's important to let them know that there are many pathways and possibilities for reaching the same end point.

Action. The action stage is next. At this point, clients are ready to take action to create positive change and reach their established goals. Therapists accommodate this stage of change by helping clients implement the strategies outlined in the preparation stage. The therapist must also modify such strategies based on the results achieved. It is important to note that many clients will move back and forth between preparing to take action and actually taking action.

Maintenance. At this fifth stage, the issue is one of helping clients maintain the changes and gains they have made and to extend them into the future. Therapists can assist clients in this stage of change by anticipating possible hurdles or obstacles that might occur down the road. This can include developing prevention strategies or plans as a means of holding course. Relapse planning and recovery in chemical dependency treatment is concerned with this phase of the change process.

Termination. The final stage is termination. Prochaska (1993) describes this stage of change as 100 percent confidence that a client will not engage in the old behavior. Miller, Duncan, and Hubble (1997) note that this is an ideal rather than a realistic or achievable state of change. They state that most clients will remain in the maintenance stage and will "continue to be mindful of possible threats to their desired change and monitor what they need to do to keep the change in place" (p. 104).

What seems to be most important is accommodating the client's motivational level and stage of change. In fact, stages of change have been found to be better predictors of outcome than variables such as age, socioeconomic status, problem severity and duration, goals, expectations, self-efficacy, and social supports (Miller, Duncan, & Hubble, 1997; Prochaska et al., 1992). Therefore, from a collaborative, competency-based perspective, clients are viewed as being motivated to differing degrees and in different stages of change. Some clients are motivated to not have to come to therapy! We don't attempt to get these clients to take action when they are in a precontemplative state of mind; instead we assume that change is possible if we accommodate their views of the therapeutic relationship. Case Example 4.5 is a brief example of how a therapist might go about working with such a client.

Case Example 4.5 *I Don't Want to Get Locked Up*

THERAPIST: What's brought you in today?

CLIENT: I don't know. They made me come here.

THERAPIST: Tell me about that.

CLIENT: My probation officer made me come. She said if I didn't go to therapy she would lock me up again.

THERAPIST: I see. So am I right in saying that you probably wouldn't be here if you weren't told that you needed to go?

CLIENT: You got that right. And besides, I'm doing fine. I don't need therapy. She's the one with the problem. I shouldn't even be here.

THERAPIST: So your sense is that she's the one with the problem and that you shouldn't be here.

CLIENT: Yep.

THERAPIST: Well, I just wanted to say that I'm impressed with the fact that even though you were told to come here, you actually made the decision to come. How did that happen?

CLIENT: I had to. I didn't want to get locked up.

THERAPIST: Sure. But people are sent to therapy against their wishes all the time with the threat of being locked up, and they don't all follow through and go. You know what I mean?

CLIENT: Yeah.

THERAPIST: If it's okay with you, I'd like to ask you another question.

CLIENT: Fine.

THERAPIST: Is it safe to say that you'd like to find a way to not have to come to therapy in the future?

CLIENT: You got that right. And I want off probation!

THERAPIST: So if we could work toward you not having to come back to therapy in the future and your ultimately getting off probation, would that work for you?

CLIENT: Sure.

For this client, the motivation was not having to come to therapy in the future and getting off of probation. Depending on the stage of change, some clients will be more invested in the change process than others. However, this is not an issue of clients being resistant or unmotivated. The therapist's task is to see where each client is in terms of change processes and work with clients in ways that match that particular client and stage of change.

Determining Progress toward Goals and Preferred Outcomes

If you've ever been to Walt Disney World or Universal Studios, it's likely that you experienced an interesting phenomenon and either didn't notice it or pay much attention to it. First, the entertainment begins once you get in line. There are television monitors showing videos, music coming out of speakers, things to look at and read along the way, and oftentimes refreshments within reach. Next, although the lines to get on rides are often very long, rarely do you stand in the same place for extended periods of time; the lines keep moving.

What the people at Disney and Universal learned is that when people get the sense that they are moving and making progress toward their preferred outcome—getting on the ride—they are less likely to become irritated, frustrated, angry, and drop out of line. Even though it still takes a long time to get on a ride, people at these amusement parks get the sense that they are progressing.

If you've ever taken a long-distance trip across the country you may have also had this experience. If the trip involves going from Missouri to California, about 1,700 miles, the thought of it can be overwhelming. However, if the trip is broken into parts (e.g., 100 miles to Salt Lake City, an hour until stopping for dinner, etc.), each delineating progress toward the destination of reaching California, the trip can seem more tolerable and possibly even enjoyable.

What do amusement parks have to do with therapy? More than first meets the eye. We've found that clients who attend therapy will sometimes respond similarly to patrons waiting for a long time to get on a ride at an amusement park. When clients get the sense that they are making progress they are less likely to become frustrated and give up. Therefore, once goals have been clearly delineated we also work to identify what will indicate that progress is being made toward the established goals. We refer to this as identifying or looking for signs of change. Here are some questions to assist with this process:

- What will be the first indication that you have begun to turn the corner with your problem?
- What will be the first sign that you have taken a solid step on the road to improvement even though you might not yet be out of the woods?
- What's one thing that might indicate to you that things are looking up?
- What will you see happening when things are beginning to go more the way you'd like them to?
- What would have to happen that would indicate to you that things are changing in the direction you'd like them to change?
- How will you know when the change you are looking for has started?
- What is happening right now with your situation that you would like to have continue?

By focusing on in-between change, therapists can help clients identify progress toward goals. This can both counter client frustration and help orient them toward exceptions and differences in regard to their described problems. This way clients are noticing what is happening that they want as opposed to what they do not.

Exploring Change through Incremental Procedures

Scaling Questions

In determining progress toward goals and preferred outcomes it can be helpful to use questions that indicate incremental change. A first way of doing this is through scaling questions (Berg & de Shazer, 1993; Berg & Miller, 1992; de Shazer, 1991, 1994; Lipchik, 1988). To use these types of questions, the therapist begins by describing a scale from one to ten where each number represents a rating of the client's complaint(s). The therapist might say, "On a scale of one to ten, with one being the worst this problem has ever been, and ten being the best things could be, where would you rate things today?"

Once the therapist is given a number, he or she explores how that rating translates into action-talk. For example, if a client rates his or her situation at a three, the therapist asks, "What specifically is happening to indicate to you that it is a three?" The next step is to determine the goals and preferred outcomes. To do this the therapist asks the client where things would need to be for him or her to feel that the goals of treatment have been met or that therapy has been successful. If the client indicates that an eight would indicate sufficient change, the therapist asks the client for a description of what will be happening when things have reached an eight.

Last, the therapist and client determine what will indicate in-between change and progress. The therapist asks, "You mentioned that things are at a three now. What will it take for things to get to a three and a half?" In determining in-between change, it's important that therapists do not suggest leaps that are too big for clients. For example, it's usually too much for a client to go from a three to a six in one session, although it's not impossible. We aim for small changes that will represent progress in the direction of goals and preferred outcomes.

Percentage Questions

A second way of determining change in incremental methods is through the use of percentage questions. To use these types of questions, the therapist finds out what percentage of the time the problem interferes with the client's life, what percentage will indicate progress toward goals and preferred outcomes, and what percentage will indicate that treatment has been successful. For example, the therapist might ask, "What percentage of time do you think things are going the way you'd like?"

Next, the therapist asks, "What percentage of time would things need to be going well for you to feel like you no longer need to come to therapy?" Last, the following question would help to determine in-between change, "What would it take to go from ______ percent to ______ percent?" Again, it's important that all percentages are described in action-based language.

Ongoing Assessment with Multiple Clients

In working with families, couples, or other situations where there are multiple clients it's important that therapists attend to each person's conversational preferences, goals, preferred outcomes, and ideas. Because there will be different ideas about how therapy should proceed (what the concerns are, what needs to change, what will indicate success, etc.), it's common to have separate complaints and goals for each client. Even though this may be the case, most often there are common threads between complaints and goals that we work to identify.

We've found it helpful to coordinate these complaints and goals through the use of acknowledgment, tracking, and linking. To do this, each person's perspective is acknowledged and restated in the least inflammatory way possible, while still acknowledging and imparting the intended feeling and meaning (Bertolino, 1999; O'Hanlon & O'Hanlon, 1999). Tracking means that we take note of each person's complaint and goal statements. These statements are linked by the word "and," as it builds on a common concern rather than opposing or competing needs or goals. Case Examples 4.6 and 4.7 illustrate this idea of acknowledgment, tracking, and linking.

Case Example 4.6 *I Need Your Help!*

ASHLEY (WIFE): He's impossible! He never helps out with he kids or around the house—I could go on and on.

JUSTIN (HUSBAND): (Sarcastically) Right, I *never* help out.

THERAPIST: (To Ashley) So it seems like he really hasn't helped out as much as you'd like.

ASHLEY: He definitely hasn't.

THERAPIST: Okay, and you really need his help because you've got your hands full with the kids, work around the house, and whatever else comes up during the day.

ASHLEY: That's right. I just can't do it alone.

THERAPIST: What about you, Justin?

JUSTIN: What am I supposed to do? Abandon my work? We have to pay the bills! **(Directly to Ashley)** If you'd just quit nagging me then I wouldn't get so mad, and I'd help out. But nooo ... you're always on my case!

ASHLEY: Famous last words.

THERAPIST: **(To Justin)** So you feel like you need to get your work done and that's important in order to pay the bills. And, it seems to you like you've been nagged about helping out and your idea is that if she would take a step back you would help out more.

JUSTIN: Exactly.

THERAPIST: So let me see if I understand you both. Ashley, you would really like for Justin to help out more with the kids and around the house—with everyday tasks. We'll get to specific things that you'd like help with in a few minutes, but in general, that would help you. **(Ashley nods her head indicating agreement)** And Justin, correct me if I'm wrong, but you seem to recognize that Ashley needs your help with some things and you're willing to pitch in more but the nagging hasn't worked for you. At the same time, you need to be able to get the work done that you bring home. So, you'd like to find a way to do both. **(Justin also nods in agreement)**

Case Example 4.7 *Finding a Way Back*

MIA (MOTHER): I just want her to return to school. It's ridiculous for her to be out. And besides, if she doesn't go she'll never get the kind of job she wants.

THERAPIST: Okay. So you're concerned because your sense is there's really no reason for a sixteen-year-old to be out of school, and because it could negatively affect her future.

MIA: Right.

LISA (DAUGHTER): What's the point? I can't stand school. Besides, if you're gonna continue to be on my case, then I'll never go back!

MIA: See, that's what I get every day!

THERAPIST: I can see that it's been rough on the both of you. And for you Lisa, you haven't found a reason to go to school and to tolerate it yet.

LISA: Yeah. School is boring and if she doesn't back off . . . then forget it.

THERAPIST: And what do you mean by your mom being on your case?

LISA: She constantly says, "You better go. You better go. You can't miss another day!" It's like she thinks that I don't have a clue! I know that I need to graduate to get a good job. Duh!

THERAPIST: Okay, and the ways that she's tried so far to get you to go haven't work so well for you?

LISA: Nope.

THERAPIST: I see. So let me see if I'm following the two of you. Mia, you'd really like Lisa to return to school, finish her education, and have a better chance of a good future. And Lisa, you seem to have dreams for yourself, and even though I haven't heard about them yet, it seems that school is a part of that in some way. So you'd like to find a way of tolerating school so that you can graduate and work toward the career you want. And maybe there are other ways that your mom can be helpful to you with that—ways that don't involve her telling you to go, because you already know that—but ways that you see as being supportive with school.

In both case examples acknowledgment, tracking, and linking were used, particularly in the last therapist response in each case. It is important to acknowledge each person and his or her perspective. Whether working with couples, families, or other multiple-client variations, clients should feel free to clarify any misperceptions or areas of discomfort until a mutually agreeable description emerges. Once this occurs, therapists can begin to flesh out the direction, goals, and preferred outcomes of treatment. This process can be done with all members present or by separating clients. As discussed in Chapter 2, clients' perspectives on how to meet will need to be taken into consideration with certain circumstances requiring that therapists assume a more directive posture.

Collaborating with Outside Helpers and Larger Systems

It is common for therapists to work in conjunction with other service providers. This can be a challenging task when there are varying ideas regarding what should happen in a particular case. Whether working with other therapists, mental health professionals, probation or parole officers, social service workers, or other outside helpers, it's important that therapists maintain a collaborative stance. This involves having conversations with outside helpers to learn about their expectations and goals. Case Example 4.8 shows how we do this.

Case Example 4.8 ***I'd Be Shocked***

THERAPIST: So that I'm clear, what specifically are you wanting to be addressed in therapy?

DEPUTY JUVENILE OFFICER (DJO): Definitely Eddie's attitude about things. He thinks he's invincible.

THERAPIST: So what has he done that's given you the idea that he thinks he's invincible?

DJO: He's assaulted people. He's stolen and he keeps thinking that he won't get caught even though he has [been caught] many times.

THERAPIST: So what would have to happen to convince you that he wasn't seeing himself as invincible anymore?

DJO: He'd have to stop assaulting people and quit stealing. He'd also have to talk more respectfully to me. He tries to intimidate me.

THERAPIST: Okay. So when he's not assaulting people, not stealing, and is being more respectful in how he talks with you, then you'll wonder if maybe he's turned the corner?

DJO: Oh yeah. But I can't see those things happening.

THERAPIST: So it would surprise you?

DJO: That's putting it mildly. I'd be shocked.

THERAPIST: And for the sake of clarity, when he does those things, will you reconsider whether long-term residential placement is the right place for him?

DJO: That's right.

The presence or involvement of outside helpers is then incorporated into therapy sessions. To do this we first ask clients, "Did ______ tell you what he/she expects us to focus on here?" If clients know then we proceed by incorporating those goals or directions into the therapy. If clients do not know then we consider using speculation: "What do you think ______ will say when I talk with (him or her)?" We want to invite clients to share their perceptions and understandings of what others may have conveyed to them.

When clients truly do not know what outside helpers' concerns are or when their perceptions are inconsistent with what we have been told by the outside helpers, we gently introduce our understandings. For example, we might say, "My understanding after talking with ______ is that (he, she) will have the sense that you're moving in the right direction when you're ______." We then follow with, "How does that sound to you?" As we do when working with multiple clients, we acknowledge each perspective, and search for continuity between the respective goals.

We also have found it helpful to invite outside helpers to attend therapy sessions. We welcome multiple perspectives and by expanding the system new possibilities and potential solutions are often generated. When outside helpers join therapy sessions, we remember that there are multiple ways of viewing situations with no one view being more correct than another. At the same time, we want to challenge perspectives that close down possibilities and promote those which can facilitate change in the direction of goals and preferred outcomes.

In this chapter we've explored how ongoing assessment procedures are important in determining client conversational and relational preferences, concerns and problems, goals and preferred outcomes, and progress toward those goals and preferred outcomes. In Part Three we will introduce ways of changing clients' views, actions, and contextual propensities associated with problems.

Summary Points for Chapter Four

- Ongoing assessment involves determining clients':
  - Conversational and relational preferences
  - Concerns and complaints
  - Goals and preferred outcomes
  - Progress toward goals and preferred outcomes
- It is important to obtain clear descriptions of client concerns and goals. Action-talk and videotalk can be helpful with this process.
- Other methods of learning from clients about their preferred outcomes and visions of the future include the crystal ball, the question, the miracle question, and the time machine.
- People tend to go through stages of change regarding therapy. These include:
  - Precontemplation
  - Contemplation
  - Preparation
  - Action
  - Maintenance
  - Termination
- Methods of incrementally measuring clients' concerns, goals and preferred outcomes, and in-between change can be useful.
- When working with multiple clients and outside helpers, emphasis is on acknowledging each person's perspective and ideas about what needs to change. We search for mutual descriptions that encompass each person's concerns.

PART THREE

Creating Change in the Realms of Viewing, Action, and Context

Bill once took a psychotherapy seminar in graduate school in which he was required to write his semester paper on the psychotherapy theorist of his choice. Since he was studying with Milton Erickson at the time, he chose Erickson as his theorist. But there was a problem. Half the paper was supposed to detail the theorist's views of psychopathology—how people developed problems or abnormalities—the other half was to be devoted to the theorist's theory of change. The problem was that Erickson had very little in the way of a theory of psychopathology—certainly not enough to fill half of a long paper. The best Bill could come up with, after extensive research into Erickson's work, was that Erickson thought people were a little too rigid in their thinking and their behavior and this led to problems. So the paper turned out to be heavily weighted toward the intervention and change side of the theory, where there was more material.

Similar to the paper that Bill wrote many years ago, we will spend some time over the next three chapters detailing how people become stuck in their problems. However, since our primary emphasis is not on *why* people become stuck and instead on helping them to become unstuck, we'll explore multiple areas for creating change with clients. These include changing the viewing, doing, and contextual propensities associated with problems.

As we address ways of creating change, we are mindful of several things. First, we all have our favorite ideas and techniques. Whether these ideas, techniques, or methods are helpful to clients depends on the extent to which they fit with clients' ways of changing and tap into their strengths. Next, the ideas that are generated must address and fit with what clients want. If ideas or techniques do not fit with clients they will discard them in some manner. Last, clients need to agree with the ideas offered and techniques suggested or utilized. A lack of collaboration on the part of the therapist in any or all of these areas can contribute to clients being viewed as resistant, unmotivated, passive–aggressive, and so on.

Therefore, counselors improve their chances of being effective when their ideas and techniques match clients' stages of change, ideas about how to achieve the goals, and preferred outcomes that have been established. Jerome Frank (1995) stated, "I'm inclined to entertain the notion the relative efficacy of most psychotherapeutic methods depends almost exclusively on how successfully the therapist is able to make the methods fit the patient's expectations" (p. 91). In addition, client expectancies about the credibility of therapeutic procedures must be taken into account. If clients believe in the efficacy of methods used they are more likely to benefit from therapy. Last, because the therapeutic relationship is paramount, any method of intervention must be respectful to clients. The realms for creating change that we will explore in Chapters 5–7 are illustrated in Table P3.1.

TABLE P3.1 Ways of Creating Change in the Four Realms

Experience	Views	Actions	Context
Give messages of acceptance, validation, and acknowledgment. There is no need to change or analyze experience as it is not inherently a problem.	Identify and challenge views that show: Impossibility Blaming Invalidation Nonaccountability or determinism Also: Offer new possibilities for attention.	Find action and interaction patterns that are part of the problem and that are repetitive. Then suggest: **1.** Disrupting the problematic patterns **2.** Finding and using solution patterns	Identify unhelpful and helpful aspects of the context, then suggest shifts in the context around the problem (e.g., changes in biochemistry, time, space, cultural habits, and influences). Explore social support systems and familial, cultural, gender, and spiritual influences.

CHAPTER

5 Changing the Viewing of Problems

Several traditional approaches to psychotherapy (e.g., Adlerian, cognitive, Gestalt, existential, reality) emphasize the role of cognition (i.e., thinking, perception, insight, awareness) in both the creation and resolution of clients' concerns, complaints, and problems. Although we agree that this is one possible area of intervention, we also believe that *cognition* offers too narrow a description of what people experience when it comes to perceptual processes. In this chapter, instead of focusing only on cognitive processes, we will offer a more encompassing perspective and explore the ways that clients view themselves, others, their lives, and their situations.

Views include the explanations that people have for their problems and where they focus their attention when they are having difficulties. In essence, when people become stuck in a problem, it's often due to rigidities in the realm of viewing. Some time ago, we came across a quote by Emile Chartiér, who summarized this rigidity well: "There's nothing as dangerous as an idea when it's the only one you have!" Therefore, our task as therapists is to help clients change the viewing of problems by developing new ideas, patterns of attention, and identity stories. By developing new views, clients can focus on new perspectives and possibilities regarding their problems.

The man who first ran the four-minute mile was Roger Bannister. Like all runners of his day, he was daunted by the prospect of breaking that four-minute barrier. Bannister decided to break the problem into smaller pieces. He concentrated on running only one-sixteenth of a second faster each time he ran. By doing this, he was finally able to break the mental barrier of impossibility. He changed his view of the situation. After Bannister broke his mental barrier, and the four-minute mile, many people ran faster miles within several years. Gaining a new perspective can help a person change their situation or solve their problem.

There are many ways of helping clients change the way they view their problems and create new possibilities. We'll offer multiple methods for doing so in this chapter. It is our hope that as you learn about these ideas and methods you will generate your own unique and respectful ways of putting them into practice. In addition, we hope that you will recognize when various therapeutic moves from other theorists and methods fall into this category.

What's in a View? Learning Clients' Theories of Change

Throughout we have emphasized the importance of learning clients' theories. Many times clients have developed views about how their concerns, complaints, and problems came about and what it will take to solve them. Sometimes these views are helpful in moving toward problem resolution. Therefore, before exploring specific methods, we've found it important to learn and attend to clients' theories about problem development and resolution. Here are some questions to ask clients to assist with this process:

- What ideas do you have about what needs to happen for things to improve?
- What theory or theories have you been considering about how this problem has come about and what might put it to rest?
- Oftentimes people have ideas not only about what is causing the problem, but also about how to resolve it. Do you have any ideas about how change is going to happen here?

By learning clients' views, therapists can better understand how such views may be of assistance in resolving concerns. After learning clients' views we can work to apply them, thereby taking more direct pathways to problem resolution. For example, if a client has an idea as to what is causing a particular concern we might ask:

- Given the ideas that you have about the problem you're facing, what do you think would be the first step in addressing it?
- What might you do differently as a result of the theory you've developed?
- What have you considered trying that is consistent with your ideas about what's causing this problem?
- If you had this theory about someone else, what would you suggest that he or she do to resolve it?

At times clients need validation from others that their theories are legitimate or viable. With acknowledgment and validation some clients will have the permission they need to move forward.

At other times, clients' views will be part of the problem. They will subscribe to rigid views that cloud the possibilities for change. These views, left unchanged, can continue to lead clients toward unhelpful ways of resolving their concerns. When clients' views are contributing to the development and maintenance of problems, there are two ways we can help them change those views: (1) changing focus of attention and (2) changing problematic stories.

Let's take a closer look at both of these.

Noticing the Unnoticed: Changing Patterns of Attention

When people are in pain, they tend to focus their attention on the pain they are feeling. Milton Erickson used to remind clients in pain that there were parts of their bodies that weren't feeling any pain at that moment. As soon as they would reorient their attention to those parts of their bodies, they would often find that they would feel less pain. Why? Because when we have problems, part of how those problems stay the same is that we fixate our attention. When we're depressed, for example, we often focus our attention on all the horrible things we've done or felt or on our past failures. Consider the following scenario as a way of further understanding the role of attention:

> A major league baseball player was having an all-star season. He was leading the league in hitting and playing better than he ever had. After the mid-season all-star break, he returned to the diamond only to find that he was struggling as a hitter. He couldn't believe that things had changed so quickly. When he continued to slump at the plate he decided to watch videotapes of the games in an effort to find out what he was doing wrong. As the player watched tapes of himself striking out and hitting weak ground balls, he noticed that he was lunging at pitches. He vowed to correct this problem, and during the next few games he worked on keeping his hands back and waiting on the pitch. However, his hitting didn't improve. The player realized that he must have missed something on the videotape, and he began to rewatch the tapes of games that he played following the all-star break.
>
> As the player watched more tapes, he noticed he was moving his feet too much. He couldn't believe that he had missed such an obvious thing. He quickly took steps to correct this habit as he played the next few games. Nevertheless, the change didn't work and the player began to get more and more frustrated. He felt like he was missing something on the tapes, so he asked the hitting coach to watch a tape with him and perhaps give a second opinion.
>
> The player and hitting coach sat down to watch a videotape. The player sat back waiting to hear the advice of the coach. After a few seconds, the coach asked, "Why are we watching this?"
>
> "What do you mean? Haven't you noticed that I'm hitting poorly? I have to review these tapes to figure out what I'm doing wrong. I thought you could help," explained the player.
>
> The coach followed, "How come you've been spending so much time watching yourself strike out and do poorly? You ought to be watching tapes of yourself prior to the all-star game, ones that show you playing the way that you're capable of. Study the tapes that demonstrate your ability."

> The player said that he hadn't thought of that, and he did as the coach suggested. Within a few games he had his swing back and was on track with his hitting again.

The baseball player's view was not wrong, just unhelpful. The coach suggested that he address his concern in a different way. By looking at things differently he was able to gain a new perspective that ultimately contributed to the improvement in his hitting. Case Example 5.1 shows the benefit of changing patterns of attention, but from a clinical perspective.

Case Example 5.1 *Give Yourself Credit*

Bill was working with a woman who was depressed. She told him that she went through phases of being very depressed. During these times she would quit her job and take to her bed. She focused fearfully on the future, convincing herself things would get even worse, perhaps resulting in her hospitalization. Then she would emerge from the depression and be able to function. Bill asked her what changed about her focus of attention when she was emerging from feeling depressed. She said that she would begin to do little things with her newfound energy (go for a walk, call a friend, apply for a job, get dressed, etc.) and then tell herself that she wasn't so bad and give herself credit for the efforts she had made.

When this woman was depressed, she fixed her attention on a possibly catastrophic future. When she began to feel better, her attention shifted to what she had done that she could give herself credit for and what she could use to feel better about herself. In an earlier publication, Bill (O'Hanlon) and Michele Weiner-Davis (1989) commented that a shift in view "can lead to changes in action and the stimulation of unused potentials and resources" (p. 126). This can be especially helpful for clients because the generation of a new view can lead to a small shift in a pattern of attention, therefore leading to new and creative ideas.

For each client, there will be a specific fixation of attention. As a therapist, your job will be like that of an anthropologist, investigating where clients' attention has been stuck at problem times and where it goes when things are better. The realms in which therapists can help clients to shift attention are varied, but the typical ones include:

- Time (past, present, or future)
- Sensory perceptions (visual, kinesthetic, auditory, gustatory, or olfactory)
- Internal or external focus
- What clients do well (rather than mistakes or problems)
- Actions (instead of explanations)

In a moment we will offer possibilities for helping clients to shift their attention. It is important to note that these methods are generic and that their use in therapy is always specific. In earlier chapters, we stressed the idea that this is not a one-size-fits-all model. We do not think there is one correct focus of attention. Other therapists may have opinions on where clients should focus their attention. We don't carry such strong ideations and don't claim to have the correct answers. We are interested in finding what works for each client, always keeping in mind that there are many pathways to the same point.

In collaborating with clients to determine what works best, we once again employ a position of conjecture. As discussed in Chapter 2, this involves asking questions, making interpretations, and offering new perspectives from a position of curiosity. This allows therapists to offer alternative views and possibilities as opposed to truths or facts. For example, we might say to a client, "The next time you notice yourself drifting back to the time of the abuse, you might consider noticing what else was happening at that time in your life." This way, clients can accept or reject what has been offered. We merely suggest possible ways that clients can change their attentional focus. We then notice and learn from clients whether these suggestions help them make progress toward their goals and preferred outcomes. Next are eight specific ways of doing this:

- **Suggest that clients change their sensory attention.**
  Suggest that clients shift from seeing things to listening, from listening to touching, or from talking to smelling. A change in sensory attention can help clients alter unhelpful patterns of attention.

  Example: A man who obsessed about his appearance had tried many things to stop obsessing, including taking medication, challenging his irrational beliefs, and getting long-term psychoanalysis. When none of these made a significant difference, he tried refocusing his attention. He decided that anytime he was obsessing, he would transfer his energy to his sense of smell, noticing anything he could smell in the room. This helped distract him and break the cycle of obsession he usually experienced.

- **Suggest that clients recall other aspects of the situation.**
  This can help clients notice aspects of a situation that they had not noticed previously, thereby bringing about a shift in perspective.

  Example: A woman who had been sexually molested by her father felt terribly guilty about not having resisted his advances. When describing the one time he had intercourse with her, she happened to remember that she had given him a little shove just as he was lifting himself off her. This changed her view that she had never resisted him, and relieved a great deal of guilt and shame.

- **Suggest that clients think of one thing that would challenge their thoughts.** By having clients challenge their own thoughts they can create new perspectives for themselves. You can also suggest to clients that every time they have recurring thoughts or obsessions that they make themselves think of at least three things they could do in the present or the future that could change their situations for the better.

  Example: A client who avoided dealing with money tended to get hit with unexpected monetary crises (car breaking down, owing unanticipated taxes, etc.). She would often wake in the middle of the night sweating anxiously, unable to fall back asleep. She agreed to get up and balance her checkbook, pay bills, or work on a budget every time she woke up and couldn't go back to sleep.

- **Suggest that clients shift from focusing on the past to focusing on the present.** By suggesting that clients shift their attention from one period of time to another they can change a pattern of viewing and perhaps gain a new perspective.

  Example: A man who was having flashbacks of his war trauma learned to diminish their intrusiveness by looking around the room he was in and noticing three things (e.g., the color of the walls, the carpet, and decorations).

- **Suggest that clients shift from focusing on the present or the past to focusing on the future.**

  Example: A client who was bored with the university courses she was taking almost quit school but got herself to stay by imagining her life in the future when she would be pursuing her career.

- **Suggest that clients shift from focusing on their internal experience to focusing on the external environment or other people.**
  By suggesting that clients orient their attention elsewhere, old patterns can be changed and new perspectives can result.

  Example: To a client who was shy and anxious it was suggested that she gaze into at least three people's eyes after entering a social setting. Then she was to look around the room and try to guess who else was anxious or uncomfortable.

- **Suggest that clients shift from focusing on the external environment or other people to focusing on their inner worlds.**

  Example: A boss who routinely got feedback that he was insensitive spent twenty minutes each day meditating and noticing his own feelings. He began to notice others' feelings more acutely when he was in touch with his own.

- **Suggest that clients focus on what has worked rather than what has not.** Many times when clients become stuck in their views it is because they're noticing what's wrong and what hasn't worked. This is a common occurrence because people are traditionally told to focus on problems as opposed exceptions. Suggest that clients focus on what they have done in regard to their problem that has worked to any degree.

  Example: A man who had been violent with his partner was asked to detail the times he felt he would be violent, but in turn did something nonviolent. He was able to discover several times that he had left the room or the house instead of losing control of his actions. This had the effect of not only convincing him that he had a choice about whether to be violent, but also to develop a plan for self-control in the future.

In working with clients to identify unhelpful patterns of attention, therapists can help them shift their attention elsewhere, notice what else may be happening, and ultimately, create new ways of viewing themselves, others, events, and situations. A shift in attention can lead to problem resolution when the client's new perspective causes a change in actions and interactions.

Reauthoring Life Stories: Changing Problematic Stories

Stories reflect the views that clients have of themselves or that others have of them. The stories that clients carry regarding themselves are referred to as *identity stories.* When clients are experiencing pain, difficulty, or trouble, they will frequently hold stories about themselves or others that are unhelpful, contribute to problem maintenance, and close down the possibilities for change. While clients' identity stories influence how they approach their lives, the stories that others hold about them will affect the ways they relate to each other. Therefore, when other people's stories about clients are problematic they may relate to clients in unhelpful or negative ways. These stories are sometimes referred to as *problem-saturated* (White & Epston, 1990).

One of the things we do as therapists is pay attention to stories that close down the possibilities for change. We then work to change those problematic stories to ones that engender hope, possibilities, validation, and accountability. Before discussing ways of promoting change, let's look at how to identify problematic stories.

The Four Problematic Stories

Some views are acceptable and some are not. There are stories involving blame, invalidation, nonaccountability or determinism, and impossibility that we have found to be troublesome for clients. We refer to these as the *four problematic stories.*

Stories of Blame. Stories of blame occur when individuals label themselves, or others label them, as having bad intentions or bad personality traits. These labels suggest that not only are people's intentions bad, but they are intentional or preconceived.

Clients who carry these types of stories about themselves will often think things such as, "It's my fault that he hit me" or "I'm bad because I was sexually abused." They either perceive themselves as damaged goods or believe they have innately bad intentions. Others can also convey these stories through statements such as, "He has no intention of changing" or "He's always playing head games and is never serious about anything."

> Example: A husband and wife came to therapy due to "constant arguments." During the initial session, the husband stated, "She's treated me that way forever. I swear she's trying to give me a heart attack."

Stories of Invalidation. Stories of invalidation are those that characterize clients as being abnormal or wrong in some way, or give them the message that they can't trust their perceptions. Oftentimes this occurs when the internal experience or knowledge of clients is undermined by others. Many clients will feel invalidated by others who say they are wrong, that they are making things up or making too much of something, or that they should move on and forget about things. Stories of invalidation can be detected through statements such as, "You shouldn't feel that way," "Just let it go," "She's too emotional," and "He needs to express his anger about his father's death; he just doesn't recognize how angry he is yet."

> Example: A single mother brought her adolescent son to therapy. She remarked, "Lots of kids have fathers who aren't involved in their lives. He needs to just get over the fact that that's the way it is."

Stories of Nonaccountability or Determinism. Stories of nonaccountability or determinism involve people not accepting responsibility for themselves and their actions. At times people will say things such as, "He made me do it," "I was drunk," or "I can't help it." We believe that people are accountable for the physical actions that they take. This is different from times when people have no choice and are intruded on without their consent. Then, the person who committed the intrusive act is accountable.

> Example: A young woman attended a party with some friends. During the evening, she became intoxicated and started a fight with another woman. She thought the woman was trying to steal her boyfriend. Later that evening as she was returning home, the young woman was raped by a man who had been at the same party.

The distinction here is that the young woman was accountable for what she did with her body and for those areas where she had choices. These included becoming intoxicated and fighting with another woman. She was not accountable for what was done to her that she had no choice in—being raped. Case Example 5.2 further illustrates this type of story.

Case Example 5.2 *Everyone's Accountable*

Bill had a client, Kim, who had come to therapy on the aftereffects of abuse. When Kim first came in, she had the view that she was responsible for all the abuse. She thought she should have done something to stop it. After some discussion, it became apparent that under the circumstances, she hadn't really had a choice in the matter. After realizing this, Kim concluded therapy. A few years later, she returned and said she had something very important and difficult to discuss. Three times (out of the hundreds of times it had happened) she had sought out her abuser and made herself available for the abuse. Bill immediately tried to reassure her, saying that she had been sexualized as a child and that she wasn't really responsible. "No," she told him firmly, "I know what you are trying to do and it won't work. Don't try to wave your therapeutic magic wand and free me from the responsibility of these incidents. I used to think I was responsible for it all, but now I'm telling you that it was just these three incidents. I was responsible for those. If you don't hold me responsible, then I can't hold him responsible for all those other times, since he was probably abused himself. It's important that you hold me accountable." Bill quickly realized his mistake and began to help her come to terms with what she had done.

Stories of Impossibility. There are also stories of impossibility. These involve ideas that maintain that clients are unable to change or are incapable of change. When stories of impossibility are present people will say things such as, "She'll never change," "He's just like his father," or "ADD never goes away."

> Example: A fourteen-year-old was referred to therapy by a school counselor due to chronic truancy. On the referral form, the school counselor had written, "This adolescent has had a history of truancy since the age of ten. Given the chronic and ongoing nature of this problem, it is extremely unlikely that she will change her behavior anytime soon."

As therapists, we want to challenge, create doubt in, and stand against stories of blame, invalidation, nonaccountability, and those that close down possibilities. Meanwhile, we seek to amplify and nurture ideas that run counter to the four problematic stories. These are stories that (1) allow for the possibility of change, (2) hold people accountable, and (3) validate. To illustrate how alternative stories that reflect these ideas can make a significant difference we offer the following:

> Years ago there was a group of young men who were part of the Flaming Arrow Patrol of Ingleside's Troop 294. Located in the Phoenix, Arizona area, the troop was supervised by various parents, one being a man named Dick Hoffman. Over time, Hoffman developed a view about one particular member of the troop. In describing the young man, he stated:

"He seemed to go in fits and starts—he would dash from one thing to another. I thought it was a disability, not being able to concentrate the way the rest of us would. I knew he was wildly enthusiastic, but I didn't think he had enough ability to analyze things.... I thought, 'When he grows up and gets into the real world he's going to have a tough time keeping up.' I didn't dream anything would come of him. Of course that was a complete misjudgment of the kid's personality." (McBride, 1997, pp. 77–78)

The story that the troop leader held of the young man influenced how he approached him and what he communicated to others about him. However, the young man himself did not subscribe to the same story. Instead, he carried an identity story that enabled him to become the director of such blockbuster movies as *E. T.: The Extraterrestrial, Close Encounters of the Third Kind, Schindler's List, Saving Private Ryan, Jurassic Park,* and *Jaws.* The young man was Steven Spielberg.

When clients enter therapy, they often have stories (ideas, beliefs, hypotheses, etc.) that contribute to their being stuck. These stories tend to be rigid and divisive. Stories are unhelpful when they prevent or get in the way of positive change. However, within every dominant, problem-saturated story are many others. These alternative stories offer different perspectives that contradict the problematic narrative. They represent validation, hope, resilience, possibilities, and accountability.

To challenge or cast doubt on problematic stories, therapists can transform the story by *acknowledging, adding the element of possibility, inviting accountability, finding counterevidence, and finding alternative stories or frames to fit the same evidence or facts.*

Transform the Story

In Chapter 2 we offered ways of acknowledging clients' experiences while simultaneously opening possibilities for change. We acknowledge and validate the current or past problematic points of view but add a twist that softens them a bit or adds a sense of possibility. For example, a mother may say of her son, "He doesn't care about our family. He just wants to do what he feels like doing, regardless of the pain it causes us." A therapist might respond by acknowledging the feelings and point of view of the parent, but then reflect it back with a softer, less global sense: "A lot of the things he's been doing have given you the sense he cares more for himself than for you or the family." Another reflection could add a sense of the possibility that things could change in the future: "You'd like to see him doing more things that show that he can put the family above his own interests at times." Here's another example of how to open up possibilities using this method:

CLIENT: My husband only thinks about himself. He doesn't care about anyone else. He only does things if they benefit him.

THERAPIST: A lot of what he's done has given you the sense that he only cares about himself.

CLIENT: Yeah, I mean, he hasn't shown me otherwise. It's frustrating.

THERAPIST: Okay, and, based on what you've seen, up until now it seems that he hasn't shown you any indication that things will be different, and that's frustrating.

CLIENT: Exactly. I'm waiting, but I may be waiting a long time.

In this example, the therapist acknowledged the client's internal experience (frustration) and then introduced the possibility that change might occur in the future. This was done by using statements relating to partiality ("a lot"), perceptions ("has given you the sense"), and past tense ("he's done," "you've seen," "hasn't shown"). These small changes in language assisted in the deconstruction of the complaint. The client went from saying that her husband "only thinks about himself," "doesn't care about anyone else," and "only does things if they benefit him" to "I'm waiting," suggesting a shift in view and the possibility of change in the future.

It has been said that language is a virus. We frequently hear clients repeat phrases that we routinely use in sessions, such as "back on track," "keep your feet moving," and "do something different." Small changes in the ways therapists use language can contribute to clients changing the ways they talk about their concerns, complaints, and problems. This can open the door for the possibility of change.

Invite Accountability

It is not uncommon for clients to carry stories of nonaccountability and determinism. Clients and others will attempt to justify an action or behavior by attributing it to a genetic, physiological, developmental, interpersonal, familial, or personality propensity, thereby removing accountability. For example, a client might say, "I have a chemical imbalance. If I don't take my medication I can't control what I do," "He's ADD. He can't help it," "My mom forgot to give me my medication so I didn't remember to call her," or "That's the way I am. That's what us bipolar's do."

We don't want to buy into these kinds of stories. While we want to acknowledge and validate internal experience, we also want to invite clients into stories of accountability, where they take responsibility for their actions and behaviors. Here are some ways of doing this:

Reflect clients' nonaccountability statements without the nonaccountability part. When clients use an excuse or explanation, therapists repeat the statement back, leaving out the part that they believe makes them unaccountable.

CLIENT: He called me a name. So I hit him.

THERAPIST: You hit him.

CLIENT: She yelled at me, so I left.

THERAPIST: You left.

CLIENT: I didn't get my medication, so I forgot the appointment.

THERAPIST: You forgot the appointment.

Find counterexamples that indicate choice or accountability. A second way to invite accountability is to search for exceptions to the actions or behavior for which the client is claiming unaccountability. Therapists can make generalizations here because it is impossible for a person to have a negative behavior at all times. Once an exception is identified it can be amplified to see how the client can become more accountable in the future. Here are three examples:

CLIENT: I was abused by my mother when I was younger. The only way I know to handle my anger is to lash out—and it's mostly toward women.

THERAPIST: I'm sorry that you were abused when you were younger. And I'm curious, because your wife said that yesterday when she told you her paycheck was smaller than usual, you got as angry as she's ever seen you. Yet you didn't take it out on her, you stomped out of the room. How did you do that?

CLIENT: The drugstore was out of my medication. What was I supposed to do? It's the thing that calms me down.

THERAPIST: I'm a little confused. You said that your medication has been changed several times in the past few months—and while that was happening you managed to go without incident at work. Even though your medication wasn't regulated at that time, how did you do that?

CLIENT: It's a family thing. My father and uncles were alcoholics. I can't stop drinking—it's genetic.

THERAPIST: So your sense is that if it runs in the family then you're predestined to have it run your life as well. You mentioned last time that there was a period of time earlier this year when you didn't drink for a month. How do you stand up to your genetics and take responsibility for yourself?

Use the word "and" to link internal experience and accountability together. We have stressed the importance of acknowledging and validating all internal experience. Although what people feel is acceptable, not all of their actions are acceptable. When therapists hear stories of nonaccountability it can be helpful to reflect what clients are experiencing internally and link it with that for which they are accountable. To do this, we use the word *and* (not *but*). Here are some examples:

CLIENT: I can't calm down with her on my case!

THERAPIST: You can feel like you can't calm down, and you can calm yourself down.

CLIENT: I get so upset that I just start cutting on my arm.

THERAPIST: It's okay to feel upset, and it's not okay to cut on yourself or hurt yourself.

CLIENT: She's always on my case. She makes me so mad that I hit her.

THERAPIST: It's okay to be mad and it's not okay to hit her.

We want to be sure to let clients know that their feelings and experiences are acceptable, but some actions are not. Although the three methods offered are relatively simple, they can help clients to make a distinction between their internal experiences and actions.

Find Counterevidence

This involves getting clients, or others who know them, to tell you something that doesn't fit with the problematic story. The therapist acknowledges the client and explores other aspects of the person's life, events, or situations to identify counterevidence. For example, to a parent who has described his son as being out of control a therapist might say, "You tell me that he's out of control, but now you're telling me that his teacher said he kept his cool when another boy taunted him in class." A therapist might say to a husband who has been violent toward his wife, "So, you tell me that you were raised in a family in which the only way to express anger was violence. But I'm curious, when you get angry you typically hit your wife and your son, but when you get mad at work do you hit your boss or the customers?" Case Example 5.3 shows another way to search for counterevidence.

Case Example 5.3 *It's Never Good Enough*

CLIENT: It doesn't matter what I do, it's never good enough for my boss.

THERAPIST: It seems to you like whatever you've done to this point hasn't been good enough for your boss.

CLIENT: Right. It just seems like I try and try and I always fall short.

THERAPIST: You've been trying and trying and somehow it seems like you haven't hit the standard he'd like yet. Is this something you would like to spend some time on?

CLIENT: Yeah, I mean I don't like it.

THERAPIST: Okay, tell me more about how this has affected you.

CLIENT: Well, it's like he gives me five things to do at the start of each day and inevitably he finds something wrong with each of them.

THERAPIST: Can you give me an example?

CLIENT: Yeah, yesterday I handed in two charts that took me all day and he just ripped me up and down about the one on cost analysis.

THERAPIST: Sounds like he was hard on you. I bet that didn't feel too good. (**Client nods in agreement**). And I'm curious, what happened with the other chart that you turned in yesterday?

CLIENT: He just glanced at it and then threw it into a pile.

THERAPIST: He didn't say anything . . . like you needed to redo it?

CLIENT: (Pondering the question) Nope. No, he just tossed it in a pile.

THERAPIST: What did that mean?

CLIENT: Well, that's kind of his way of saying that the work is acceptable.

THERAPIST: I see. So he's not the kind of person who really gives out the accolades. He just lets you know that the work is acceptable by putting it into a pile and not saying much to you about it.

CLIENT: Right. (**Pauses**) I guess sometimes my work meets his stringent criteria.

THERAPIST: Sometimes your work is up to par in his eyes—not as often as you'd like—but on occasion he's as pleased as he's going to be.

CLIENT: Right.

In this particular case the client held a story that reflected impossibility. The view he held was that his work was never, and would never be, good enough for his boss. The therapist did two things. First, the therapist acknowledged the client and interjected the idea of possibility into otherwise impossibility-laden statements. Next, the therapist searched for and was able to find that there were times when his work was acceptable to his boss. This represents counterevidence. Let's look at another example of this in Case Example 5.4.

Case Example 5.4 *She Never Goes by the Rules*

FATHER: Jennifer never goes by the rules. In fact, I don't know why we even have rules. She doesn't think they apply to her.

THERAPIST: It seems that Jennifer really hasn't been following the rules. Tell me a little about the particular rules that she's broken that have been most bothersome.

FATHER: Well, she doesn't do her chores. That's the main problem. I just can't get her to lift a finger.

THERAPIST: I see. It seems like she hasn't helped out as much as maybe she should.

FATHER: Not at all. I'd settle for any effort at this point.

THERAPIST: Okay, and when was the last time you can remember her pitching in?

FATHER: I don't know. Maybe a month ago she helped her mother with the dishes.

JENNIFER: A month ago! I did them yesterday! Are you blind?

FATHER: Wonders never cease! You should have done them anyway.

THERAPIST: (To Jennifer) Do you sometimes do other things too and pitch in more?

JENNIFER: My room is always clean.

THERAPIST: Really? How do you manage to keep it clean?

JENNIFER: It's easy, I just make sure I have it straightened before I go to bed.

THERAPIST: Terrific. What else do you do sometimes?

JENNIFER: I take the dog out every morning.

THERAPIST: (To the father) Is that accurate?

FATHER: Well, yeah, she does. But she's responsible for doing those things.

THERAPIST: Right. There are some things that she's responsible for and it's been frustrating to you when she hasn't done them all. Is it safe to say that with some rules she shows more responsibility than others?

FATHER: Yeah, that's true.

In this example the therapist once again began by acknowledging the father and tuning into his use of statements that reflected impossibility. The therapist then made subtle changes to introduce possibilities and began to search for counterevidence. As counterevidence was found, the problematic story began to dissolve.

In searching for counterevidence we've found it helpful to start in the present and work backward. The more recent the evidence that counters the problematic story, the more powerful it tends to be. Sometimes therapists will have to go back a few weeks, months, or even years to find such evidence. The idea is to be persistent and work toward finding exceptions to problematic stories that represent abilities that have been covered up or have gone unnoticed. These abilities are important because it's generally easier to get clients to do what has worked for them in the past instead of trying to teach them something completely new. If it is an ability they've already used sometime in the past then they don't need to learn a new skill.

For example, Bob works with many adolescents. Parents will sometimes say things such as, "He's always been a poor student," "He's never been able to apply himself," or "He's too hyper to concentrate long enough to do the work." In turn, adolescents will say things such as, "I've never been a good student," "I'm ADD so I can't focus," or "I'm too stupid. I can't do it." These stories are laced with blame, invalidation, nonaccountability, and impossibility. If therapists accept these stories at face value then they're likely to become as stuck as the clients.

As a result of hearing such stories, many therapists will assume that the adolescent (or other person) needs to be taught to be a better student, to concentrate better, to focus, and so on. As with exceptions, counterevidence is a way of orienting clients to times when things were a little different in regard to the problematic story. When working with an adolescent who is struggling with grades, a therapist might search for counterevidence by assuming some past ability, saying:

> You know, when most people were very young, maybe in early grades like third, fourth, and fifth, they did okay in school. You see, one thing that I know about you is that you've been learning for many years. If that weren't true you never would have learned your left hand from your right or the alphabet. You wouldn't have learned how to form words, to make sentences, or to read and write. Somehow you learned these things even when you thought they were so hard that you'd never figure them out.

The therapist can then ask, "When was the last time you remember doing better in school?" This is followed with questions such as, "What do you remember doing that helped you learn things that you didn't think you would ever learn?" "How did you manage to learn things that you didn't think you would be able to learn?" and so on. Although these questions often go unanswered, they reorient people to times when things were different regarding the problematic stories that have been dominating their lives. Here are some questions that can assist with this process:

- What was different before the problem began to have such influence in your life?
- Tell me about a time when things went a little different in regard to the problem.
- How far back would you have to go to find a time when things went just a little better in regard to the problem you're facing?

These questions help clients notice what was different about times when they had some influence over the problem. They can be followed up with inquiries as to what the person did differently at those times. This can help identify actions the client took as the result of a different view. Oftentimes clients can then begin to use past actions that were helpful to manage the problem and to move in a preferred direction.

Find Alternative Stories

At times clients' interpretations, explanations, and evaluations of themselves, others, events, or situations close down the possibilities for change. This is because clients are acting in ways that are consistent with such rigid views. In these cases it can be helpful to offer a different point of view in an effort to dissolve the problematic story. It is essential that therapists do not state these points of views as facts or truths. We want to give clients the space to accept or reject all or some of the therapists' interpretations. Once again, the use of conjecture can aid in this process.

To offer alternative stories or frames of reference we give the facts a more benevolent interpretation. For example, a therapist might say, "You get the sense he only wants to do what he wants, when he wants. I'm wondering if he's trying to find a way to be independent and make his own decisions. When you come down hard on him, perhaps the only way he feels he can show his independence is to rebel and resist you, even if it gets him in trouble." In more traditional approaches to therapy this is sometimes referred to as reframing. Case Example 5.5 shows one way to offer a new perspective to a client.

Case Example 5.5 *Exploring New Territory*

JAMES (ADOLESCENT): My mother doesn't have a clue about what's going on. She thinks she does. What a joke! All she does is ground me and make rules and try to make my life miserable. If she wants me to hate her she's doing a good job.

THERAPIST: It seems to you that your mother's mission is to put restrictions on you and make your life miserable.

LAUREN (MOTHER): I've tried to raise him to be respectful of others and look at the result! It's a rare day when he goes by the rules. All he does is fight with me. I'm very bitter about it.

THERAPIST: You've tried hard and it seems that your efforts to teach him so far haven't been as successful as you'd like. I can see how that might make you bitter.

LAUREN: I am.

THERAPIST (To James): You know, your mom hasn't raised a fifteen-year-old boy before, and you haven't been a fifteen-year-old before. I wonder if your mom is doing what she thinks is best for you. Maybe she will need some further education about what it's like to be a teenager in this day and age. **(To Lauren)** You mentioned before that you have a seventeen-year-old daughter who is doing well. Perhaps you're finding out that it can be different raising daughters and sons. Some of the things you've tried haven't worked and some have. I'm wondering if you're still making the adjustments to raising a fifteen-year-old son versus a fifteen-year-old daughter.

A new interpretation of the same evidence or facts can lead to a new perspective for clients. If clients change their frames of reference, their actions are more likely to be in accordance with those views. For example, if a father believes that his son's behavior is a result of manipulation, the father will act in one way. However, if the same father sees his son's behavior as an indication that he needs more affection, the father is likely to respond in another way. We want to help clients subscribe to views that will generate creativity, change, and possibilities.

Sometimes problematic stories become so embedded in clients' lives that it becomes hard for them to see anything but the problems. When people seek or are referred for therapy, one of the major concerns is that they start to organize their views of themselves and others' views of them in terms of their illness. Pathologized people behave pathologically. The job of the therapist is to help such clients change their views and see and experience themselves as capable and accountable. Case Example 5.6 demonstrates that a shift in a therapist's view can lead to new ways of acting and interacting, thereby affecting the clients' view of themselves. Being treated with dignity can make all the difference, as was the case with the client we call "Mrs. Terror."

Case Example 5.6 *Mrs. Terror*

(This case example is from Birgitta Hedstrom, Sundsvall, Sweden)

The caseworker was at her wit's end. Two or three times a day, without an appointment, the woman would appear in the social services office, demanding to see her case worker, Mrs. Johanssen. She would swear and bang things if she was told she would have to wait because Mrs. Johanssen was in a meeting, with another client, out to lunch, or off work that day. Other clients had learned to clear out of the waiting room because they had been hit, sworn at, or threatened by this unkempt, wild woman. She had come to be known as "Mrs. Terror" by all in the social service office.

When Mrs. Johanssen was finally available, Mrs. Terror would begin the meeting with a threat, yelling and banging around the office. Mrs. Johanssen had become a nervous wreck and was afraid of Mrs. Terror. Coming to work was getting harder and harder. In desperation, she brought up the situation to Birgitta Hedstrom, the consultant for the social services office. She had little hope Mrs. Hedstrom could offer any real help. Birgitta is a possibility thinker, but hearing about this situation was a challenge even to her optimism.

As she discussed the situation of Mrs. Terror with the entire staff they discovered two intriguing features of the situation that seemed to offer some possibilities. One was that even when she was swearing and threatening, Mrs. Terror always used the polite form of address (Mrs., Mr., etc.). Most of the clients in social services came to call the staff by their first names. The second interesting fact was that although visits to Mrs. Terror's apartment revealed that it was generally a mess, with garbage, broken furniture, and clothing strewn about, she kept one beautiful Chinese vase intact and well cared for.

Birgitta became intrigued and asked more about Mrs. Terror. The staff said that she had come to Sweden from a place in another country that also happened to be the place where the Queen of Sweden, much beloved by Swedes, came from. Birgitta asked the staff to think about how they would treat the Queen if she happened to drop by unannounced one day. She suggested they treat Mrs. Terror the same way the next time she came in. They laughed and quickly got into the fun of it. The receptionist, Mrs. Andersson, who could tolerate many unusual behaviors in a calm manner, was especially keen on this idea. It was agreed that Mrs. Andersson would take on the task of making Queen Terror feel welcome the next time she appeared in the office. Mrs. Andersson prepared a special brew of nice coffee and kept it in a thermos next to her, along with two beautiful ceramic cups she brought from home to substitute for the usual styrofoam cups used in the office.

When Queen Terror arrived, instead of the usual brusque manner she used with the woman, Mrs. Andersson quickly jumped up and greeted her like an old friend. "Hello," she said. "Welcome. I assume you've come to see Mrs. J. She's busy right now, but can I get you a cup of coffee while you are waiting?" Queen Terror appeared confused and uncertain in response to this atypical greeting. "Coffee would be nice, Mrs. Andersson," she said softly. When Mrs. Andersson appeared with the beautiful mugs of delicious coffee, she sat down and began to chat with the Queen about this and that. The Queen responded enthusiastically to this talk and spoke quite normally. After her coffee was finished, she promptly announced that she did not need to see Mrs. Johanssen after all. "Are you sure?" asked Mrs. Andersson. "I'm sure she won't be long. Won't you please wait?" But the Queen waved her off. "No, it's okay."

Several succeeding days saw a repetition of this scene, with the same outcome. Soon, the Queen began to skip days and only show up on the day of her appointment, now behaving and speaking much more civilly.

During an appointment not long after, the Queen asked Mrs. Johanssen for her help in being able to keep her apartment. It seemed that she had previously terrorized many of the tenants with the same kind of behavior that she had shown in the social service office, and was subsequently being evicted. Mrs. Johanssen, impressed with the dramatic change in Mrs. Terror's behavior, agreed to be her advocate and intercede with the landlord. Mrs. Johanssen got the reluctant landlord to agree to a joint meeting at the social services office.

He arrived, belligerent, with lawyer in tow, ready for the worst. But Queen Terror arrived and did not throw the angry scene the landlord expected. Instead, she softly told him that the eviction notice had caused her much pain. The landlord softened a bit and told her that he could understand that. She told him that it had also hurt her when he had gotten her committed twice to a psychiatric hospital. Tears ran down her face as she softly told him of the humiliation she had faced being taken away in front of the neighbors. He apologized for her pain, but said that he had felt it was the only option he had. She told him that she understood. She also said that she had visited every neighbor in the apartment building, asking them if they thought she deserved a second chance. They had unanimously agreed, and had also agreed to vouch for her to the landlord if necessary. She also asked the landlord to admit that many of the other tenants had behaved in a similar manner, disrupting their neighbors' lives. He admitted that this was true. Why was she being singled out then, she asked. The landlord had no good answer for this. She asked him if he could see his way to giving her a second chance. He agreed.

Mrs. Johanssen ended the meeting and called Birgitta Hedstrom. "I now believe in miracles," she said. " I have seen one today." Several years of follow-up has shown that when treated like a queen, the former Mrs. Terror could behave with grace and dignity.

Here are some further ways of finding alternative stories or frames or reference:

Identify a valuing witness. Search for people who do not view the client as disabled, incapable, or crazy. Find at least one person who can see beyond the problem or who can remember the client before the problem arrived in his or her life. We call this person the *valuing witness.* The valuing witness can be an old friend or family member. If the witness is available, we often invite them in to get some evidence for this more hopeful, healthy view of the client. If the witness is not available in person, you can ask the client to stand in for the witness. For example, "If your best friend were here, what would he be able to tell me about the Jim who was here long before schizophrenia? What kind of person is that Jim?"

Look for hidden strengths. Find out about hidden or nonobvious aspects of the person or the person's life that do not fit with their disempowered (hopeless, helpless, or stuck) views about themselves or the problem. Ask the person, or his or her intimates, how they explain the incompatibility.

When you listen with ears of hope and possibility, you'll often hear something during the course of a conversation or session that contradicts the view that this person is out of control, can't change, isn't responsible, or whatever the case may be. It's a bit like finding a picture of a polluted urban scene and noticing a pristine mountain lake in the middle. Train yourself to notice what is right with the picture (that is, what doesn't fit with the problematic story).

Normalize and de-stigmatize. One of the insidious things about any problem—especially psychotherapy problems—is that clients begin to think of themselves as different from others in a bad way. They begin to feel isolated and actually be isolated. Connecting these clients with others who have experienced similar struggles and have found alternative ways to think about them or deal with them can be very helpful. These types of connections can be made through books, tapes, letters, or support groups. Whatever the mode, these connections can help normalize the experience.

Reauthoring Stories through Externalizing Conversations

Throughout this chapter we have discussed the implications of clients' views of themselves, others, events, and situations. We've also emphasized the role of stories in peoples' lives. Stories are social constructions of meaning and understanding that can vary greatly (Berger & Luckmann, 1966). As clinicians we are mindful that because stories are socially constructed, they are changeable.

In some cases problematic views and stories seem to take on a life of their own. In this way the person becomes the problem. As discussed in Chapter 3 with labels, the person identifies himself or herself as the problem, or others refer to the person as the label or problem. This implies that the person is characterologically flawed or bad.

Another way to change these stories and the viewing of problems is to use the narrative therapy idea of *externalizing* (White & Epston, 1990). This method is especially useful when people already have diagnoses and labels, particularly those that haven't been empowering, validating, or facilitative of the change process. Narrative therapy, an approach cocreated by Michael White and David Epston, holds that people live in stories. They are influenced by stories about their lives, where they have come from, where they are, and where they are going, as well as who they are. These stories are never exact representations of their lives and often leave out crucial details and distort others. Narrative therapists work to reauthor people's lives in ways that honor them and open up possibilities for change.

The hallmark of the narrative approach is the credo, "The person is never the problem; the problem is the problem." Through use of externalization (their most well-known process), narrative therapists are able to acknowledge the power of labels while both avoiding the trap of reinforcing people's attachment to them and letting them escape responsibility for their behavior. Externalization offers a way of viewing clients as having parts of them that are uncontaminated by the symptom. This automatically creates a view of the person as undetermined and as accountable for the choices he or she makes in relationship to the problem.

While externalization is the main way that narrative therapists go about creating change, we view it as a process, not a technique. It is a way of having conversations with clients whereby they are able to view themselves as separate from problems in order to challenge actions, interactions, and ways of thinking that are blaming or unhelpful. In this way they can experience their association with problems differently, and allow the emergence of a new view and story. Now let's explore this process.

Create a Name for the Problem

The therapist begins by having a conversation with the client(s) whereby the problem is given a name. This collaborative process involves attentive listening by the clinician because the name of the problem typically evolves from the conversation. For example, if a parent says, "He's always in trouble," a therapist might begin the externalizing process by saying, "So Trouble has made its way into your son's life." A therapist might ask a child who has been having temper tantrums, "So, Anger has been convincing you to throw yourself on the floor and kick your feet, huh?" To a person who has been having paranoid hallucinations, you could ask, "When Paranoia whispers in your ear, do you always listen?" At first, the client and others may persist in attributing the problem to the person, so the therapist may need to gently persist in the other direction, linguistically severing the person from the problem label. Then clients themselves soon begin to take on the externalized view of the problem.

Most of the time, the names that are given to problems will be a direct reflection of the name itself. Examples might include Anorexia, ADD, Fighting, Violence, and so on. With younger clients there will be more room for creativity. Here are some examples of creative names that our clients and their families have come up with:

- Temper Tantrums—Mr. or Ms. Tantrum
- Truancy—Mr. I. B. Truant
- Incomplete Homework—Ms. Ing Homework
- Trouble Sitting Still—Ants N. Mypants

Personify the Problem

The next step in the process involves the therapist talking with the person or family as if the problem were another person with an identity, will, tactics, and intentions that are designed to oppress or dominate the person or the family. Often, the therapist will use images that help bring the process to life for the client. For example, "How long has Anorexia been lying to you?" or "How does the Alcoholism Bully push your family around?"

This starts to free the client, and those around him or her, from identifying himself or herself as the problem and evokes motivation to change. For example, if you are working with a client experiencing anorexia who continues to identify herself as an anorexic, she would have to defend herself against any attempt to change as an attack on her and her autonomy. Externalizing questions both separate her identity from Anorexia and attribute bad and tricky intentions to Anorexia, so she can use that defensive energy to stand up to the problem. Here are some questions that can assist you with this next part:

- How long has ______ been trying to convince you to lead a life you don't agree with?
- When did ______ first come over to visit without permission?
- When did you first notice ______ lingering around and making noise?

Investigate How the Problem Negatively Affects the Client

Before the therapist tries to create change with the situation, he or she finds out how the client has felt influenced by the problem to do or experience things he or she didn't like. The therapist might ask anyone in the room about the effects of the problem on the client and on him or her. This both acknowledges the client's suffering, and the extent to which his or her life and relationships have been limited by the problem, and provides further opportunities to create the externalization by asking more questions. For example, a therapist might ask, "When has Jealousy convinced you to do something you regretted later?" or "What kinds of tricks does Anorexia use on your daughter to alienate her from those she loves?" or "What kind of lies has Depression been telling you about your worth as a person?" Here are some other general questions that can be of assistance at this point:

- How has ______ come between you and your (family, friends, etc.)?
- When has ______ recruited you to do something that you later got in trouble for?
- What intentions do you think ______ has for you?

It's important to note that the language used here is not deterministic. The problem never causes or makes the person or the family do anything, it only influences, invites, tells, tries to convince, uses tricks, tries to recruit, and so on. This language highlights people's choices and creates an assumption of accountability, rather than blame or determinism. If the person is not the problem, but has a certain relationship to the problem, then the relationship can change. If the problem invites rather than forces, one can turn down the invitation. If the problem is trying to recruit a client, he or she can refuse to join.

This step also increases motivation. The person, couple, or family come together with the therapist in their common goal of overthrowing the dominance of the problem.

Discover Unique Outcomes to the Problem

At this point the therapist talks with the person, couple, or family about moments of choice or success that there have been in regard to the problem. These moments represent times when the person and others haven't been dominated or cornered by the problem and experienced things they didn't like. This tack, involving a search for unique outcomes (White & Epston, 1990), is akin to the solution-based method of searching for exceptions to the problem. However, whereas a solution-based therapist might ask, "What was the longest time you have gone without drugs?", a narrative therapist would ask, "So what's the longest time you have been able to stand up to Cravings?" No matter how the question is answered, the assumption that the problem is separate from the person has been reinforced. Gradually, a new reality begins to be created. Typical questions during this phase of the interview are: "Tell me about some times when you haven't believed the lies Anorexia has told you?" or "When have you seen Johnny stand up to the Temper Tantrum Monster?" Here are some other possible questions:

- When have you been able to take a stand against ______?
- When has ______ whispered in your ear but you didn't listen?
- Tell me about times when ______ couldn't convince you to ______?

This step shows that change is possible, highlighting moments when the problem has not happened or when it has been successfully overcome. Again, language is a virus. By now the virus of externalizing the problem is running quite rampant through the therapeutic system.

Find a New View of the Person

This is where the process of externalizing gets interesting. Here, the client's identity and life story begin to be rewritten. This is the narrative part. The previous steps have been used to prepare for rewriting clients' stories about themselves. Narrative therapists use the evidence of discovered competence as a gateway to a parallel universe, one in which the person has a different life story, one in which he or she is competent and heroic. To keep this from being merely a glib reframing of the person's life, therapists ask for stories and evidence from the past to show that the person was actually competent, strong, and spirited, but that he or she didn't always realize it or put a lot of emphasis on that aspect of him- or herself. The therapist gets the client and the family to support and flesh out this view.

This aspect of the externalizing process involves finding out about the resilient qualities of the client or others, which have allowed them to stand up to the problem. This represents a change or shift in self and the client's identity story. To find out about qualities we ask questions that reflect the overall question, "Who are you?" Here are some examples:

- What qualities do you think you possess that help you to stand up to ______'s plans for you?
- Who are you such that you were able to reject ______'s taunting?
- How do you explain that you are the kind of person who would lodge a protest against ______?

It is also important to root this new sense of self in a past and future so bright the person will have to wear shades. Typical questions might be: "What can you tell me about your past that would help me understand how you've been able to take these steps to stand up to Anorexia so well?" and "Who knew you as a child who wouldn't be surprised that you've been able to reject Violence as the dominant force in your relationship?" Here are some other questions to consider asking clients:

- What do you think ______ would say if he/she could hear you talk about standing up to ______?
- Who is someone who has known all along that you had the ability to take your life back from the grasp of ______?
- What is it about your experiences in life that have aided you in rejecting ______'s advances?

Speculate about the Future

Next, the therapist helps the person, couple, or family to speculate on what future developments will result now that the person is seen as competent and strong, and what changes will result as the person keeps resisting the problem. For example, "As you continue to stand up to Anorexia, what do you think will be different about your future than the future Anorexia had planned for you?" or "As Jan continues not to believe the lies that Delusions are telling her, how do you think that will affect her relationship with her friends?" This step is designed to further crystallize the new view of the person and his or her life. Here are some questions to help with this:

- As ______ continues to stand up to ______, how do you think that will affect her relationships with family members?
- As you continue to keep the upper hand with ______, what do you think will be different about ______, compared to what ______ had planned for you?
- How do you think your strategy with ______ will help you in the future?

Find an Audience for the New Story

Since the client developed the problem in a social context, it is important to make arrangements for the social environment to be involved in supporting the new story or identity that has emerged. This can be done by writing letters, asking for advice from other people suffering from the same or similar problems, and arranging for meetings with family members and friends. Some questions might be: "Who could you tell about your development as a member of the Anti-Diet League that could help celebrate your freedom from Unreal Body Images?" and "Are there people who have known you when you were not under the influence of Depression who could remind you of your accomplishments and that your life is worth living?" Here are a few others:

- Who else needs to know about the stance you've taken against ______?
- Who needs to know that you've made a commitment to keep ______ from hanging out without permission?
- Who could benefit from knowing about your enlistment in the ______ club?

The therapist keeps using this process until it is clear it has taken in the client's life. This is when the client (or his or her family) reports that things are changing for the better in relation to the problem. This is also reflected when the client starts to see himself or herself in the new, more competent, choice-saturated view, even when outside the therapist's direct influence. This may happen within a few sessions, but can also be a more extensive process.

Having just given you this formula for externalizing, we must give you a warning—if externalization is approached purely as a technique, it will probably not produce profound effects. If you don't believe to the bottom of your soul that people are not their problems and that their difficulties are social and personal constructions, then you won't be seeing the same results that the best narrative therapists routinely get.

Additionally, some clients will struggle with this different use of language. If it doesn't work for them, try something else that fits better with their ways of talking about problems, possibilities, and solutions. It's also okay to use the unique way of using language without subscribing to the entire process. Although you will not be externalizing the problem, subtle changes in language can help clients to gain a different view on problems.

The Resilience Factor: Tapping into Qualities Within

In the last section we referred to qualities of clients and how they allow them to manage, negotiate, and move through difficult times and adversity. Researchers have referred to this as resilience. Michael Rutter (1987) defined resilience as "the positive role of individual differences in people's responses to stress and adversity" (p. 316). Resiliency relates to adverse situations people have lived or grown up in (i.e., low economic resources, underprivileged circumstances, high crime areas, abusive environments) and have managed to survive (Herman, 1992; Higgins, 1994; Katz, 1997; Wolin & Wolin, 1993). Case Example 5.7 illustrates the idea of resilience.

Case Example 5.7 ***Standing Up to Adversity***

Bob worked with a twelve-year-old boy at a local hospital who had been seeing psychiatrists, psychologists, and psychotherapists for over six years. He had been assigned multiple diagnoses and his was deemed a chronic case. His mother had also been diagnosed with several psychiatric disorders and was emotionally unstable. Additionally, his father was a severe alcoholic with an assortment of ongoing health problems. The family also had housing and financial problems.

The twelve-year-old had a remarkable ability to take care of himself, and at times, others in the family as well. He routinely sought out those people who he knew he could count on for support and help: teachers, neighbors, friends, and mental health professionals. He reminded his mother of his appointments and dealt with her erratic behavior on a daily basis. He helped his father even though he was frequently embarrassed by his episodes of drinking. As if growing up wasn't hard enough, the young boy took on the day-to-day challenges that life presented him.

The young boy became legendary at the hospital for continually overcoming adversity. Over and over he survived conditions that were unimaginable to most people. He somehow mined his own resourcefulness to survive, and in doing so, taught his parents how to do the same.

In many cases clients continue to move from day to day despite the odds they face. However, they don't always notice those qualities and actions that enable them to do so. By orienting clients toward these aspects of themselves, it is possible to help them to change the views they have of themselves and their situations and help them to use those resources to deal with future adversity.

In tapping into reliance, we do two things: (1) search for resilience qualities and (2) find out about actions that have resulted from being resilient. Here are some questions to assist with each of these parts:

Resilient Qualities

- What qualities do you possess that you seem to be able to tap into in times of trouble?
- What is it about you that allows you to keep going?
- What is it about you that seems to come to the forefront when you're facing difficult situations/problems?
- Who are you that you've been able to face up to the challenges that life has presented you?
- What would others say are the qualities that you have that keep you going?

Actions Informed by Resilient Qualities

- What have the qualities that you possess allowed you to do that you might not have otherwise done?
- Given the type of person that you are, what do you do on a regular basis to manage the challenges you face?
- In the midst of all that has happened, how have you managed to keep going?
- Tell me about a time when you were able to deal with something that could have stopped you from moving forward in life. What did you do?

These questions are designed to evoke clients' inner qualities and the actions they've taken. We are not trying to convince clients of anything. We are not saying, "Don't you see all the wonderful qualities that you have?" That's invalidating to people who are suffering and in pain. Instead, clients are convincing us by answering our questions. They are doing self-inventories and tapping into their personal resources. This allows clients to shift their views and attribute change or control to their personal qualities, internal abilities and resources, and actions.

That Reminds Me of a Story: Stories and Metaphors as Healing Rituals

For hundreds of years, stories have captivated people. Stories, including fairy and folk tales, myths, and metaphors, are a universal means of communicating and are an accepted part of nearly all walks of life. In many instances stories shape our vision of the world. Although the degree to which they are used varies between societies and cultures, the healing value of stories is widely recognized.

What is it about stories that makes them so healing? First, they engage people and hold their attention. Listeners wonder what is going to happen next and how the story is going to end. When listeners' attention is captured, it is more likely that they will gain some meaning from the story. In addition to capturing attention, stories also allow people to create new meanings and understandings that can lead to possibilities. We think of stories as a way of accessing multiple pathways that can help clients feel less stuck in their problems. Some of the ways stories do this are by:

- Normalizing the experiences of clients
- Acknowledging realities and experiences
- Offering hope
- Offering new perspectives and possibilities
- Bypassing everyday conscious ways of processing information
- Reminding clients of previous solutions and resources

Stories can help normalize because they convey the sense that others have had similar experiences. Stories that normalize, but do not invalidate or downplay experiences, can help clients feel a little less shameful and a little less isolated. Therapists can use stories as a way of acknowledging clients' experiences and letting them know that they have been heard. This can strengthen the client–therapist relationship. Case Example 5.8 shows one way that attention to a client's metaphor frame facilitated the therapeutic relationship and alliance.

Case Example 5.8 *Roller Coasters and Riverboat Rides*

Bob met with a family consisting of a mother, her fifteen-year-old daughter, and her twelve-year-old son. The mother requested therapy after her daughter and son had taken her car out for a joyride in the middle of the night. While on their excursion they caused an accident with another vehicle, abandoned the car, and left the scene. In addition to this incident, the mother reported that her daughter and son had been stealing from her and were constantly in trouble.

During the session the mother was very tearful and distraught. She said, "It's all too much. I feel like I'm on a roller coaster."

"If you could get off the roller coaster and change rides what would you choose?" inquired Bob.

The woman pondered the question then replied, "Well, I've never liked roller coasters. I prefer the calm rides—maybe a riverboat ride."

"How might a riverboat ride be different from a roller coaster?" inquired Bob.

"Roller coasters move too fast and they go up and down too much. There's just too many hills and dips," she continued. "Riverboat rides can be bumpy, but not too bumpy, and they're slower."

Stories can also offer hope. One way that this occurs is by highlighting alternate ways of viewing and doing things. Clients get the sense that things can change and that there are possibilities in the future. Hope and an expectation of change are embedded in some stories. Stories also offer new perspectives and possibilities for clients and can remind them of previous solutions and resources. Stories serve as a way of helping clients shift their patterns of attention to create new, hopeful narratives.

There is a Hassidic story of a rabbi who is consulted by two men who are having a conflict. The rabbi listens to the first man, who advocates his point of view in the matter. When the first man finishes, the rabbi declares, "You are right." The second man objects, and proceeds to relate his view. The rabbi says, "Yes, you are right." The rabbi's assistant, who has been listening, interjects, "Wait a minute, Rabbi, they can't both be right!" To this, the rabbi responds, "And you are right." As therapists, our view of stories is similar. There is not a single, correct meaning that comes from a story. Each person can get something different from a single story.

Different types of stories resonate with people in different ways. Interestingly, the stories that we believe are the most profound may not affect our clients. Sometimes the stories we think are simple and unsensational can have deep effects with clients. They will come back months later and say, "That story you told me about the boat, that really made a difference for me!" (At that moment, you might be struggling to remember what story that was.) Stories reach clients at the different levels of experience. What we want to do is pay attention to the verbal and nonverbal responses of clients to stories. Their responses tell us how to proceed.

The stories that we use in therapy come from a variety of contexts. We file them away until something a client says triggers one of the stories. We then use them when they may offer clients a pathway to healing in one of the aforementioned ways. For example, here's a story we often tell in therapy when parents are having trouble setting clear limits for their kids:

> Just before Bill's father died he came down to Arizona, where Bill was living at the time, for a visit. The elder O'Hanlon had cancer, and he was reflecting on his life in a casual conversation. He said that he had learned one thing from raising eight kids. That got Bill's curiosity going. What was the one thing he learned?
>
> "What I learned is that each of my kids has to hit a brick wall, and that is how they learn about life."
>
> "What do you mean *brick wall?*" Bill asked.
>
> "When one of you kids was messing up and about to do something that could negatively affect your future, like using drugs or alcohol, getting into trouble with the law, getting involved with a bad group of kids, or getting bad grades, it was like you were riding a motorcycle aimed for a brick wall. As a parent, I saw the brick wall. For your two oldest brothers, I stood between them and the wall, flailed my arms, and yelled, 'Hey, you are headed for a brick wall. You are about to mess up with that drinking. You are getting bad grades at school and won't be able to go on to college. You are involved with someone who is clearly taking advantage of you or is going to break your heart.' They would rev up the motorcycle, give me a rude gesture, and crash headlong into me and we'd both hit the wall. Then we somehow got ourselves back up and limped back into life."

After getting sandwiched between the hypothetical motorcycle and emotional brick wall many times with his first two kids, Mr. O'Hanlon wised up a bit. Rather than stepping off the curb, he held his perch on the street's edge and loudly warned the next several children. This method produced the same results—minus the serious damage to the father. The kids still sped up, gestured rudely, and pounded into the brick wall. Finally, after watching six children slam into countless brick walls, Mr. O'Hanlon got the message.

"I finally realized this is how kids learn," he said. "I would take a seat on a curbside bench and tell my youngest two kids, 'Look. I'm an old man. I've been around for a while. I think there is a brick wall up there. I think you're headed for it. You probably think I'm full of it, and you probably won't listen because you think you know better than I do. Here is your opportunity to learn whether you do or not.' When I'd say it that way, they would slow down, the rude gesture would drop out, and they would still hit the brick wall. That is the way kids learn that there are limits in life, that there are consequences, and that they are accountable for what they do.

"If I thought they were going to die, I would reach over and try to pull the key out of the motorcycle. But I couldn't follow them around every minute, so at those times I just hoped I raised you kids with some common sense, or that you would be lucky, or that my prayers would protect you. You know, it never got any easier to see my kids hit the brick wall. I always wanted them not to. I finally just realized they all would in one way or another. It would tear my heart out to see them get hurt. But I learned that kids have to hit brick walls, and that is how they learn about life and responsibility."

Telling this seems much more effective than giving the parents a talk on the importance of setting and keeping limits and letting kids learn from their own mistakes. We've had parents (and kids, surprisingly) come back to the next meeting telling us that the story had helped them take a entirely different and more effective approach. Such is the power of stories.

Future Pull: Creating or Evoking a Compelling Future and Finding a Vision for the Future

As discussed in Chapter 4, we often think that the past determines the present and the future. From a collaborative, competency-based perspective the past is not a determinant, but an influence on the present and the future. We often help people connect to a preferred imagined future and then work backward to the present to guide both the therapy process and the person's life. As in earlier sections on assessment, we cannot very well proceed with the therapy unless we know where people want to go and how they will know when therapy is over. Otherwise there is a danger that we would be imposing our own ideas and preferences on their lives and on the therapy.

Another major use of this future orientation is to help create a sense of hope and possibility for clients. Focusing on a future in which things are better can give people the energy to deal with current problems and struggles. At times merely shifting the focus (or the viewing, as we have called it) from the past or the present to the future may be therapeutic. It can also be helpful in another way. Just as Viktor Frankl did years ago, we can help clients mine the future for a direction and then work backward to the present to determine (from that direction) what the next step might be. If Frankl was going toward a future in which he was going to give a lecture in post-war Vienna, what did he need to do next to move toward that future? He needed to stand up and take a step.

Likewise, if a client who is shy envisions a future in which he is in a romantic relationship, what is an appropriate step to take the next time he meets someone he is interested in? Perhaps instead of his usual strategy of looking away and getting quiet, he might make eye contact and say "hi." Maybe he could attend a social event rather than staying home as usual. He could take a course in public speaking to start to overcome his reluctance to speak in social situations. The point is that if he is beginning to get a new sense of his future, new actions would probably arise out of that new sense.

In our experience, the lack of a future vision can have extremely debilitating effects. For example, many clients experiencing suicidal ideations have no vision of the future without pain and suffering. The same can be true for clients who have been sexually abused or traumatized in some way. They won't want to go on because of the intense pain and lack of hope they are experiencing.

For other clients the absence of a vision for the future will simply leave them going nowhere fast. For example, in the motion picture *Good Will Hunting,* Will Hunting seems to have little sense of the future. He appears to meander from day to day. In one particular scene, his therapist, Sean McGuire, asks Will what he wants. Will's response is, "I want to be a shepherd." He continues to play games until the therapist has had enough and tells him to leave. Interestingly, Will later gains a vision of the future and what he wants. He then takes steps to put that plan in motion.

Similarly, we can help clients create or rehabilitate a future where pain and suffering are diminished or have gone away completely. This can influence their views of the present and the past. Once that vision has been established we can help them determine what steps are necessary to move toward that preferred future.

How does the therapist help shift clients' views toward a preferred future? One way is by asking questions and using methods that encourage a focus on the future. For us, then, there are three aspects of this technique that bring a preferred future alive in therapy. The first is to help clients to connect with and articulate a preferred future. Next, there are barriers, either internal (stories, beliefs, fears, self-imposed limitations, restricted views of one's identity, etc.) or external (lack of money, lack of skills, lack of knowledge, prejudices or biases in the world, etc.). In order to make the preferred future a reality, the next step is to make a plan to overcome the barriers and to begin to move toward that future. We refer to this overall process as *future pull* (Bertolino, 1999; O'Hanlon & Bertolino, 1998).

For example, we wanted to write a textbook about collaborative, competency-based counseling and therapy. That was the future vision. However, there were barriers. First we went on a search for a publisher. After we secured a publisher we created an outline that we both agreed upon. Then we had to sit down and write (and rewrite and rewrite and rewrite and rewrite and...you get the idea).

To utilize each aspect of future pull, and to help clients create a compelling future and move toward it, we have included some questions you could ask. They can be changed to fit both your style and your particular clients.

Finding a Vision for the Future

The following list of questions can assist therapists in helping clients to create a vision of the future and what they want for themselves and, perhaps, for others around them.

- What is your life purpose?
- What is your vision of your preferred future?
- What dreams did you or do you have for your life?
- What are you here on the planet for?
- What are human beings on the planet for, in your view?
- What area of life could you make a contribution in?
- What is your bliss?
- What kinds of things compel you?
- What are your hobbies and interests?
- What is your goal or direction in therapy?
- How will your life be different when therapy is successful?
- How will you be able to tell that you are heading in the right direction or getting results from therapy?
- If we could wave a magic wand and your problem was gone, what would you be doing differently?
- It's five years from now and you have made a decision to go in a particular direction (e.g., stay in your marriage or leave it). How does that feel and look to you?

Dealing with and Dissolving Barriers to the Preferred Future

When clients have a sense of where they want to go with their lives, sometimes they will perceive barriers as standing in their way. Some will feel or think that they are inadequate to the task of making their vision happen. Others will believe that certain things must happen before they can pursue their preferred futures and dreams. The following questions can assist with identifying and negotiating perceived barriers.

- What, in your view, stops you from realizing your dreams or getting to your goals?

- What are you afraid of?
- What do you believe must happen before you can realize your dreams?
- What are the actions you haven't taken to make your dreams and visions come true?
- What are the real world barriers to deal with to realize your dreams and visions?
- What would your models, mentors, or people you admire do if they were you in order to realize this dream or vision?
- What are you not doing, feeling, or thinking that they would in this situation?
- What are you doing, feeling, or thinking that they wouldn't?

Making an Action Plan to Reach the Preferred Future

For some clients, simply having a vision of the future will not be enough. They will need to do something to make that vision a reality. This involves a plan of action. The questions below can assist with helping clients to clarify what steps they need to take to make their preferred futures happen.

- What steps could you take in the near future that would help you realize your visions and dreams?
- What would you do as soon as you leave here?
- What would you do tonight?
- What feeling would you have in your body as you took those steps?
- What would you be thinking that would help you take those steps?
- What images or metaphors are helpful to you in taking these steps?
- Will you make a commitment to me or someone else to take those steps by a specific time?
- Who would be the best person to keep you on track, to coach and monitor you?
- When will you agree to take these steps and how will the follow-up happen to ensure that you have?

With many clients, orienting their gaze from the past or present to the future will be a major shift in attention. It can open up pathways with possibilities that were not apparent to them previously. It can also provide information regarding directions for treatment, introduce meaning and purpose into clients' lives, and lead to a restoration of hope (Bertolino, 1999).

Reflecting, Conversational, and Consulting Teams: Constructing Therapeutic Conversations

The tradition of using the one-way mirror in family therapy is a long-held one. For years clinicians have used it as a vehicle for teaching and training therapists and for developing interventions to shift dysfunctional patterns of interaction with families. This was sometimes accomplished with a supervisor giving a directive to a therapist who would then deliver it to a family. In other cases a team would develop a consensus regarding the best idea and deliver it to a family along with a task, as a way of facilitating change.

As discussed in the Introduction, a shift from interactional and problem-focused approaches to collaborative, competency-based approaches ushered in new ways of understanding individuals, couples, and families. Instead of seeing family systems as essentially stable, with governing homeostatic mechanisms, therapists began to see them as evolving and changing. In addition, people were seen as having resources within themselves and their social systems to solve problems. This new view represented a significant deviation from past ways of thinking, and brought with it new therapeutic approaches. These focused more on how clients' changed due to the creation of new meaning through language and interaction.

One of the most novel contributions during this shift in the field was Tom Andersen's (1991) idea of the reflecting team. This concept offered therapists an entirely new way to use the one-way mirror as a vehicle for facilitating change. Reflecting teams helped flatten the hierarchy between clients and therapists, making treatment more collaborative and conversation-oriented. They also ushered in new ideas and a format, which at that time was considered revolutionary.

Perhaps most important about this new reflecting process and way of using the mirror was that clients were no longer offered what was deemed to be the *best* idea by a supervisor or team. Instead they would hear all of the team's reflections and choose which ones fit best for them. Andersen (1993) stated, "Reflecting processes ... are characterized by the attempt to say everything in the open. Everything the professional says about the client's situation is said so that the client can hear it" (p. 306).

Consistent with social-constructionist thinking, the idea behind the reflecting team was to have the team highlight differences and events that did not fit with the old, problem-saturated story. It was hoped that the introduction of new ideas would lead to the creation of new meanings for clients, thereby allowing them to reauthor their life stories. These new stories of hope and possibility could then pull clients toward their preferred futures. In addition, it was hoped that in some instances therapists themselves would gain new perspectives and ideas for working with clients.

The original view and uses of the reflecting team have changed and evolved since its inception in the early 1990s. We now have conversational and consulting teams as well, which are very similar and have been created to fit the needs of mental health professionals and their clientele. These team approaches can be used at any point in the treatment process, or as a method of crisis intervention, for training therapists, and for therapist consultations. Their most common use is with clients who have become stuck in their problem-saturated stories. It is believed that by generating new ideas, clients can begin to view their lives differently and reauthor new life stories.

Introducing the Idea of the Reflecting Team to Clients

There are a variety of ways to introduce the idea of the reflecting team to clients. In Bob's clinical practice, it is offered to clients in the following way:

> Sometimes when things seem stuck it helps to get a few more ideas. We have the idea here that three (or four or five) heads are better than one. So I'd like to offer you the opportunity to be part of our reflecting team process. This will take about the same amount of time as one of our therapy sessions, and we'll go into a room where there is a one-way mirror. There will be a team of three to five therapists behind the mirror who will listen to our conversation. After about a half an hour or so, we'll switch places, and all of us will go behind the mirror and the team will come into the therapy office. The team will then talk about what they heard and noticed. This will take between five and ten minutes. Last, we'll switch once more and you'll have the opportunity to talk about anything that stood out for you.

Most often we hear comments such as, "Great, we get four therapists for the price of one!" or "We'll try anything." Other times there may be some apprehension as clients are leery about what the team members might say. We've found that such apprehension is typically due to clients not understanding that the team will be helping to generate new ideas, not criticizing or judging them. We detail the process as much or as little as necessary, depending on the client(s) inquiry.

Basic Premises

Although there have been changes, many of the basic premises remain much the same. Here we offer some fundamental ideas associated with reflecting, conversational, and consulting teams:

- We each create our own new meanings or truths based on the distinctions we draw from our own experiences, beliefs, and social contexts.
- In the therapeutic system, the therapist is a participant in the social construction of the therapy system's reality.
- Meanings and behaviors interact recursively. Each can change and influence change in the other.
- Positive connotation is extremely important. It is difficult for people to "leave the field" or to change under negative connotation.
- A stuck system needs new ideas. Thus, our goal is to provide a context where clients can see and hear differently so they can understand their situations differently.

The Posture of the Reflecting Team

Upon entering the session, the therapists on the team do not have any previous information on the clients. They have not read files or case notes, nor have they been briefed. Their job is to only respond to what occurs in the room. Andersen (1987) stated:

> The reflecting team has to bear in mind that its task is to create ideas even though some of those ideas may not be found interesting by the family, or may even be rejected. What is important is to realize that the family will select those ideas that fit. (p. 421)

The team also adheres to the following operational ideas:

- We base our comments on what actually happens in the room, wondering about and giving personal responses to what happens in the session.
- We situate our ideas in our own experience believing that this invites family members to adapt what we say to fit their personal experience.
- We strive to keep our comments nonevaluative. We wonder about or focus on differences or new occurrences around which family members may choose to perform meaning.
- We have a conversation to develop ideas rather than a competition for the best idea.
- We address ourselves to other team members rather than through the mirror to the family.
- We try to respond to everyone in the family.
- We don't talk behind the mirror, believing that this keeps our conversations fresher and more multifaceted.
- We aim for brevity, especially if there are small children in the family.
- We try not to instruct or lead the family. Instead we try to bring forth many perceptions and constructions, so family members can choose what is interesting or helpful to them. (Freedman & Combs, 1996)

Basic Format

Even though reflecting teams have gone through quite an evolution since they were first used, the basic format tends to be consistent. The idea is that a team of therapists observes the therapy session, usually from behind a one-way mirror, but occasionally in the same room, on tape, or by phone. The team usually consists of three to five clinicians. In our experience, if there are too few or too many clinicians the process doesn't work as well and can become bogged down.

During the initial part of the session the therapist meets with the individual, couple, or family for fifteen to forty-five minutes. The therapist begins by introducing each family member or invites each person to say his or her name. (Note: It's important to not forget this part. If it's not done the team members may not know how to refer to each person during the period of reflection.) Next, there are two basic questions that are asked by the therapist to the clients:

1. Could you tell me a little bit about how this meeting came about (who had the idea, how was the decision made, etc.)?

2. Who would like to talk about how we can best use this time? (Andersen, 1991)

The therapist then follows these questions with his or her usual process of working with the individual, couple, or family. At the end of this time, the therapist can say, "I wonder what the team heard or noticed about our conversation. If it's okay with you, I'd like to invite them to switch places with us so that we can listen to their conversation." When the clients have agreed, they are told, "As you listen, choose what you feel comfortable with and leave the rest behind." Then the therapist remains with the family and they switch places with the team.

The team members first introduce themselves by name, then engage in a conversation with one another about what stood out for them. The reflections include new perspectives and punctuations from a positive frame of reference that tap into clients' strengths, resources, positive attributes, and good intentions. The reflections in the conversation are speculations and are tentative offerings. They are not evaluations or judgments. To remain nonevaluative, the team members use conjecture and curiosity. Here are some examples of how this is done:

- "I noticed that...."
- "I wonder if...."
- "I was curious about...."
- "I was struck by...."
- "When I heard ______ say, I wonder if he/she thought...."
- "I wonder what would happen if...."
- "Perhaps it is...."

To illustrate the conversational process that takes place, we offer a brief interchange between members of a reflecting team.

THERAPIST 1: I was struck by what George said about trying to get the family back on track. He said, "I'll do whatever it takes." I wonder where that strength comes from.

THERAPIST 2: I wondered that as well. And I was curious as to whether the others had some of that strength—Kelly mentioned that she got a job after being laid off for six months. I wonder how she got herself to do that and if they would consider that a step toward getting back on track.

THERAPIST 3: I was impressed with how Gina supported Kelly even though there have been some rough times between the two sisters. I wonder if that's a sign of maturity and growing up on her part.

THERAPIST 2: And perhaps that's part of getting things going in a better direction. Maybe the little changes that they're making on their own and as a family will build into larger ones.

THERAPIST 1: That really struck me as well... I wonder how they will keep that momentum in the future and make it work for them.

Sometimes the team asks questions of the therapist or clients and sometimes they just reflect the experiences, feelings, or perspectives they had while observing. In the collaborative, competency-based tradition, these conversations are not supposed to determine the correct diagnosis or the proper course of treatment, but are used to both validate and encourage the therapist and clients and also to widen the viewing of the situation. Hearing the perspectives of many people almost invariably shows that there are multiple valid ways of viewing and construing the situation.

We tell therapists who are part of a reflecting team for the first time to trust in the process. Conversations tend to evolve in two ways: (1) Based on what each team member has written down to highlight and (2) what has just been stated. Some comments will be taken directly from what a team member wrote down while behind the mirror while others will be created as a result of hearing what another team member stated. This process makes for spontaneous and creative conversations.

After the team has taken five to ten minutes to have a conversation and offer reflections, they thank the clients for allowing them to be part of their lives and wish them well. The team then once again switches places with the family and therapist.

The therapist then invites the clients to share any thoughts or comments that they might have as a result of experiencing the team's conversation. The therapist might ask questions such as, "What was your experience like with the reflecting team?" "What did you hear/see/feel/notice?" "What stood out for you about the process?" "What made sense to you?" or "What stood out for you?" Therapists should avoid having families fall back into problem-talk and focus on what they experienced. This process should take about five minutes or less. In subsequent sessions, more exploration of and discussion can take place around the experience.

Reflecting teams offer a flexible alternative to therapists and clients and can be used in a variety of contexts and formats (Friedman, 1995). Most important, from the perspective of clients, research has supported the efficacy of reflecting teams (Katz, 1991; Sells, Smith, Coe, Yoshioka, & Robbins, 1994; Smith, Yoshioka, & Winton, 1993). Further, therapists training from this perspective have reported it to be helpful (Bertolino, 1998).

In this chapter we offered multiple pathways for working with clients to create change in the viewing of problems. This is but one area of change that therapists can work within. In the next chapter we'll explore ideas for helping clients to do something different as a result of changing their viewing of problems. We refer to this as *changing the doing* of problems, which includes clients' patterns of action and interaction.

Summary Points for Chapter Five

- ♦ There are two main ways of creating change in the viewing of problems:
  1. Changing focus of attention
  2. Changing problematic stories
- ♦ Ways of Changing Focus of Attention:
  - ■ Suggest that clients change their sensory attention.
  - ■ Suggest that clients recall other aspects of the situation.
  - ■ Suggest to clients that they think of one thing that would challenge their thoughts or cause doubt about them.
  - ■ Suggest that clients shift from focusing on the past to focusing on the present.
  - ■ Suggest that clients shift from focusing on the present or the past to focusing on the future.
  - ■ Suggest that clients shift from focusing on their internal experience to focusing on the external environment or other people.
  - ■ Suggest that clients shift from focusing on the external environment or other people to focusing on their inner worlds.
  - ■ Suggest that clients focus on what has worked rather than what has not.
- ♦ Ways of Changing Problematic Stories:
  - ■ Transform the story by acknowledging and adding the element of possibility.
  - ■ Invite accountability.
  - ■ Find counterevidence.
  - ■ Find alternative stories or frames of reference to fit the same evidence or facts.
- ♦ Further methods for changing the viewing of problems include:
  - ■ Utilizing externalizing conversations
  - ■ Tapping into resilience
  - ■ Using stories and metaphors
  - ■ Using future pull
  - ■ Reflecting, conversational, and consulting teams
  - ■ Changing focus of attention

CHAPTER 6 Changing the Doing of Problems

In the last chapter we explored how the views that clients have of themselves, others, events, and situations can become problematic. In a similar way, behavioral, marital, and family therapists have long explored the ways in which patterns of action and interaction play a role in the development and maintenance of problems. We refer to this as the *doing of problems.* Some clients will repeat unhelpful patterns and seemingly become stuck without a way of escaping. Therefore, in this chapter we'll explore ways of changing and disrupting problematic patterns of action and interaction.

Problems as Patterns

We don't think about problems as things. Instead, we think of what people call *problems* as patterns. Modern physics has told us that the things we see are not quite as solid as they appear. Chairs, tables, desks, even the book you are holding in your hand are not quite as fixed as we might imagine. They are all made up of patterns of energy, of vibrating subatomic particles. If we heat those things enough, they change form, becoming gas or some other less solid form. We think of human problems in the same way. They are not as solid and set in form as they initially appear. Of course, they appear solid and set, so we must find a way of thinking of problems as more changeable.

One of the ways this can be done is to think of problems as patterns of actions and interactions. One can think of problems more as hot air balloons than as blimps. The hot air balloon requires constant pumping of gas for it to keep its shape. A blimp has a structure that keeps its shape even when no gas is being pumped into it. Problems, in this view, require the constant input of the patterns of behavior and interaction that help maintain their shape in order to exist.

To change or dissolve a problem, one could change the patterns that continually maintain its shape. We call this changing the doing of the problem. The watch phrase of changing the doing is: "Insanity is doing the same thing over and over again and expecting different results." It is as if some logs get jammed up in a bend in the river and this method helps remove the fewest number of logs to break up the logjam. We don't have to take every log out of the river, or catalog when it fell into the river (or which parent it resembles). We also don't have to get into the river and push the logs down the river every week. We merely need to help break up the pattern that keeps the logs stuck.

Years ago, Bill was having a conversation with brief therapist John Weakland of the Mental Research Institute (MRI). He told Bill that we had been naïve when we first came up with psychotherapy. We thought we could make people's lives problem-free if we just gave them good enough and long enough therapy. But after one hundred years of therapy, we found that was too utopian a goal. That's because life, as the old saying goes, is just one thing after another. Just when you think you've got everything sorted out, you move into a different developmental stage and life hands you new dilemmas. However, for the people who seek therapy, life has become the same thing over and over. Bill thought about what John Weakland said and finally realized that our job as therapists is to move people from the same thing over and over back to one thing after another, and then get out of their lives.

Identifying Problematic Patterns in Context

Milton Erickson was fascinated with clients' problems and how they did them. In fact, he would often map out the details of their problems. Richard Bandler, the cocreator of Neuro-Linguistic Programming (NLP), and John Grinder (1975; Grinder, DeLozier, & Bandler, 1977) meticulously studied Erickson's work. They often asked clients, "If I were you, how would I do your problem?" What Erickson, Bandler, and others have taught us is the importance of learning from clients how they do their personal patterns.

In a previous publication (O'Hanlon & Bertolino, 1998) we discussed the role of therapists in identifying clients' problematic patterns:

> We explore with clients the negative problem patterns that seem to be inhibiting or intruding in their lives. We seek to be geographers, exploring the topography and the coastline of Problem-Land. We want to know the details of the problem or symptom, *and* help the client to find ways of escaping it. (p. 66)

Therapists elicit detailed, sensory-based descriptions to learn about clients' patterns. Action-talk and videotalk can be helpful here in moving clients from vague descriptions to clear, observable ones. We then listen to these descriptions and search for any aspect of the problem that repeats, indicating a pattern. To do this we explore the following areas:

- How often does the problem typically happen (once an hour, once a day, once a week)?
- What is the typical timing (time of day, week, month, year) of the problem?
- How long does the problem typically last?
- Where does the problem typically happen?
- What does the client, and others who are around, usually do when the problem is happening?

It's sometimes helpful to think of a complete description of the symptom by answering the following questions: How often does it happen? In what rooms of the house? Sitting or standing? Who else is around? How much? How often? When exactly? What happens first? What about after that? And then what happens? One would thus be able to describe the blow-by-blow sequence of events, behaviors, and circumstances of the problem's occurrence. Case Example 6.1 shows how a therapist might begin to learn about a problematic pattern.

Case Example 6.1 ***I Eat Too Much!***

THERAPIST: You mentioned that you'd like to work on eating less and losing weight. Tell me a little bit about your eating habits.

CLIENT: Well, I just eat too much at each meal.

THERAPIST: It seems that you've been eating too much. Is it the same or different at each meal?

CLIENT: It's the same.

THERAPIST: Tell me more about that.

CLIENT: Well, when I sit down to eat... I eat real fast. I'm always done before everyone else, so I eat more.

THERAPIST: Okay. So when you sit down to eat, you take a regular size portion, but you eat it quicker than the others who are eating with you?

CLIENT: Exactly.

THERAPIST: And then you get another helping....

CLIENT: ...Yeah I may have two or three more helpings.

THERAPIST: Is it only with specific foods?

CLIENT: It's really with all foods. I'm not choosy.

THERAPIST: And how fast is eating fast... how long does it typically take you to eat that first portion?

CLIENT: Oh, about five to seven minutes.

THERAPIST: What about the second and if there's a third?

CLIENT: The same. I just keep eating until everyone else is done.

THERAPIST: How long does that typically take?

CLIENT: About twenty minutes or so.

THERAPIST: Where do you usually eat your meals?

CLIENT: Mostly at home, but at work I eat with my coworkers.

THERAPIST: At home, do you eat in the kitchen?

CLIENT: Yeah.

THERAPIST: Is anyone with you?

CLIENT: My husband and two kids.

THERAPIST: Do they stay the whole time?

CLIENT: Oh yeah, they can't be excused until we are all done.

THERAPIST: What do they do while you are eating?

CLIENT: Nothing really. They just eat too. I think they're used to it.

THERAPIST: How often do you eat alone?

CLIENT: Rarely.

THERAPIST: Is there anything different about how quickly you eat or the amount of food you eat when you're alone as opposed to with others?

CLIENT: No, not that I can think of.

THERAPIST: And in regard to work, do you bring extra food?

CLIENT: No, I don't have to because there's always goodies sitting around—donuts, cookies, cake....

THERAPIST: And do you eat at the same rate at work?

CLIENT: Yep, and when I'm done I grab cookies or whatever else is around.

THERAPIST: How much time do you have to eat lunch at work?

CLIENT: A half hour, but I wind down after about twenty-five minutes so I can clean up and get back to my desk.

THERAPIST: Other than your regular meals, do you eat more than you should at other times?

CLIENT: No, not really. I don't really snack much. It's really just a matter of me eating too much at meals.

This case example reveals information about how the client does her problematic pattern. For example, there are time elements associated with her eating. She eats quickly for approximately twenty to twenty-five minutes whether at home or at work. We also learn that she continues this pattern three times a day, but only at meals. There are a few places to intervene with this woman. Once a problematic pattern is identified, we then find some place in that pattern in which the client can do something differently. We'll revisit this case example a little later in this chapter.

Changing Problematic Patterns

There are two main ways to change patterns:

1. *Depatterning:* Altering repetitive patterns of action and interaction involved in problems
2. *Repatterning:* Establishing new patterns in place of problems by identifying and encouraging the use of solution patterns of action and interaction

Let's explore each of these.

Depatterning: Altering Repetitive Patterns of Action and Interaction Involved in Problems

Depatterning involves disrupting the patterns involved in or surrounding the problem and then noticing whether the problem changes or not. There are no correct methods. There are only possibilities. Although we will offer multiple methods in this chapter, the best methods are the ones that work for clients. Therefore we strive to be creative with clients and will sometimes give them examples of things that others have tried or tell them a story to help them to think more out of the box. For example, in the last chapter we discussed the value of stories. So here's a story that we've told to clients to get the creative juices flowing:

> A retired man bought a new home near a junior high school. The first few weeks following his move brought peace and contentment. Then the new school year began. The afternoon of the first day of school three boys came walking down the street, beating on every trash can they encountered. This continued each day until the man decided to take action.
>
> One afternoon, the man walked out and met the young percussionists and said, "You kids are a lot of fun. I like to see you express your exuberance like that. Used to do the same thing when I was your age. I'll give you each a dollar if you promise to come around every day and do your thing." The boys were elated and agreed to continue their drumming. After a few days, the man approached the boys, and with a sad smile said, "The recession's really putting a big dent in my income. From now on, I'll only be able to pay you 50 cents to beat the cans." Although the boys were displeased, they agreed to continue their banging.
>
> A few days later, the retiree again approached the boys and said, "I haven't received my social security check yet, so I'm not going to be able to give you more than 25 cents. Will that be okay?" "A lousy quarter?" the drum leader exclaimed. "If you think we're going to waste our time, beating these cans for a quarter, you're nuts! No way, mister. We quit!" The man went on to enjoy peace once again. (Gentle Spaces News, 1995, pp. 297–298)

Some traditional first- and second-wave theorists would take a directive approach and tell clients what to do to change their problematic patterns. However, we collaborate with clients and learn what they think will work best for them. In order to do this we need to be sure we know what they have tried to solve or resolve their concern in the past. We also want to know what they feel might work before giving any suggestions. Furthermore, before changing patterns of action and interaction we want to be sure that clients are at a preparation or action stage of change and are ready to do something different. If they are not, we are more likely to gear our efforts toward helping them to change some aspect of their viewing of the problem. This would involve more observing and noticing. As discussed earlier in the book, we want to work in ways that are consistent with clients' stages of change and theories of change.

In a metaphorical sense, for many clients, it's as if their trains are stuck going round and round on a circular track. This method involves us pulling the switch to help them get off the circular track and move on in their journey. Within every problematic pattern, there are typically several places to pull the switch to alter or disrupt it. Let's now explore eleven different ways of doing this:

- **Change the frequency or rate of the complaint.**

  Example: A wife stated that when her husband argued with her she would become very upset and start talking rapidly. After a few moments, her husband would then tell her that he couldn't understand what she was saying, and would start becoming even more upset and would raise his voice. The wife stated that if she could keep from talking so fast she would be able to clearly say what she had to say. It was suggested that the next time she found herself in an argument with her husband she was to look at her watch and say no more than one word every five seconds, thereby slowing down her rate of speech.

- **Change the location of the complaint.**

  Example: A couple was having intense, unproductive arguments that they would both later regret. It was suggested to the couple that the next time they started to have an argument they should proceed straight to the bathroom. Once there, the husband was to take off all of his clothes and lie down in the bathtub. The wife was to remain fully clothed and sit on the toilet. If they could, they were to continue the argument. They couldn't.

- **Change the duration of the complaint.**

  Example: A young boy would throw screaming fits each time he didn't get his way. These fits would last between five and ten minutes. Following a consultation with a therapist, the next time the boy began to scream she informed him that he was to scream for no less than twenty minutes to be sure that everyone who needed to hear his complaint was duly informed. When the boy stopped after two minutes she notified him that he had eighteen more minutes to go. He refused to resume screaming.

- **Change the time (hour, week, month, time of day, or time of year) of the complaint.**

  Example: A mother brought her twelve-year-old son to therapy because he would sneak out late at night. It was suggested that she schedule a sneak out time for each morning. She was to wake her son up at 5:00 AM every morning and sit on his bed until he got up and went outside for at least fifteen minutes. Her son was annoyed by being woken up so early each morning that he quit sneaking out at night.

- **Change the sequence of events involved in or around the complaint.**

  Example: A woman was trying to get her mother to stop giving her advice on life. Her mother would call each evening and ask for a run down of the day's events. Then she would proceed to criticize her daughter for the decisions and actions she had taken each day. It was suggested to the woman that she tape her mother's next rant. Then, on the following occasion she should beat her mother to the punch by playing the tape back to her over the phone.

- **Interrupt or otherwise prevent the occurrence of the complaint.**

  Example: A teenager would come home from school each day, throw her books on the floor, and say, "I'm not going back! I hate school." Her mother would then have problems getting her to do her homework and getting her to attend school the next day. It was suggested that the mother change the sequence of interaction with her daughter. She was to meet her at the front door and before the daughter could say anything, she was to blurt out, "I can't believe the day you've had! How did you make it through?" The first time the mother tried this the daughter was surprised and said, "Mom, it wasn't that bad." The second time, the daughter responded with, "Mom, get a life." The problems with school ceased.

- **Add a new element to the complaint.**

  Example: A mother was growing tired of her son calling her every name in the book when he didn't get his way. In fact, she claimed that she had heard his "whining dissertation" so many times that it stuck in her head like a song. It was suggested that the next time her son started in on her with the name calling, that she hum a song along with his words.

- **Break up a whole element of the complaint into smaller elements.**

  Example: A husband and wife were having disagreements over a variety of household concerns. Each time they would try to discuss a topic, it would turn into an argument. It was suggested that they get a timer, set it for two minutes, and allow each person that amount of time to state his or her point of view. Once the timer went off, it was the other person's turn. The couple was to argue one point at a time.

- **Reverse the direction of striving in the performance of the problem.**

  Example: A man would become anxious, sweating profusely and stuttering when his boss approached him. He was worried that others would notice his strange behavior, which made him more self-conscious. It was suggested that he practice producing his anxiety at home so he could become anxious with every person he met. This way he would relate to each person the same way and no one would be able to notice the difference. The man abandoned his anxiety.

- **Link the occurrence of the complaint to another pattern that is a burdensome activity.**

  Example: A fourteen-year-old was failing five out of six subjects at school, was late to class, was not completing homework, and was breaking curfew. It was suggested that each night, his parents count how many minutes he was late for curfew. When he returned home, they were to go to his room and read to him for the amount of time that he had exceeded his curfew. No matter what time he came in, they were to read to him, making sure that he got his education. Since the boy didn't bring books home they were asked to read from encyclopedias. They agreed that any education that he could get from the reading would be beneficial since he had been doing poorly at school and not completing homework. The parents informed the teenager of their plan, but they never had to use it. He stopped coming in late, as he did not want to be bothered by his parents reading to him at all hours.

- **Change the physical performance of the complaint.**

  Example: A woman would cut on her arms when she became upset or anxious about things in her life. She said that she did this to release the pain. She would proceed until she drew blood. Instead of cutting on herself, it was suggested that she use a red lipstick to mark on her arm.

To change the doing of the problem, the therapist usually arranges for the client to alter the performance of the complaint in some small or insignificant way. A small change is often all that is necessary to change a problematic pattern. The work of Milton Erickson contains many examples of this type of contextual intervention. Erickson (as quoted in Rossi, 1980b) held the view that:

> "...maladies, whether psychogenic or organic, followed definite patterns of some sort, particularly in the field of psychogenic disorders; that a disruption of this pattern could be a most therapeutic measure; and that it often mattered little how small the disruption was, if introduced early enough." (p. 254)

To alter or disrupt a pattern, Erickson might direct a compulsive hand washer to change the brand of soap he uses to wash his hands. He might get a person who smokes to put her cigarettes in the attic and her matches in the basement. He told a thumb sucker to suck her thumb for a set period of time every day. He once directed a couple who argued about who was to drive home after a party (at which they'd both had a few drinks) that one was to drive from the party to one block before home, then they were to stop the car, switch places, and the other was to drive the rest of the way home. Erickson once worked with a man who had insomnia. He had the man wax floors all night (a task he hated) if he wasn't asleep fifteen minutes after he went to bed. After the third night of waxing, the man never had trouble going to sleep again.

To further illustrate this approach, let's return to Case Example 6.1 concerning the woman who eats too much. The most likely areas to intervene with this case are in the timing and duration of the problem. However, we have stated throughout that clients often have ideas about how their problems developed and what might work in resolving them. So the first thing we do is to summarize what we have heard from clients and ask them if they have any ideas based on the ways they do their problems. In this case a therapist might say:

> From what you've described, it seems that you eat your meals quickly—usually in five to seven minutes per serving. Since you generally eat for between twenty and twenty-five minutes you can eat at least two or three servings. As I'm summarizing what we've talked about so far, is there anything that stands out for you? Do you have any ideas about what you might do differently?

If clients have ideas we explore them in-depth, learning from clients what they feel might work. Case Example 6.2 demonstrates this.

Case Example 6.2 *No Classical Music*

Bob consulted with a woman who was upset because her eleven-year-old son would grab on to her clothes and yell at her when he would not get his way. In fact, she reported that he would not let go of her clothes until she gave in. Her clothes were getting ruined and she was at her wits end. During their conversation, Bob and the woman talked about many different things, including her position in a symphony orchestra and her love of music.

Bob asked the woman, "What does your family think about you being in the symphony?"

"My husband loves it, but my son can't stand classical music," she replied.

"That must make it hard to practice at home," followed Bob.

The woman smiled and said, "No it doesn't because I don't practice at home. I practice at our rehearsal site."

"Well how do you know that he doesn't like classical music?" asked Bob.

"Because every time I turn it on at home he leaves the room. I should say, he runs out of the room," she answered.

At that moment the woman laughed and the light bulb went on. She said, "I know what to do. The next time he grabs my clothes I'll just pull him into the living room and turn on classical music." Being the astute observer, Bob replied, "Sounds great!"

At the next session the woman described how her son went through his ritual of grabbing on to her clothes after she refused to let him go to a friend's house after dark. She was able to pull him into the living room and turn on the stereo. When the classical music came on, the boy let go and yelled at her, "Turn that crap off!" He then lunged back at her to try and reestablish a grip on her clothing. Whereas in the past she would have withdrawn and moved away from his attempts to grab her clothes, this time she moved toward her son and said, "Do you want to dance? I love to dance and your father's not here...." She proceeded to grab his arms to dance with him. The boy immediately pulled his arms back and said, "What are you doing? You're a freak!" and ran out of the room.

The woman then turned the music off and started to leave the room. As she did, her son came back around the corner and went after her. She again pursued him and said, "I don't need music to dance. C'mon!" Once again, the boy ran from her and stood behind the kitchen table where she could not reach him. From that point the pattern of him grabbing on to her clothes had been broken.

It's important to encourage clients to consider any new idea and not worry about finding the right one. Further, we are mindful that clients are typically more interested in trying something new if they have made a contribution to the development of the idea. If a client has an idea we have them elaborate on it:

- Tell me more about that idea.
- How might that work for you?
- What do you need to do to make that happen?
- What will be your first step in putting this idea in motion?
- What, if anything, can others do to help put this idea into motion?

If clients don't have any ideas we can explore the pattern further to see what ideas might be generated. A second possibility is that if the therapist feels he or she has enough information about the problematic pattern, he or she can offer ideas by using conjecture. To do this, the therapist can tell one or more stories offering metaphorical possibilities and solutions, offer straightforward anecdotes about how other clients solved similar problems, or make suggestions based on how he or she understands the client's problematic pattern. Let's refer back to Case Example 6.1 to explore some possibilities.

One possibility might be to suggest to the client that she position herself where she can see a clock. Then she would take just one regular size bite of food every minute—no more, no less. Another might be to have her eat in sequence with another person at the table. For example, when that person takes a bite, she takes a bite. This might alter the timing around the problematic pattern. Further, it might be suggested that if she's right-handed that she eat left-handed (or vice versa), thereby changing the physical performance of the problem.

Further exploration about how the client does her problematic pattern would reveal other ways of altering or disrupting that pattern. The ideas discussed here, as well as others that might be generated, are only ideas. That is, clients can accept or reject them. We always bear in mind that if what we are doing isn't working, we need to try something else.

Repatterning: Identifying and Encouraging the Use of Solution Patterns

In addition to (or instead of) depatterning, we also help clients repattern their actions and interactions around problems. To do this we elicit previous solution patterns, including abilities, strengths, and resources. The idea is not to convince clients that they have solutions and competencies, but rather to ask questions and gather information in a way that shows them that they do. For example, we wouldn't say, "You can do it! Look at all your strengths!" This would be invalidating to clients who are experiencing difficulty and pain. Instead we ask questions such as, "How were you able to do that?" and "What did you do differently at that time?"

Emphasis is on evoking a sense of competence and an experience in being able to solve problems. Often when clients become caught up in their problematic patterns, they do not recall the wealth of experience they have available. We search in various areas to find this sense of competence and to identify previously successful strategies for dealing with or resolving the particular problems the client has brought to therapy. What follows are some methods that therapists can use to gather information about solutions and to evoke them.

Find out about previous solutions to the problem, including partial solutions and partial successes. We are always curious about times when clients have had some sort of influence over the problem at hand. Even when clients appear to be stuck, there have been times when they were not experiencing their problems in full force. These are exceptions to the problematic patterns. Here are some sample questions a therapist might ask to learn about these exceptions:

- Tell me about a time when the problem happened and you were able to get somewhat of a handle on it. What was different about that time? What did you do?
- You've had trouble getting to sleep three of the last four nights. How did you manage to get to sleep at a reasonable time on that one night?
- You mentioned that you and your wife have argued a lot recently about the bills. Yet when you received a gas bill that was higher than usual it didn't start a fight. What happened so that the situation didn't reach an argument? What did you do? What did your wife do?
- Johnny, your mom told me that you've run away three times in the past week. Even though you had the chance and may have thought about it, how did you manage to keep from taking off on the other four days?
- From what I understand, you usually back down from intimidation, but you didn't that one time. What did you do that was different this time? How did you get yourself to do it?
- You didn't cut yourself as much last night. How did you keep yourself from doing what you usually have done? What did you do this time instead of continuing to cut?

Notice that we are not asking *if* there have been times when things went better. We are presupposing that there *were* times when things were better. We aim to gain clear action descriptions of what clients did at those times. This involves finding out what happened, when it happened, and what needs to happen in the future so that the solution pattern occurs more deliberately and with more frequency. This is demonstrated in Case Example 6.3.

Case Example 6.3 *Calling a Friend*

THERAPIST: You said that there have been times in the past when you've been so upset that you've said things that you later regretted. But last weekend, when you were told that you weren't going to get the raise you were expecting, you didn't say anything to your boss that you might later regret. How did you do that?

CLIENT: I was still mad.

THERAPIST: Right. You were still mad and that's okay. Yet you didn't react as maybe you have in the past. I'm curious about what was different about this time.

CLIENT: I can't lose my job so I didn't go off.

THERAPIST: Is that what you told yourself? "I can't lose my job."

CLIENT: Yeah.

THERAPIST: And even as angry as you were, what did telling yourself that do to help you through that moment?

CLIENT: Well, it helped me remember that I have kids to feed, bills to pay.

THERAPIST: I see. You remembered your kids and bills. Then, what did that allow you to do instead of going off?

CLIENT: I called my friend Melanie. She's always there for me.

THERAPIST: Okay. So then you called Melanie. How is that different than what you've done at other times?

CLIENT: Well, I don't always talk to people when I get mad. I usually just go off and by calling her I didn't blow my top and risk my job.

It's not uncommon for clients to have difficulty identifying what they did differently or what worked for them. By asking questions about these exceptions, clients will temporarily reorient their attention toward their influence over the problem versus the influence that problem has had on them in the past. It also can be helpful for therapists to offer multiple options to clients to see if something that came out of a conversation resonates with the client, and to offer other possibilities for future situations. For example, a therapist might say, "I'm curious as to whether it was thinking about your kids and bills, or calling Melanie, or something else that made a difference for you." Clients will often affirm one of the choices or respond, "No, what really helped me was ______."

It's important to note that we don't say, "Tell me about a time recently when you didn't have the problem" or "When were things better?" Clients' responses to such inquiries are not surprising: "I always have the problem" or "It's never better!" As discussed in Chapter 4, that's too big a leap for most clients. Since their orientation will generally be toward the problem and what is not working, it will be too much for them to turn 180 degrees and look at times when the problem was completely absent and notice what was working. Therefore, we search for small indicators of success. For example, we might say, "Tell me about a time recently when things went a little better" or "What has been different about those times when the problem has been a little less dominating?" Smaller increments of change will typically be more palatable for clients and will be easier for them to identify.

In the event that clients continue to struggle to notice any solutions, including partial ones, therapists should consider the following:

- Make sure clients feel acknowledged and validated. Read clients' reflections. Are we hearing what clients want us to hear? Do they feel understood?
- Make sure that we are working with clients in ways that they consider to be helpful and consistent with their theories of change.
- Work from worst to best. Start with understanding how bad the problem is before exploring any shades of difference regarding the intensity of the problem.

Case Example 6.4 shows how to work from worst to best.

Case Example 6.4 *Trying to Tame Tantrums*

THERAPIST: You've said that Scott's behavior has been very bad lately and that you're most worried about his tantrums. During these tantrums he has scratched and kicked you. Tell me about a time recently when he seemed a little more manageable.

CLIENT: I don't think you understand. His tantrums are always bad. They're very bad. They just go on and on.

THERAPIST: Okay. Help me to understand what you've been going through with Scott because I think I'm off base here.

CLIENT: Well, it's just flat out frustrating. He just seems to be getting worse.

THERAPIST: It's been very frustrating to you. How have you managed to hang in there?

CLIENT: It hasn't been easy.

THERAPIST: That's what it sounds like... and I'm wondering, because you've been through so much, how you think I might be able to help you with this?

CLIENT: If we could just see any change with him then I think I would have some hope.

THERAPIST: I see. If it's all right with you I'd like to ask you a few more questions to help me better understand how it's been with Scott.

CLIENT: Sure.

THERAPIST: So which day this week was the worst regarding Scott's scratching and kicking you?

CLIENT: Thursday. Definitely Thursday,

THERAPIST: What happened on Thursday?

CLIENT: He kicked me so hard that he bruised my arm. It also took me a long time to calm him down once he got going.

THERAPIST: Are you okay?

CLIENT: Oh yeah. It'll go away.

THERAPIST: I'm sorry that Thursday was such a difficult day.

CLIENT: Thanks. I'm guess I'm used to it.

THERAPIST: Well, I appreciate your persistence. And I'm curious as to how the other days stacked up against Thursday, because that was the worst day.

CLIENT: You know, Tuesday wasn't quite as bad.

THERAPIST: What happened on Tuesday?

CLIENT: He slept a little more and the one time he started to get riled up he calmed down pretty quickly.

THERAPIST: How did that happen?

CLIENT: I think maybe I caught him as he was getting riled up and I distracted him with a puzzle.

In this particular case the therapist went back and made sure that the client felt heard and understood, attended more to the problem, then searched for a small opening from which to build.

In searching for previous solutions and successes there are many types of questions that therapists can ask. Generally speaking, we've found it helpful to distinguish between using conversations that search for changes with problems and using solution-talk. A therapist searching for changes in the problem is more likely to ask, "Tell me about a time when the problem wasn't quite as bad." In contrast, a therapist using solution-talk would ask, "Tell me about a time when things were a little more manageable for you." Although both types are useful, one orients clients toward problems, the other toward possibilities and solutions. We've found that by using solution-talk we find out more about what's working as opposed to drawing attention to the problem. Ultimately, we work to match our language to fit our clients. If we were using one or the other and it was not working for a particular client, we would change what we were doing.

Find out what happens as the problem ends or starts to end. The problems that clients experience have beginnings and endings. In fact, their problems all come to end, even if for only a short period of time. By exploring these moments solution patterns may be identified. To learn about this we can ask the following questions:

- How do you know when the problem is coming to an end?
- What is the first sign that the problem is going away or subsiding?
- How can your friends, family, coworkers, and others tell when the problem has subsided or has started to subside?
- What have you noticed helps you wind down?
- What will you be doing when the problem has ended or subsided?
- How do these problem-free activities differ from what you do when the problem is happening or present?
- Is there anything that you or significant others have noticed that helps the problem subside more quickly?

Case Examples 6.5 and 6.6 illustrate therapists learning about how problems end or start to end.

Case Example 6.5 *The Cold War*

Bill worked with a couple in marital counseling who reported that several times they had experienced a cold war between them. When things would start to get tense, the couple would exchange words, but this would often lead to more tension and both of them withdrawing into silence for days at a time. Bill asked them how the cold started to thaw. The wife traveled frequently on business, and they told him even if they were in the midst of a cold war they always seemed to be able to talk on the phone and begin the process of thawing out. Perhaps it was the physical distance, the absence of the visual component, or something else that made a difference. In any case, Bill suggested to the couple that they experiment using two separate phone lines in their house to call one another within an hour after a cold war had commenced. The couple did this and found that this process often helped them to thaw much more quickly.

Case Example 6.6 *Pictures of You*

Bob worked with a woman who was having flashbacks and would replay over and over again the experience of being raped. During these flashbacks she would experience physical memories and would cry uncontrollably. Bob asked the woman what brought the flashbacks to an end. She stated that she envisioned her mother.

Her mother was the one who discovered her following the rape and even though she had passed on, she was a continuing source of comfort. Bob asked the woman if she had a small picture of her mother. She said that she did, and he asked her to make multiple copies of it. She was then asked to place copies of the picture in her purse, the glove compartment in her car, on her desk at work, and in other places where she was likely to have flashbacks. When she started to feel herself experiencing a flashback she could look at the picture of her mother and bring the flashback to an end.

The information gained about how a problem ends or starts to end can provide immediate solution patterns that can then be used to alter or disrupt problematic processes. Clients can then intervene earlier in problematic sequences as opposed to letting them play out.

Find out about any helpful changes that have happened before treatment began. For some clients the road to positive change has started prior to the first therapy session. As discussed in Chapter 3, researchers refer to this phenomenon as *pretreatment change*. Studies have indicated that nearly two-thirds of clients coming to their first session report positive changes regarding the complaint that brought them to therapy (Lawson, 1994; McKeel & Weiner-Davis, 1995; Weiner-Davis, de Shazer, & Gingerich, 1987). To find out if there has been any pretreatment change, therapists ask clients what they noticed happening between the time that they made the appointment for therapy and the first session. This can often help to identify solution patterns. Case Example 6.7 illustrates how inquiring about pretreatment change can be helpful.

Case Example 6.7 *How about a Phantom Appointment?*

Abby had been feeling down in the dumps for quite some time. After talking with friends, she finally agreed to make an appointment to talk with a therapist. One day about two weeks later Abby was having lunch with a friend. Her friend inquired, "How did it go with your therapist?" To this Abby shouted, "Oh no! That appointment is in twenty minutes!" Abby rushed over to see the therapist. After sitting down she said, "I made this appointment a few weeks ago when I was really down. But things have changed. It's weird." The therapist asked Abby what had happened between the time that she had made the appointment and the actual appointment. Abby stated that she had changed jobs and started journaling again. She hypothesized that making the appointment had jump-started her life again. Before ending the session, the therapist talked with Abby about how she might jump-start herself again in the future if she felt herself slipping back into her old patterns. Abby said, "I could just make a phantom appointment!" The therapist followed, "Terrific! And I'll send you a phantom bill!"

Sometimes therapists don't give their clients enough credit. At times, clients may have already begun to solve the problem before they seek help. Just focusing on the problem enough to seek therapy can help clients make changes. It may be that the sense that they will get some help gives them enough hope and energy that they begin to make changes. Clients may also begin to direct more attention and effort to the problem—similar to the way we floss more often in preparation for a visit to the dentist. Asking about positive pretreatment changes of this sort can yield important information about how clients solve their problems or make changes. In turn, clients can learn to use this information more deliberately in the future.

Here are some further questions to assist with identifying pretreatment change:

- What's been different between the time you made the appointment and now?
- What have you noticed that's been just a little better?
- What ideas do you have about how this change came about?
- What difference has the change made for you?
- What will it take to keep things going in a better direction?
- What will you need to do?
- What else?
- What, if anything, can others do to help you to continue to move forward?

Search for contexts in which the person feels competent and has good problem-solving or creative skills. Although clients may be experiencing difficulties in specific areas of their lives, they often have strengths and abilities in other areas that can be helpful in solving the problem at hand. Areas where clients have special knowledge or abilities (e.g., school, sports, clubs, hobbies, work) can be tapped into as resources for solving problems. We refer to these as *contexts of competence.*

Therapists also search for exceptions to problems. This includes identifying situations in which the problem would not occur (maybe at work, at a sporting event, etc.). We can also find out about times when the client, or someone he or she knows, has faced a similar problem and resolved it in a way that he or she liked. Case Example 6.8 demonstrates this idea.

Case Example 6.8 ***Training a Husband***

Bill was consulted by a woman named Rebecca who was unhappy with her marriage. She decided that instead of seeking marital therapy she would go to therapy alone and do the work herself. Rebecca described her husband as moody—which meant that he would yell at her and call her names. Because at one point he had been physically abusive and had stopped, Rebecca told Bill that she couldn't ask him to make any more changes and it was unlikely that he would change anyway. Bill disagreed and told Rebecca that he thought her husband could change his moodiness just as he had his violent behavior. She did not agree with him.

Bill proceeded and told Rebecca that the friend who had referred her to him said she was an extraordinary horse trainer. The woman said this was true. Bill asked her what she would do if someone brought her a horse that was impossible to train. She responded by telling him that there was no such thing as an impossible-to-train horse. Bill persisted, "What if someone told you that a particular horse was impossible to train?" Rebecca responded, "I wouldn't accept it." "How would you train such a horse?" he inquired. She went on to explain four principles of horse training including:

1. Don't try to teach the horse more than one thing in each training session.
2. If you get upset with the horse, get off the horse and take a walk, or come back later when you're fresh and not upset.
3. If the horse fights with you, drop the reins. Once the horse calms down pick up the reins again and reestablish who is in charge.
4. Once you have selected the approach you're going to use, stay with it.

To correspond with each of these principles, Bill wrote on a piece of paper:

1. Go for small changes and once the horse has learned one thing, give it a rest.
2. Don't get upset or you'll be punishing rather than training.
3. Give up the small control to stay in charge.
4. Choose a consistent approach and stick with it.

Bill then tore off the piece of paper on which he had written, handed it to Rebecca, and said, "Pretend your husband is a horse. I'm an expert on husbands just as you're an expert with horses and I think your husband is trainable." At that moment, the lightbulb came on for Rebecca. She left the session with a clear plan for training her husband.

Case Example 6.9 illustrates this approach with an adolescent.

Case Example 6.9 *From the Field to the Classroom*

BOB: How's it been going at home?

SHANE: Bad....

BOB: How so?

SHANE: My parents won't get off my case about the fights. They just need to leave it alone and everything would be fine.

BOB: They've been on your case a lot lately... mostly about the fights at school.

SHANE: Yep. They don't get it. If people say stuff to me at school I'm gonna stand up to it. That's the way it is.

BOB: I can see how that might get to you.

SHANE: It does.

BOB: So that's what happens in school. What about on the football field?

SHANE: What do you mean?

BOB: Well, I haven't heard about you getting ejected from a football game for fighting. In fact, have you ever even had a personal foul?

SHANE: No way.

BOB: How come?

SHANE: I can't get kicked out the game—that's what happens when you get a personal foul in high school sports.

BOB: So what? Haven't you been so mad that you felt like going after another player?

SHANE: Oh yeah, all the time.

BOB: What do you do when there's an opposing player who is talking trash or when someone shoves you after a play?

SHANE: I just ignore it and get back to business.

BOB: How do you do that?

SHANE: I just focus on getting the next play done and I let it go.

BOB: That's interesting. Tell me more about how you focus.

SHANE: I just focus in on the game and eliminate everything else.

BOB: It sounds a bit similar to what I used to do when I was in high school. I played baseball and on the days that I was pitching people would say that it was like I was in a trance or something. I was just focusing.

SHANE: Exactly! I do that too—it's kind of hard to do anything on game days.

BOB: That's actually a very good skill that serves you well on the field. It also raises my curiosity about you. What if you were to get suspended from school for fighting during football season—what would happen?

SHANE: I'd miss a game—at least.

BOB: Are you willing to risk that?

SHANE: No way.

BOB: Okay, so what I'm wondering is how do you get yourself to focus on the field in those moments when you really need it?

SHANE: It's the bigger picture. I've got a job to do—to help my team to win.

BOB: What about at school? What's your job there?

SHANE: I guess to get an education.

BOB: So fighting hasn't interfered with your job on the field, but it has with your job in the classroom.

SHANE: Yeah.

BOB: So how could that ability you have to focus on the field be helpful to you when you're in school?

SHANE: I see what you mean. Yeah, I think I just have to remember what my job is on and off the field.

BOB: Your dad told me that you want to play college ball. Is that right?

SHANE: Yeah, I've got some colleges looking at me.

BOB: That's terrific. And adding a new element to your overall game wouldn't hurt—showing the ability to focus in and out of school. That's why we have academic all-American athletes each year in college sports. They do well in academics and in sports. I bet many coaches would find the ability of being able to focus to be a wonderful quality in a player—and perhaps a sign of maturity.

SHANE: That's what my dad would say. I know I can focus better in school and I'm not going to ruin going to college because of some idiot who knows he can get me riled up.

BOB: It's not worth losing your dream, is it?

SHANE: No way.

An ability in one context of a client's life can sometimes be helpful if used elsewhere to solve a problem. Although our clients often have abilities we don't always ask about them. For example, many parents will say things such as, "He's horrible at home, but the neighbors think he's the most wonderful kid!" or "I don't get it, he's fine here but at school all he does is get in trouble." People have abilities, strengths, and resources that come to light in different contexts. One of our tasks as therapists is to assume that clients have some abilities. It is a matter of asking questions to identify those competencies and then link them to problem contexts. Here are some questions to assist with this process:

- How have you managed to keep the problem at bay when you're at ______?
- What do you do differently when you're ______ as opposed to ______ that helps you to manage your life a little better?
- How can being able to ______ when you're ______ be helpful to you in dealing with ______?
- How can you make use of that ability in standing up to ______?

Find out why the problem isn't worse. Problems vary in intensity. They get better then worse then better again and so on. Sometimes when problem situations don't seem to be improving, clients have mechanisms in place to keep them from completely bottoming out. These mechanisms in the form of abilities, strengths, and resources can be useful in altering the direction of change. There are many questions that therapists can ask to evoke these sensibilities. These are sometimes referred to as *coping sequence questions* (Berg & Gallagher, 1991):

- Why isn't your situation worse?
- What have you done to keep things from getting worse?
- What steps have you taken to prevent things from heading downhill any further?
- What else has prevented things from deteriorating further?
- How has that made a difference with your situation?

One way to explore this idea is to have the client explain, in comparison to the worst possible state a person could be in, why his or her problem isn't that severe. This normalizes and helps put things in perspective. This gives therapists information about how clients restrain themselves from getting into more trouble. Another way to do this is to ask the client to compare any incident of the problem to the worst manifestation and explain what is different about the times the problem is less severe. Case Example 6.10 demonstrates this.

Case Example 6.10 *Working the Plan*

Bill worked with a man named Omar who had weighed as much as 280 pounds. Omar told Bill that his eating and weight were out of control. Bill asked him why he didn't weigh 350 pounds. After giving him a funny look, Omar told Bill that he wouldn't be able to stand it if he weighed that much. Bill acknowledged him and asked what he did to make sure that he didn't gain an extra seventy pounds. Omar reported that whenever he reached 280 pounds, he would modify his eating habits and begin to exercise more. He essentially had a method in place to keep things from getting worse.

Bill and Omar focused on helping him to change his pattern of eating and exercising before he reached 280 pounds. Omar already knew how to lose weight, but he wasn't implementing his ability early enough. So he began to practice his strategies of modifying his eating and exercising habits when the scale showed 270 pounds instead of 280. In this way Omar was able to implement what he already knew about losing weight earlier, allowing him to gradually decrease his weight.

When clients are asked why things aren't worse they're often caught off guard. They simply haven't viewed their situations from that perspective. Bob often tells his supervisees and students, "The clients you're working with have had experiences dealing with all sorts of concerns and conditions. Some of those things were present before you got involved and some will occur later. Consider asking your clients, 'How have you managed to keep things from getting worse when they could have?' 'How have you stayed afloat and what will allow you to keep going when we're finished meeting?'" These, and questions offered earlier, can orient clients to whatever aspects of themselves, others, or their situations have worked to any degree. These preventative mechanisms can help to build hope for clients when they feel or think that nothing is going right.

Therapeutic Rituals: Action Methods with Meaning

Another way to change the doing of problems is to help clients create or develop rituals. We generally use two types of rituals in therapy: (1) continuity and stability rituals and (2) transition rituals. In the next sections we'll look at each of these.

Continuity and Stability Rituals: Balancing Security and Change

The first type of ritual is one that helps develop a certain stability or sense of continuity in clients' lives. When people are confronted with problems, they often find they stop doing regular stabilizing activities, like exercising, writing in a journal, having dinner with the family, going out for an evening with one's partner, and so on.

Steve and Sybil Wolin (1993) conducted research on the resiliency of children from alcoholic and abusive families. The researchers wondered why all children who were raised in alcoholic families don't turn out to be alcoholics or don't have Adult Children of Alcoholics (ACOA) syndrome. Some do, but many don't. They were interested in the exceptions.

One of the key things they found from their research was that a child whose family rituals were not disrupted by the alcoholism or abuse did not develop as many dysfunctional patterns in adulthood (Wolin & Wolin, 1993). Everyday routines and activities remained a constant in these children's lives. We are both from large families. At dinnertime, everyone would gather together at the same time each evening. Although things may have been chaotic with lots of kids running around and many different activities going on simultaneously, everyone knew that dinner was at the same time each night. It was a stable activity in our everyday lives.

Along with the daily dinners, we also had daily, weekly, monthly, seasonal, and yearly rituals. These regular activities helped us connect with ourselves and inoculate us from some of the troubles that can plague children from dysfunctional homes. The Wolins found that children whose rituals were disrupted didn't do as well. We would like to share the following story to illustrate the importance of rituals:

> When Bob was in the fifth grade he made friends with a boy named Will. The two lived within half a mile of each other and Will would visit Bob and his family frequently. In fact, Will's visits came to be routine and predictable. Most evenings he would show up at the backdoor of Bob's home precisely as the family was beginning to have dinner. What Bob and his family came to understand was that while Will's home life was chaotic and unpredictable, at Bob's home things tended to be

routine, predictable, and consistent. Each evening Bob's mom would make enough food for a small army (which was necessary with seven children), and there was always plenty of food, conversation, and camaraderie. Will could blend in as one of the family. Will's routine remained consistent for several years until Bob and his family moved to Massachusetts when Bob was in the eighth grade.

Years passed, and after Bob graduated high school, he and his family moved back to Missouri. One day, Will spotted Bob's sister Mary on the highway. Although approximately four years had passed, he recognized Mary, turned around, and followed her home. From that point, Will began to come around regularly again, and even lived in the home for a while. It seems that Will had found his stability again.

Will found continuity and stability in his life through rituals. He sought consistency in his life through relationships with others. At Bob's house, Will knew he would not be made fun of, would have enough to eat, and would be around people who enjoyed his company. Many people who come from chaotic, abusive, alcoholic, or other detrimental environments need rituals that connect them to others. These rituals provide consistency and can help people deal with adversity.

As therapists, we can help clients who have experienced disruption by encouraging them to restore old rituals that have been interrupted by their life changes, or by helping them create new ones. We refer to these as rituals of *continuity* or *stability.* These are habits that help establish some balance in their lives.

Any disruption or trauma can disconnect people from their rituals of continuity or stability. This disruption does not have to be something traumatic such as a death or an illness. As with Will, it could be ongoing instability or chaos in one's life. It also could be a desirable event, such as the birth of a child or a new job. For example, say a married couple had a ritual of going to dinner together once a week to talk. Then they have a baby and they find that they no longer are spending the time together that they used to. They lose the ritual of connecting. In times of change—positive or negative—it is particularly important to maintain old stability rituals or create new ones. Stability rituals can be ones that connect one to others or one to oneself. Case Example 6.11 illustrates this idea.

Case Example 6.11 *Bedtime Rituals*

Bill worked with a woman, Marcia, who had been abused. As an adult, Marcia had created the ritual of locking the door to her house and the door to her bedroom every night, which made her feel safe. She would also hold a teddy bear, light incense, listen to new age music, and drink herbal tea at bedtime. This ritual engaged all of her senses. Marcia would then write in her journal to connect with what she had experienced that day. After doing this ritual for awhile, anytime Marcia began to feel disconnected, all she would have to do is put on the music or light the incense and she would be reminded to reconnect.

Our colleague Steve Gilligan (personal communication, 1992) has the idea that when organisms are traumatized they naturally withdraw. If a dog has been hit by a car on the highway, but not killed, he might move away from or snap at the proferred hand of a passing stranger. This can be true with people too. When traumatized, they withdraw from aspects of themselves and sometimes don't reconnect. Our job as therapists is to help them reconnect to themselves or to others. Anthropology is rife with descriptions of the kinds of rituals people do to connect and stabilize their lives. Table 6.1 provides a summary of some of the connection and stability rituals that we've used to help people reconnect.

Transition Rituals: Leaving Old Roles and Pain Behind

The second type of ritual that therapists can use with clients is a transition ritual. Transition rituals are helpful when clients have identity stories or unfinished business that they feel a need to leave behind. Transition rituals offer these people a physical way to disrupt old stories and move on to new stories and gain a new sense of themselves. Transition rituals include rites of passage, rites of mourning, and rites of exclusion, as shown in Table 6.2. To utilize this kind of ritual, we help clients find symbols. Symbols represent the unfinished experience within the

TABLE 6.1 Types of Connective/Stability Rituals

Activities Clients Can Count On—Daily, weekly, monthly, seasonal, holidays.

Continuity Rituals—Restoring previous rituals.

Connecting Rituals—Prescribing rituals that restore or make connections to people or situations.

Rituals of Remembering—Rituals that help connect with memories, the past, and disconnected resources.

Rites of Inclusion—Designed to make people part of a social group or relationship.

TABLE 6.2 Types of Transtion Rituals

Special Activities Marked Out from Everyday Life—Special times, places, clothing, foods, scents, activities; restricted to special people.

Rites of Passage—Designed to move people from one role or developmental phase to another and to have that validated and recognized by others in their social context.

Rites of Exclusion—Designed to eject or bar people from a social group or relationship.

Rites of Mourning and Leaving Behind—Designed to facilitate or make concrete the end of some relationship or connection.

clients. Symbols should be physical objects that can be carried around, burned, or buried.

Case Example 6.12 ***The Light within the Darkness***

Bob worked with a young woman named Felicia who would burn her legs with a lighter. Felicia said that the black burn marks represented all the darkness in the world. She was an artistic young woman and very poetic in her descriptions of things. Although she was not suicidal, her persistent self-mutilation was beginning to create scars and present medical problems, because her wounds didn't always heal enough before she burned her legs again. Her father was a pediatrician, and prior to her seeing Bob, he had his daughter hospitalized four times in six months for the self-mutilating behavior.

After establishing an agreement with Felicia not to burn herself, Bob asked her if she felt that all the darkness and blackness the world had shown her was all that life had to offer her. She said that there were other colors too, but that black was mainly what she saw. Since she enjoyed painting, Bob suggested that the next time she felt the impulse to burn her legs, she work to capture the color she was trying to describe on canvas. Felicia's first paintings were very dark black with specs of gray and white. She said that those specs represented "the light that sometimes shows through the black." Her paintings gradually became lighter in shade with less and less black present. She abandoned the self-mutilating behavior and began to paint pictures of nature settings for other people.

During the final therapy session Felicia said, "I can still see the light even if there's darkness." The painting served as a symbol for Felicia—she manipulated the paint on the canvas rather than burning her legs. In so doing, she was able to make the transition from darkness to light.

Symbols can help clients recognize and express what they are experiencing without harming themselves physically or mentally. When we do symbolic work, we ask clients what symbol they think will work for them. We will also offer possibilities that other clients have used or that have been a result of the therapeutic conversation. These might include using a picture, a doll, a plant, a rock, and so on. We've found that many clients will choose to write something as at least part of their ritual, but it depends on the person.

Phases of Creating Rituals

Next are the steps that we use to create healing rituals:

1. *Introduce the idea of a ritual.* Clarify what the purpose of the ritual is and what is still unfinished for the client. Brainstorm what kind of symbol might be used for the ritual.
2. *Prepare the client to do the ritual.* Make sure that clients are emotionally and psychologically ready. The clients need to decide who is going to do the ritual (a family member, friend, the therapist, etc.), or whether they want to do it alone.

3. *Have the client(s) do the ritual.*
4. *Create a respite experience.* There is usually a transition from doing the ritual back into everyday life. The person goes away from the ritual and does something else. This can be some kind of getaway that could include, but is not limited to, meditation or praying.
5. *Celebrate reintegration to everyday life.* The final step in the ritual process should be a celebration—something that symbolizes that the person has moved on and has entered a new phase in life.

Some rituals combine both transition and continuity. Having clients choose both problem symbols that they are going to leave behind and solution or resource symbols they are going to carry with them is a way of combining both. Rituals give people something to do about the unfinished or disconnected feelings they have inside. Rituals can also help them reconnect with their social environment after they have been disconnected by trauma or change in their lives. Rituals are also a combination of changing the doing and changing the viewing of the problem situation. By performing some action that is imbued with meaning and symbolism, both aspects are addressed.

Class of Problems/Class of Solutions Model

Some years ago, Bill studied with Milton Erickson. Bill was perplexed by the seemingly endless creativity as well as effectiveness of his interventions. Erickson rarely used the same intervention for similar problems, but at the same time, he did not seem to be random in his creation of these interventions. To try to emulate some of Erickson's success, Bill created a model that he has since found useful in helping clinicians to think creatively and specifically about how to intervene in therapy problems. He called this model the Class of Problems/Class of Solutions Model (O'Hanlon, 1987).

The first step in using this model is to derive from the specific presenting problem an abstraction that is a *set* of the kinds of problems that the problem exemplifies. The class of problems is not to be an explanation of the problem (e.g., to keep the parents from discovering their conflict, to get attention, or secondary gain); rather, it is to be descriptive. An abstraction that includes the kind of abilities that people have to solve that sort of problem is then devised. From that set of abilities (the class of solutions), a specific intervention is derived.

The intervention is a parallel communication and treatment agent for the specific presenting problem. The specific intervention is usually a metaphor of some kind (an anecdote or analogy), a task assignment, an interaction, or one of the trance phenomena. These are designed to access or develop the ability that is needed to solve the problem. We have included Table 6.3 for a graphic representation of this process. Perhaps the best way to understand the model is to look at examples of its use with some problems. The examples used here are from Erickson's work.

TABLE 6.3 CLASS OF PROBLEMS/CLASS OF SOLUTIONS MODEL

Specific Presenting Problem	——►	Specific Intervention *Analogy* *Anecdote* *Trance Phenomenon* *Task* *Interpersonal Move*	——►	Transfer to Problem Context
D E R I V E		E V O K E		
Class of Problems	——►	Class of Solutions (Pattern of experience) (Resource/skill)		

Treating Enuresis (Bed-Wetting)

Erickson described a number of cases in which he used parallel treatment devices to treat enuresis. The specific problem is bed-wetting. The class of problems here might be described as lack of muscle control. A class of solutions might be automatic muscle control. There may be other classes of problems and classes of solutions which could be abstracted (for example, another class of problems could be staying asleep when bladder is full, and a concomitant class of solutions could be automatically waking up when bladder is full), but what we are searching for here are ones that are descriptive and lend themselves readily to interventions. In the cases that follow, Erickson works toward the goal of automatic muscle control through such parallel interventions as analogies, task assignments, and interactions.

Case Example 6.13 ***Erickson Case Example 1***

A twelve-year-old boy was brought to Erickson for bed-wetting. Erickson dismissed his parents and immediately began talking to the boy about other topics, avoiding a discussion of bed-wetting altogether. Upon learning that the boy played baseball and that his brother played football, Erickson began to describe the fine muscle coordination it takes to play baseball compared to the gross uncoordinated muscle skills used in football. The boy listened raptly as Erickson described in some detail all the fine muscle adjustments his body made automatically in order to position him underneath the ball and to catch it. The glove has to be opened up just at the right moment and clamp down again just at the right moment. When transferring the ball to another hand, the same kind of fine muscle control was needed. If one lets go too soon when throwing the ball, it doesn't go where one wants it to go. Likewise, letting go too late leads to frustration. Letting go just at the right time gets it to go where you want it to go and that constitutes success ... in baseball. (Haley, 1985, Vol. 3)

Class of Problems/Class of Solutions Model

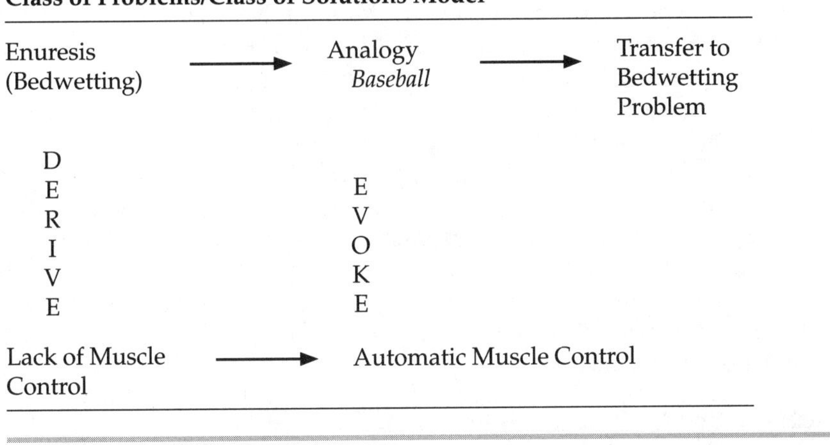

Case Example 6.14 ***Erickson Case Example 2***

A twelve-year old boy was in an intense struggle with his mother over his continued bed-wetting. Erickson gave the mother the assignment of waking up at 4 or 5 a.m. every morning to check whether her son's bed was wet or dry. If it was dry, she was to go back to bed without waking the boy. If it was wet, she was to get the boy up and have him practice his handwriting (which was very poor) until 7 a.m. Not only was the symptom resolved, but the boy's relationship with his mother and his grades at school improved. (Zeig, 1980)

Class of Problems/Class of Solutions Model

Enuresis (Bedwetting) → Task Assignment *Handwriting Practice* → Transfer to Bedwetting Problem

D E R I V E   E V O K E

Lack of Muscle Control → Automatic Muscle Control

Case Example 6.15 *Erickson Case Example 3*

An eleven-year-old girl had been cytoscoped so many times for her urinary tract problems that she had lost her ability to control her bladder sphincter. She would wet her pants if she ran or laughed during the day and she wet the bed at night. Her sisters, the neighbor kids, and the kids at school had discovered her weakness and took delight in making her wet her pants. She was miserable about the situation. Erickson told her that she already knew how to have dry beds and dry pants. She told him he was wrong. He told her that she already knew but that she did not know that she knew. She was perplexed by that.

He asked her in a rather dramatic fashion what she would do if she was sitting on the toilet urinating and a strange man poked his head in the bathroom. She replied that she would freeze. Erickson agreed and told her that this is what she knew that she did not know that she knew. All she had to do, he said, was to use this ability and to practice starting and stopping when she was urinating. She developed her muscles rapidly and was having dry beds and pants within a short time. (Rosen, 1982; Zeig, 1980)

Class of Problems/Class of Solutions Model

Enuresis (Bedwetting)	→	Interpersonal Evocation *Surprising to evoke muscle freezing*	→	Transfer to Bedwetting Problem
DERIVE		EVOKE		
Lack of Muscle Control	→	Automatic Muscle Control		

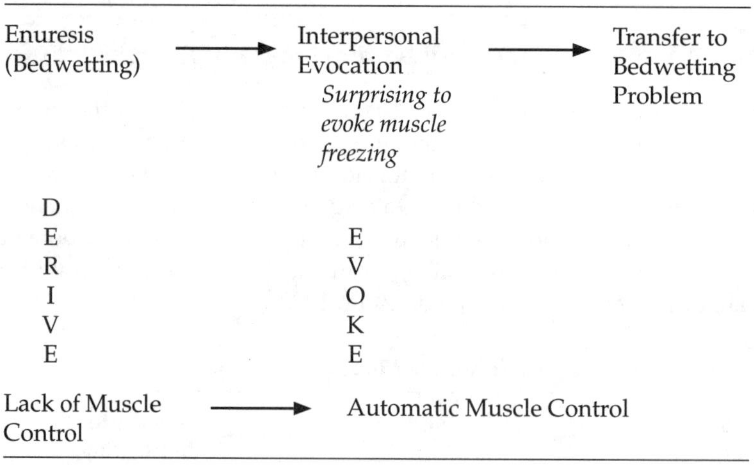

We hope you are starting to get the idea by now. While several of these cases are similar in their presenting problems, the interventions seem, on the surface, quite different. When examining them through the lens of the Class of Problems/Class of Solutions Model, however, one can clearly observe the structural similarities to the interventions.

We must take a moment to stress here that we are not providing a model for finding the true problem or correct intervention, only that we have found this model useful in generating relevant and useful interventions quite often. And as discussed earlier in this book with Erickson's work, it's not the story or technique that is important, but finding ways of evoking the inner abilities that clients possess by tailoring interventions to fit with them. Here's one further example of this.

Parallel Treatment of a Husband and Wife

In this last case illustrating the Class of Problems/Class of Solutions Model, Erickson provides parallel treatment of a husband with phantom limb pain (pain experienced where a limb has been amputated) and his wife with tinnitus (ringing in the ears). He mainly speaks to the wife, giving her anecdotes for her tinnitus. At the same time, however, he is providing a parallel treatment for the husband's phantom limb pain, since the class of problems and class of solutions are the same for both problems in this case.

Case Example 6.16 *Erickson Case Example 4*

A man sought Erickson's help for persistent pain in a leg that had been removed. His wife had also reported that she had tinnitus. Erickson began the session by telling the couple about a time when he was traveling around during his college days and he spent the night in a boiler factory. During the night, as he slept, he had learned to blot out the sounds in the factory and by morning he could hear the workers conversing in a normal conversational tone. The workers were surprised by this, as it had taken them much longer to master this ability, but Erickson said he knew how quickly the body could learn. Next Erickson told about seeing a television special the night before about nomadic tribesmen in Iran who wore layers of clothing in the hot desert sun, but who seemed very comfortable. During the session he told a number of stories illustrating the ability that people have to become habituated to any constant stimulus so that they could tune it out after a while. (Erickson & Rossi, 1979)

Class of Problems/Class of Solutions Model

Tinnitus
Phantom limb pain → Anecdotes
Ability to tune out stimuli → Transfer to Tinnitus or Phantom Limb Pain

DERIVE (from Tinnitus / Phantom limb pain down to Noxious sensory stimuli)

EVOKE (from Anecdotes down to Tune out irrelevant sensory perceptions)

Noxious sensory stimuli
Tinnitus = sound
Phantom pain = sensation → Tune out irrelevant sensory perceptions

We hope we have given you enough examples for you to begin to practice and become proficient at using this model in your own clinical work. Remember that the key is getting a description of the concern or problem that allows you to think of it as a process (not as a thing). If you do not do this, the method will not serve you well. As a way to get us to think in terms of process instead of fixed or set things, we sometimes think to ourselves: If we could create this problem, how would we do it?

Perhaps as a practice, you could start with the relatively common problem of anxiety. Think of how you would do anxiety if you were to try to create it right now. (This may be easy for those of you who have to take a test on this material.) Perhaps your heart rate might speed up. You might think of all those times you felt stupid and thought you would never understand something and would look bad. Perhaps you could focus on the future and how you might never become a counselor or therapist because it is all too hard for you.

Next, think of what category these actions might fit in. This would lead to a class of problems. Then think of something that would be a natural antidote or opposite experience or process. If you chose increased heart rate, this would be slowing down your heart rate. That would constitute the class of solutions. Then you would have to find a way to slow your heart rate through an anecdote, an analogy, a trance experience (if someone would hypnotize you or you knew self-hypnosis), by performing a task, or by having someone interpersonally evoke an experience of slower heart rate. That would constitute the intervention. Then somehow you would have to link the evoked resource or class of solution to the problem situation (anxiety).

Getting Clients to do Something Different through Action Plans and Task Assignments

We strive in each and every interaction to convey to clients that we believe in their capacity to change in preferred directions. Even though we are optimistic, we do not suggest to clients that if they believe enough or have enough faith that their problems will blow away with the wind. Similarly, some clients come to therapy expecting change to happen simply from attending sessions. While we are not surprised when change happens very quickly, in our experience most clients will have to take some action to ensure that the change they are seeking happens in their lives.

We work with clients to go beyond our therapeutic conversations and put their knowledge, ideas, actions, and interactions, whether old or new, into play. We don't direct clients to do anything. We collaborate with clients to see what fits with them. Once again this involves understanding clients' stages of change. For example, if we were working with a client that was in a precontemplative or contemplative state, we would not suggest anything that required them to take action.

Instead we might ask that they become involved with the viewing of themselves, others, events, or situations. We might say, "Between now and the next time we meet, we'd like you to notice what is different about those times when things seem to be going a little bit better for you."

For other clients who are in more of a preparation or action state, you can help them to take some form of action. One possibility is to orient clients toward taking action by using the "do something different" task (de Shazer, 1985). Clients are told, "Between now and the next time we meet, I would like each of you (or you alone) to do something different, no matter how strange, weird, or off-the-wall your action might seem" (parentheses added) (p. 123). This prompting can help clients be spontaneous and creative and can be enough for some to break out of the monotony of problematic patterns.

In our experience it's usually helpful to be more specific with tasks. We can help clients determine what their first step might be to move toward their goals and preferred outcomes. By encouraging them to take action in their lives we are looking for small steps that will get the ball rolling in the direction of the change they are seeking. We sometimes make an analogy to clients that they are at the starting line and we are like coaches standing on the sidelines. When the starting gun has been fired, the coach cannot do anything to help them reach the finish line except give them encouragement. They must take action to reach the finish line. To make it more likely that clients take action, we often work with them on making a between-session action plan. Planning action is important because:

- Clients often forget the precise ideas and instructions given or mutually decided on.
- Clients are often in such pain, anxiety, or confusion when visiting a therapist, they aren't always at their best intellectually.
- When a specific plan is decided on, people are more likely to follow through than when the plan is vague or general.

Action plans involve clients performing tasks. Tasks are meant to help bring about changes in doing (action and interaction), changes in viewing (perceptions, attention, and frame of reference), or changes in the context (time, space, gender-based patterns, cultural patterns, family of origin patterns, and biochemical and physiological aspects) of the situation involving the complaint or problem in therapy. Tasks are directed toward having clients make changes outside the therapy session. Tasks can be helpful in breaking up patterns. We can help clients find the places where patterns seem especially repetitive and predictable and direct assignments to making the smallest noticeable difference.

In our experience, the more that clients are involved and invested in the creation of a plan or task the more likely they will be to try it. Therefore, we listen very closely to their ideas about what they've tried and what they think might work. As discussed earlier, we also offer different ideas to clients, always being mindful that they make decisions as to whether or not the ideas discussed fit with their theories of change.

To further increase the likelihood that tasks will be done, we recommend writing them down, with the therapist and client each keeping a copy. This ensures that tasks are clear and understandable. It also serves as a reminder for clients to do tasks and for therapists to follow up on them. This is essential because when therapists follow up in future sessions they are communicating to clients that tasks can be of assistance in facilitating positive change. As an example of how to write out a task, we have provided Table 6.4.

We prefer the term *task* versus *homework* as the latter can sometimes evoke negative experiences of bad memories for clients. It can bring out recollections of meaningless, time-consuming assignments. For some clients you will need to create a different word to describe them doing something between sessions. We also frame tasks as experiments and as a way of trying different things.

If the assignment isn't done between sessions, we don't assume resistance. In fact, the most effective tasks are sometimes the ones that aren't done. The mere act of creating an action plan and task can change a problematic pattern. We recommend that therapists discuss the matter with clients and, if necessary, abandon the idea or make adjustments in the task until one emerges that works for all parties. If clients still don't perform assignments, make sure they are interested in the issue the task is designed for, or find another intervention.

If clients make it clear that they don't have the time or don't see taking action as a priority, be sure that you are working with them in ways that they see as helpful. This can be a good opportunity to ask more about what you still don't know about the client's situation and theory of change. We can ask:

TABLE 6.4 Action Plan/Task Sheet

Therapeutic Collaborations Therapy Center
56 Hope St.
Possibility City, VC. 11111

Date: ____________________

1. Between now and the next session, interrupt any arguments you have and take five minute breaks.
2. During that five minutes, think about one action you could apologize for and take responsibility for that was part of what led to the argument or contributed to escalating it.
3. Both of you acknowledge responsibility for that one thing and apologize before carrying on with the argument.

Date of Next Session: ____________________

- We discussed the idea of you trying out something new in between sessions and it didn't materialize. I'm getting the sense that I'm missing something about you or your situation. What is it do you think that I haven't yet understood about your situation?
- I'm getting the sense that maybe I'm not being as helpful as I could be. Can you tell me a little bit about what I'm doing that's working or not working for you?
- I'm wondering if you have some ideas about how to fade this problem from your life that I haven't already heard about or understood clearly enough. What can you tell me that might help me better understand how to approach your concern more effectively?

Getting clients to do something different may start the ball rolling in a preferred direction. Again, we aim for small changes because they can lead to bigger ones.

In this chapter we explored a variety of methods for helping clients change the doing of problems. In retrospect, changing the doing often results in a change in the views that clients have of themselves, others, events, and situations, and vice versa. Change in one can affect change in the other. In the next chapter, we will take up another aspect of the change process, *changing the context.*

Summary Points for Chapter Six

- People can become stuck or frozen in problematic patterns of action and interaction.
- Problematic patterns can be identified and changed by determining the following criteria:
  - How often does the problem typically happen?
  - What is the typical timing of the problem?
  - What is the usual duration of the problem?
  - Where does the problem typically happen?
  - What does the person, and others who are around, usually do when the problem is happening?
- There are two main ways to change problematic patterns:
  1. Depatterning—Altering repetitive patterns of action and interaction involved in problems
  2. Repatterning—Establishing new patterns in place of problems by identifying and encouraging the use of solution patterns of action and interaction
- Ways of Depatterning:
  - Change the frequency or rate of the complaint.
  - Change the location of the performance of the complaint.
  - Change the duration of the complaint.
  - Change the time of the complaint.
  - Change the sequence of events involved in or around the complaint.
  - Interrupt or otherwise prevent the occurrence of the complaint.
  - Add a new element to the complaint.
  - Break up any previously whole element of the complaint into smaller elements.
  - Reverse the direction of striving in the performance of the problem.
  - Link the occurrence of the complaint to another pattern that is a burdensome activity.
  - Change the physical performance of the complaint.
- Ways of Repatterning:
  - Find out about previous solutions to the problem, including partial solutions and partial successes.
  - Find out what happens as the problem ends or starts to end.
  - Find out about any helpful changes that have happened before treatment began.
  - Search for contexts in which the person feels confident and has good problem-solving or creative skills.
  - Find out why the problem isn't worse.
- Therapeutic rituals can help clients establish or reestablish continuity and stability in their lives or to leave old roles and painful experiences behind.
- The Class of Problems/Class of Solutions Model offers different possibilities for working with the same problem concern.
- Action plans and task assignments can help clients put their new ideas to work in vivo.

CHAPTER

7 Changing Contextual Propensities Associated with Problems

Problems are influenced by what we refer to as contextual propensities. These include social, environmental, political, economic, cultural, ethnic, gender, biochemical, spiritual, and other propensities. We believe that contextual propensities are influences (not causes) that can either be problematic or helpful. For example, a client may have a biochemical context that suggests a predisposition toward obsessiveness or schizophrenia, but that does not cause him or her to act in a particular way. One may be subject to hallucinations, but that does not cause him or her to run down the street naked or hit someone. If a man is from a cultural tradition where males are trained not to express feelings this doesn't mean he is or will always be unable to express feelings.

Sometimes, as a way of helping people reduce self-blame and to facilitate change, we highlight a cultural, biochemical, or familial pattern or influence, for example. Realizing that your mother suffered from depression in her forties, as you are now, can help normalize this experience. Learning that women are more likely to suffer depression might help alleviate some of the feeling that it is caused by some personal failing.

Every human being is a relative matrix of experience that has been contextually influenced. Therefore, in addition to the ideas of assessing and changing the viewing and the doing of problems, we also focus on changing contextual propensities associated with problems. To do this we will present several ways to minimize the biases and blind spots that clients and clinicians face, and to bring out contextual influences, both positive and negative. Let's first look at some further implications of context.

The Context of Context: Attending to Contextual Propensities

There has been considerable change in the way psychotherapy is practiced, compared to how it was practiced in the early 1960s. During that time and since, our culture and the psychotherapy field has been subject to critiques and questions from various quarters. In the 1960s, there was a growing ecological awareness that helped people see that we are all connected in an environmental context. If someone dumps chemicals into the river, ocean, or groundwater, it can have a wide effect on the environment. Using lots of carbon-based fuels and fluorocarbons can cause changes in the atmosphere that can affect climate and cancer rates.

Out of this ecological sensibility came the idea that psychological, emotional, and behavioral problems do not occur in a vacuum—they are influenced by the environment in which they occur. One of the forms that this environmental influence took was systemic therapy, and more particularly, family therapy.

In his book *King Solomon's Ring,* Konrad Lorenz (1997), the Nobel Prize–winning ethologist, tells a story about his first real-world proof of his theory of imprinting. Lorenz made the observation that goslings would follow anything that made quacking noises and was less than a certain height that appeared in front of them hours after they hatched. He had some geese on his farm in Austria. He isolated all the objects that could fit the imprinting criteria before the critical imprinting period, after the latest group of goslings hatched. He became their parent by parading in front of them, crouching and quacking. They began to follow him. He became so excited that he began wandering around his farm, transported by the excitement of finally demonstrating his theory. Hours later, he looked up to notice that a tour guide and a group of tourists were observing him with concern. He realized that he had wandered into a field of tall grass in which the goslings could not be seen. All the observers could see was a seeming madman crouching in the grass making quacking noises and every once in a while leaping about in joy, clapping his hands and yelling in excitement.

Family therapy was based on the idea that when an individual presents his or her problems, one can never know what context these problems may make sense in. Therefore, it was important to investigate the interpersonal setting in which this behavior was occurring (in effect, look for the unseen goslings). The initial investigation involved the patient's family.

This widening of the inquiry and focus was a major step forward in not assigning a simplistic single cause to people's distress. However, in its initial form it mostly consisted of blaming families for individuals' troubles. Concepts like "schizophrenogenic" mother and "dysfunctional" family became popular. The good news is that this was challenging the monolithic individual psychodynamic explanation for problems; the bad news is that it kept the pathologizing bias of that earlier approach.

Later waves of critique came from the biochemical psychiatrists, who maintained that assuming that family background or psychology had anything to do with psychiatric problems was wrong and blameful. Most disorders, in their view, arose from some biochemical dysfunction, usually genetically based.

Then came the feminist critique. It argued that a male bias created many more psychological and emotional problems for women. (Indeed, women have always been the primary consumers of therapy services.) Psychotherapy has pathologized women's desires to nurture and connect (*codependency*), to have clitoral stimulation during sex (*immature orgasms*), and to not get married or have children. Not only that, but male biases in treatment meant that many women did not get heard, validated, or helped during treatment. Further, by not recognizing or including patriarchal and sexist influences from society, some women were convinced that their problems stemmed solely from issues inside them.

The same could be said of sexual preference issues. As discussed in Chapter 3, until the mid-1970s, homosexuality was considered to be a deviant and abnormal condition to be corrected by psychotherapy. The heterosexual bias was pervasive in the field. Bisexual, homosexual, and people who prefer not to be categorized found little place for themselves within psychotherapy until recently and still run into bias and misunderstanding.

Gender issues, both male socialization and female socialization, and including all the shadings and mixtures of gender (transgendered, cross dressing, transvestitism), also began to decry therapy's unnoticed biases and oppressive pathologizing of what they experienced as valid choice or experience. In addition, cultural biases became apparent as cross-cultural therapy training began to be standard in the field. Therapy was clearly biased toward Western European ideals and modes of communication.

Collaborative, competency-based therapies are not based on normative theories and models. Therefore, they are not looking for evidence of deviation from the norm, so there is inherently less inadvertent oppression in them. But therapists practicing these approaches are subject to the blind spots of cultural and personal assumptions and values. "Often all one must do to acquire a disease is to enter a country where the disease is recognized—leaving the country will either cure the malady or turn it into something else," writes Lynn Payer (1996).

To counter biases and blind spots we attend to and listen to clients' stories. We've learned that each person is a conglomeration of many different influences that separate that person from the next. Although we all carry some general understandings and beliefs in relation to contextual influences, our approach is to let clients teach us what it is like to be them.

In earlier chapters we discussed the importance of stories. Clients' stories also play a vital role in exploring the influences of context. In the movie *Amistad*, John Quincy Adams and Mr. Joadson have a conversation in which Mr. Joadson tries to convince the former president to defend the captives who were aboard the vessel, *La Amistad*. Although John Quincy Adams initially declines this plea, he offers Mr. Joadson some advice. The dialogue is as follows:

JOHN QUINCY ADAMS (JQA): What is their story, by the way?

MR. JOADSON (MJ): Sir?

JQA: What is their story?

MJ: Why they're, umm ... from West Africa ...

JQA: ... No, what is their story?

MJ (Looking puzzled): (Exhales)

JQA: Mr. Joadson, you're from where originally?

MJ: Why, Georgia, sir.

JQA: Georgia.

MJ: Yes sir.

JQA: Does that pretty much sum up what you are? A Georgian? Is that your story? No. You're an ex-slave who's devoted his life to the abolition of slavery, and overcoming great obstacles and hardships along the way I should imagine. That's your story, isn't it?

MJ: (Smiles)

JQA: (Laughs) You and this young so-called lawyer have proven you know what they are. They're Africans. Congratulations. What you don't know—and as far as I can tell, haven't bothered in the least to discover—is who they are. Right?

In learning about clients' lives through their stories we ask, "Who are you?" and "What's your story?" and "What's it like to be you?" These questions privilege the voices of clients as opposed to any normative theoretical position. They allow us to learn from clients how they've experienced the world and about the contextual influences that have shaped their lives. We can then explore the effects of such influences and how they move clients forward and how they may facilitate or restrain positive change. Let's now discuss how to create change in the realm of context.

Into the Matrix: Drawing on Contextual Propensities

We explore and work with contextual influences in the following two ways:

1. To help clients recognize contextual patterns and elements that contribute to problems and make them worse
2. To search for helpful contextual patterns and influences

In exploring contextual influences we intertwine both aspects—finding what works and what does not. This relies on clients being the experts on their lives and, as mentioned earlier, teaching us about how they conceptualize themselves and their worlds. In addition, therapists help identify areas in which possibilities may exist, but perhaps are lying dormant. Oftentimes there are resources available to clients that have gone unnoticed or have been forgotten.

Recall that in Chapter 1 we discussed the importance of client factors. As much as 40 percent of the variance in outcome can be attributed to client factors. Therefore, we are always searching for ways of facilitating change processes by working with clients to identify the previously unnoticed aspects of the context as well as new perspectives on propensities that have not been viewed as helpful in the past. This can include their families, social support systems, relationships, community, ethnic and cultural propensities, spiritual supports, and any other influence on problems. Although this continues to be an evolving area for the entire field of psychotherapy, we will explore a few areas for creating change within the realm of context, from a collaborative, competency-based perspective.

The Inheritance Factor: Exploring Generations and Patterns of Resiliency and Competency

For many years mental health professionals have studied family histories. For example, some have explored patterns of alcoholism in an effort to empirically support the single gene theory. Others have searched for a genetic linkage relating to the transmission of mental illness. Family therapists however, including systemic and intergenerational thinkers, have explored how dysfunctional patterns can emerge within families and can be transferred through relationships to future generations.

A staple in the field of family therapy in exploring intergenerational patterns has been the genogram (McGoldrick & Gerson, 1985). Genograms have helped therapists identify and outline patterns that may be influencing current problems and may affect future ones. Although a very useful tool, genograms have typically been used to identify what is wrong with clients and their families. They lend focus to the inheritance of negative traits or the duplication of dysfunctional patterns.

In recent years, some clinicians have introduced ways of using solution-oriented genograms with clients (Kuehl, 1995). Instead of only exploring problematic patterns therapists investigate exceptions and previous solutions to the type of problem in family backgrounds. This shifts attention to the resilient qualities in families that have enabled them to stand up to adversity. This way therapists learn about the influence of problems over clients and families, and clients' and families' influence over problems.

Exploring clients' historical and familial roots can be particularly useful when clients feel or think that their problems are a result of their families. We investigate contextual influences in the same way that we would search for exceptions and solutions with problematic stories. For example, with a family where alcoholism has appeared to be a significant influence we might say, "So there has been quite a history of alcohol abuse and dependency in your family. Mom, your mother was an alcoholic until a few years ago. Dad, three of your uncles died from drinking while in their thirties. How did your mother stop drinking, Mom? And Dad, who in your family didn't succumb to the invitations of alcohol?"

It's important to learn about both sides—when the problem happened and with whom, and when it happened less or not at all and with whom. Remember, there are always exceptions. It's a matter of asking questions that invite clients into conversations about differences. Case Example 7.1 illustrates how generational patterns of competency can lead to the reauthoring of stories.

Case Example 7.1 *What Is a Real Man?*

Bob was asked to assist a colleague, Nick, as a cotherapist in the treatment of a family consisting of a single mother and her two teenage sons. The mother brought her two sons to see a therapist because both had been violent with schoolmates and each other. During the initial session the therapist also learned that the boys had assaulted their mother on multiple occasions, yet no reports or charges had been filed. The reason, according to the mother, was that she did not want her sons to get in trouble with the law. It was then learned that the mother herself was a police officer, assigned to office duty. Further exploration of the family found that the boys' father, two uncles, and grandfather were also police officers.

The boys appeared to be very hostile, arguing with their mother, calling her names, and denying responsibility for their actions, saying things such as, "She needs to shut her mouth and everything will be fine" and "I warned her. She knew what was coming." On several occasions, because of their behavior, the therapist had to separate the boys from their mother and from each other.

Bob joined the therapy in the third session. He asked the mother what she had hoped to see happen as a result of coming to therapy. She said that she wanted the boys to stop hitting her and to learn to be respectful of people. The boys were each asked the same question. Kevin, the oldest at fourteen years of age, stated, "I don't care. This sucks." The other teen, Kris, who was thirteen years old, pointed at his mother and answered, "That lady needs to get a life and get out of mine."

BOB: Where do you think the boys got the idea that violence and aggression are the way to handle things?

MOTHER: I know where they got it. That's what they've been told for years by their father.

BOB: What have they been told by their father?

MOTHER: To stand up to people. Don't let anyone walk over you. You have to be a real man.

KEVIN: **(Raising his voice)** Shut up!

BOB: Kevin, you can be upset and you don't have to agree with your mom but it's not okay to tell her to shut up or to be mean to her. Now, I'd like to ask you how you learned to deal with anger.

KEVIN: **(Silence)**

BOB: It's okay if you don't feel like talking right now. I sometimes feel that way. **(To Kris)** Kris, do you have any ideas about that?

KRIS: You've got to take care of yourself and don't let anybody walk on you. Especially girls.

NICK: Where did you learn that?

KRIS: My dad always says that.

BOB: I see. And what do you think he meant by that?

KRIS: He meant that you have to be tough.

BOB: What does that mean to you?

KRIS: If people say stuff or make you mad you have to stand up. So that means fighting back.

BOB: Okay. If you had to guess, where do you think your dad got the idea about having to be tough?

KRIS: He's a cop. They have to be tough.

NICK: So he learned it through his training to be a cop?

KRIS: Yeah, but my uncles are cops too and my grandpa was one. I think they told him to be tough.

KEVIN: (Interjects) Cops have to stand up.

NICK: Sometimes they do.

BOB: Kris, you mentioned that it's especially important to not let girls walk on you. What did you mean by that?

KRIS: Men are in charge. Girls can't tell you what to do.

BOB: Did you hear that from your dad as well?

KRIS: My dad, my uncle Vic, and my grandpa.

BOB: So there are several men in your family that believe that to be true.

KRIS: Yep.

KEVIN: Yeah, they're right too.

BOB: I'm curious about a few things. Can you teach me some more about your family?

KRIS: What do you want to know?

BOB: Well, you mentioned that you have two uncles who are police officers. One is your uncle Vic. Who's the other?

KRIS: Steve. He's cool.

BOB: What does Steve think about the idea that you have to be tough and stand up to people, especially women?

KRIS: I don't know. He doesn't talk about it.

KEVIN: I don't know either.

MOTHER: He's a very nice man and always treats his wife, Sharon, great... his kids too—he's got two girls.

KEVIN: Yeah, Katy and Diane. They're nice.

NICK: So do you get along with your aunt Sharon and your cousins Katy and Diane?

KEVIN: Yeah.

NICK: What would you do if you didn't agree with them about something?

KRIS: I know I would just talk to them.

KEVIN: Yeah, because uncle Steve would get mad at us if we argued with them.

BOB: So your uncle Steve would step in. What do you think he would say?

KEVIN: Don't fight. You don't need to fight.

BOB: I have to admit that I'm really confused here. It really sounds like your uncle Steve believes that girls and women should be treated with respect.

KRIS: He told me that *everyone* should be treated with respect.

BOB: Really?

KRIS: Yep.

BOB: Help us to understand here. It sounds like even though some members of your family think that you should stand up to people and in particular, girls and women, some of them don't believe that. How is that some of your family members have been able to stand up to aggression and disrespect?

KRIS: Well, I think they just don't like it.

BOB: I agree, and I'm getting the sense that part of you doesn't like it and doesn't really believe that you should be aggressive and disrespectful to girls and women. Is that right?

KRIS: I don't want to be mean.

BOB: What do you want your mom to know about how you feel about her?

KRIS: I love her.

KEVIN: So do I!

BOB: Well, help me to understand how assaulting, threatening, and verbally abusing her lets her know that you love her.

KRIS: (Crying) I'm sorry mom.

MOTHER: (Crying) I know... but it really hurts me when you're mean to me.

KEVIN: (Tearful) We do love you. I'm sorry.

BOB: You know, we all inherit different things from our families. I'm getting the sense that maybe you've inherited some of that compassion for others that your uncle Steve has. Now is the time to bring that out and use it and stand up to the other ideas that have been hurting you and your family. What do you think?

MOTHER: I've always known that the boys had it in them. I've seen traces of it here and there.

BOB: So how can you two begin to make use of those inherited family qualities of being respectful and kind more often in the future?

KEVIN: I just have to be nice. I know I can be.

KRIS: I can be nice too.

The therapy continued for five more sessions. Kevin and Kris were able to draw on their familial qualities of being respectful to others. The violence with their mother ceased and both boys improved their relationships with others. The most noticeable change occurred with Kris whose relationship with his female teachers changed dramatically. In fact, the mother was contacted by one of his teachers who said to her, "I don't know what has happened with Kris, but he has become quite a gentleman." The mother said that that was the first time she had pictured Kris as a gentleman. Her story about him had begun to change.

We've found that there are many ways that can help therapists learn about the influences of familial patterns. Here are some prompts and questions that can help find exceptions to problems:

- Given the circumstances of your family life, describe what you would like to see change in the future.
- How have you or other family members kept this problem from completely taking over your lives?
- How are you dealing with this problem differently than your ______ did?
- Who in your family has successfully dealt (to any degree) with this problem?
- How did they do that?
- What qualities do your family members possess such that they are able to stand up to adversity?
- What does that tell you about your family?
- What qualities or traits do you think that you've inherited from your family that can help fade this problem from your life?
- What does that tell you about yourself?
- (When change has been identified) How are you benefiting from these changes?
- How are others in your family benefiting from these changes?
- As these changes continue, what will be different in your family ______ (e.g., 6 months, 1 year, 2 years) from now?
- What do you think all of this says about your family?

A major benefit of using the aforementioned questions is that therapists do not have to physically create a genogram; they can simply ask clients questions that explore these aspects of context. These questions can be used at any point in treatment where clients' stories indicate familial influence.

Without the Family: Inheriting Familial Influences

As illustrated with Case Example 7.1, oftentimes therapists can work with clients in attributing some positive familial qualities to themselves. However, there are times when clients know little or nothing about their biological families. Further, sometimes what they do know is viewed as negative. For example, we've heard clients say things such as, "My mother was an alcoholic," "My father was a drug dealer and a womanizer," and "My family was full of crazy people." The implication of these stories is that clients will sometimes hold the idea that they are predisposed to or have inherited these negative qualities.

We've found that even when clients know nothing about their families of origin or have made generalizations about themselves and their families based on little bits of information, there are ways of shifting the perceptions of familial influences. This idea is illustrated in the motion picture, *The Mighty.* In the movie, two boys who are very different befriend each other. One of the boys is Max, who witnessed his father murder his mother years earlier. Throughout the movie, Max encounters reminders of his father, such as other kids chanting, "Killer Kane, Killer Kane, had a son who's got no brain," a friend of his father's, and a picture of his father. Each of these reminders reinforces the story he holds that he is just like his father. Young Max is emotionally tortured by this story.

There are several instances in the movie where others offer different perspectives, to gently challenge Max's view of himself and his father. In one particular scene, Max finds a picture of his father and begins to cry. His grandmother goes to check on him and finds him upset. The scene eloquently depicts the idea of the differences between inheriting negative and positive familial traits.

GRANDMOTHER: **(Knocking on door)** Max? You okay? **(Enters room)**

MAX: **(Crying)** I'm just like him.

GRANDMOTHER: **(Whispering)** Just like him? **(Walks over to Max and sees him holding a picture of his father)** Oh, Lord. I thought I'd gotten rid of every last picture.

MAX: I look in the mirror and I see him. I hear my voice and I hear his. It's no use. You are who you are, and nothing else. **(Repeats the chanting children)** "Killer Kane, Killer Kane, had a son who's got no brain!"

GRANDMOTHER: Listen to me. You are nothing like him! You will never be like him. You know why? Because you have your mother's heart. You're my noble knight. That's what you are.

While Max was paying attention to how he might be more like his father, his grandmother saw it differently. She saw that he had inherited the qualities his mother possessed. In a similar way, therapists can help clients to identify positive qualities with those clients that know little or nothing about their biological families or their caregivers. Case Example 7.2 further illustrates this point.

Case Example 7.2 *To Be or Not to Be Like My Mom*

Bob worked with a nineteen-year-old woman who had been adopted when she was three months old. During her second session with Bob she stated, "I don't want to turn out like my mom. She was a bad mother. She was an alcoholic, she was promiscuous, and she died young. I mean, it was good that she gave up her children because she knew she couldn't care for them, but she was bad otherwise."

Bob inquired, "You don't want to be like your mom in that way—battling alcoholism and promiscuity—and yet there seemed to be this redeeming quality your mother had—she cared about you and knew she needed to have someone else care for you when she couldn't. Do you think that you've inherited the quality of caring about your children?" "Absolutely. I know I have. I would do anything for my children, so I guess I got that from my mom." Bob then asked, "And what else has contributed to you becoming the terrific mom that you are?" "My (adoptive) mom has taught me a lot. She's had to deal with a lot and isn't perfect, but she's a great mom," replied the woman. Bob followed, "So you've had the benefit of drawing on the qualities of two mothers." "I sure have," answered the woman. Bob then asked, "What does that say about the type of person you are?" "I'd have to say that I've taken the best of both worlds and I left the rest behind."

For this woman, there were qualities from her biological mother as well as her adoptive mother that made contributions to who she was as a person. The identification and amplification of internal qualities can shift a problematic story to one of hope and possibilities. Let's look now at another way of exploring the influences of family.

Creating Meaning through Speculation

As mentioned, some clients will know nothing about their biological families. This does not stop the process of speculating about what one's parents might have been like. People without knowledge of their families, and parents in particular, will create perceptions even without information. In our experience, some people will spend their lives trying to find out something about their families and establish a connection with them. In many cases they never find them. However, this does not stop them from forming views about their parents and other family members. We can help them with this process.

What we first do is work with clients to identify their qualities, skills, and actions that they find valuable in some way. For example, during the course of a session we may find out from a client that he feels he is a good mechanic. Later we learn that he is a warm and caring father to his children. These things can be identified at any point of treatment. We then consider how the person's parents or family might have influenced that quality. To do this we begin to speculate, as in Case Example 7.3.

Case Example 7.3 ***My Parents***

THERAPIST: You mentioned earlier that you really care about your children and love to spend time with them. Is that right?

CLIENT: Definitely. There's nothing more important to me than my kids. I wish I could be with them more than I already am.

THERAPIST: I'm glad that they have you and that you have them.

CLIENT: Thank you.

THERAPIST: This makes me wonder, because you mentioned that you never really knew your parents. You were adopted when you were a baby....

CLIENT: Yeah, I've tried to find out about them but have found no record. I've been trying for eighteen years with no luck.

THERAPIST: I'll keep my fingers crossed that you find something out about them.

CLIENT: I keep thinking that someday I'll get word.

THERAPIST: This is the part I'm wondering about. Even though you don't have any recollection of your parents and haven't been able to obtain any information on them thus far, given the type of person that you are—friendly, caring, a loving father and husband—what do you think your parents might have been like?

CLIENT: Wow. Well, I have wondered about that. It's funny you should ask.

THERAPIST: Any ideas at this point?

CLIENT: I keep thinking that my mother must have been caring. I know that I just see a child and my heart melts. Maybe I learned that, but I just think that she must have seen no other option or thought that adoption was the best way to go, because my family (adopted) is the greatest. I couldn't have had a better life growing up. So I wonder if I am like my real mom.

THERAPIST: And what about your dad?

CLIENT: Well, maybe this is stereotypical, but I think my ability to think in a mechanical way might have come from him. Of course, I could have it backward—maybe my mom was the mechanical one and my dad was the caring one or they both had a little of each. Who knows? But that's what I think, anyway.

THERAPIST: And like you said, part of it could be learned or related to something else. It does seem like with all the terrific qualities you have that there is a good chance of a biological connection here.

CLIENT: I've always thought that.

We've found this approach to be particularly helpful with children and adolescents who are in residential treatment centers, foster homes, runaway shelters, and other placements. Some of these youth have never known their parents and never will. Yet they continue to wonder and speculate about their parents, and search for a connection to them. Because they are already creating their own stories, which are sometimes problematic, we explore with them the possibility that their personal characteristics and qualities might be related to something positive that their parents passed on. This can help to diffuse anger and negative feelings that youth have carried around in their stories about their parents. We've also created some questions that can help with this:

- What qualities do you think you inherited from your family?
- What do those qualities say about the kind of person you are?
- How are they an asset to you?
- Given the type of person that you are (caring, kind, honest, etc.), what do you think your parents might have been like?
- What qualities do you think they passed on to you that help you to move through life?
- What qualities would you like to pass on to your children? Why?

Oftentimes clients are already speculating about their parents before we engage them in conversations about them. As discussed in Chapter 5, if these views become problematic they can stifle clients and their attempts to move toward their preferred futures. In such cases, we gently offer alternative views where clients can find value in themselves and in relation to those qualities that may have been passed on.

The Multicultural Influence: Learning the Ways of the World

There is no definition or description that can encompass the vast array of multicultural diversity and experience in the world. For the purposes of this section, we refer to Arredondo and D'Andrea's (1995) description:

> Diversity refers to other characteristics by which persons may prefer to self-define. This includes, but is not limited to, an individual's age, gender, sexual identity, religious/spiritual identification, social and economic class background and residential location (i.e., urban, suburban, rural). (p. 28)

Although we strive to be as informed as possible, our views as therapists will be limited. Therefore, as we have stated throughout this book, we learn from our clients what it is like to be them. We claim no preconceived knowledge about their experiences. We assume a not-knowing position whereby we are always learning from clients what we still don't know about them and their experiences (Anderson & Goolishian, 1992). William Madsen stated (1999):

> Just as anthropologists (or more accurately, ethnographers) immerse themselves in a foreign culture to learn about it, therapy from an anthropological stance can begin with immersing ourselves in a family's phenomenological reality in order to fully understand their experience. (p. 41)

It can be said that we practice multicultural curiosity. In this way we challenge our own values and beliefs and work with clients to do the same in ways that are respectful and open up possibilities. To do this we listen to clients' stories. Clients are our best teachers and their firsthand experiences can help us understand the influence of context.

In listening to clients' views and stories, we often hear of multicultural propensities that are supportive and serve as a rich resource. To illustrate this we once again refer to the movie *Amistad*. In preparing to go before the U.S. Supreme Court, John Quincy Adams talks with Cinque, the spokesperson for the captives, through a translator. As the translator translates English to Mende and Mende to English, John Quincy Adams learns from Cinque that his rich cultural background is a source of strength that he never could have imagined:

> **JOHN QUINCY ADAMS (JQA):** Cinque, look. I'm being honest with you. Anything less would be disrespectful. I'm telling you, I'm preparing you I suppose, I'm explaining to you that the test ahead of us is an exceptionally difficult one.
>
> **CINQUE (C):** We won't be going in there alone.
>
> **JQA:** Alone? Indeed not. No. We have right at our side. We have righteousness at our side. We have Mr. Baldwin over there. [points to Mr. Baldwin, who is sitting nearby]
>
> **C:** I meant my ancestors. I will call into the past, far back to the beginning of time, and beg them to come and help me at the judgment. I will reach back and draw them into me. And they must come, for at this moment, I am the whole reason they have existed at all.

Cinque knew the inner strength he needed was already present within him, in the form of his cultural background. He could use this resource to help him through whatever obstacles he might face. This way he would not face any hardships alone.

There are other times when multicultural influences become constraints for people and contribute to their problem situations. We ask clients to teach us how these influences are helpful and how they may be restrictive. We claim no expertise on the experiences of others so we ask questions to elicit that experience. To illustrate this we offer Case Example 7.4.

Case Example 7.4 *Teach Me*

Bill was teaching a workshop on collaborative therapy in London a few years back. At the end of the first day of the workshop, a woman from the audience approached him and told him that she had enjoyed the workshop. She was having a particular problem in her workplace and wondered if Bill had any ideas.

She worked at a shelter for battered women in central London. The women who came to her shelter were a mixture of women who had been raised in England, and Pakistani immigrants. The English women would enter the shelter and at least make an attempt to change their situations—they would attend educational courses, therapy groups, and so on. Occasionally, they would leave their violent partners. The Pakistani women seemed much more resigned to their situations. They accepted that violence was part of their lot in life and that there was no escape. If they defied their husbands, they could be instantly divorced and shunned from their communities, a price that few of them were willing to pay. The counselor wanted to know how Bill's approach would solve this problem.

Bill excitedly replied that this was the beauty of the collaborative approach—he didn't have a clue how to solve this challenging problem. But he did have an idea of how to find a solution—ask the Pakistani women themselves. Bill advised the counselor, who was going to the shelter that evening after the workshop, to ask some Pakistani women from the shelter to be her consultants. She was to tell them that because she knew little about the Pakistani culture, and they were experts, she needed their help. She wanted them to tell her about any Pakistani woman they knew or knew about who had ended violence in her marriage successfully.

When the counselor arrived at the workshop the next morning, she pulled Bill aside and told him that his suggestion had worked. She had gotten her group of consultants together and they had come up with two examples of Pakistani women who had successfully ended violence in a marriage. Although the situations of these two women were different, they had something in common. Both of them had told someone in their family about the violence and their father and brothers had visited the violent husband and told him that if he continued to be violent with their daughter or sister that they would return and beat him. In one case, the brothers and father actually had to return and beat the husband before he stopped, but in the other, the warning was sufficient.

The counselor, upon hearing these stories, was a bit discouraged. This solution had worked back in Pakistan, she told the women, but because their families were almost all back in Pakistan, how could it possibly work here in England? The Pakistani women were not discouraged at all—they were rather excited. Finally one of them said, with a twinkle in her eye, "Yes, our families are back in Pakistan, but mine is coming to visit me next month. I think I shall have a talk with them."

The point here is that there are patterns of sexism, patriarchy, oppression, injustice, and violence toward women in Pakistani culture. There are also solution patterns in this culture to prevent or stop violence toward women. In each culture, there are problem patterns and solution patterns, pathologies and strengths. Here are some further questions to assist with learning about problematic patterns and solution patterns in regard to multicultural influences:

- Tell me more about the influence that (culture, race, gender, sexual identity, economics) have played in your life. What is most important for me to understand about that?

- What can you tell me about your background that will help me to better understand you?
- What aspects of your background have been most influential in your life?
- What has it been like for you to grow up in ______?
- What has it been like for you to be ______?
- What has it been like to grow up as a man/woman in this world?
- What has it been like to grow up as a (Caucasian, African American, Native American, etc.)?
- How have you been able to draw on that strength?
- What challenges have you faced?
- What do people like me need to know about you to better understand the influences of your background?
- What, if anything, about your background has posed difficulty for you?
- How have you dealt with that?
- What aspects of your background can be a resource for you in times of trouble?
- What resources are you most likely to draw on in times of need?
- How is that or can that be helpful to you?

These questions can be helpful in highlighting multicultural influences that have been existing sources of support. In contrast, we can learn about those that have contributed to problems. In the latter, we work to find out more about what we still don't know or understand, and generate questions that deconstruct problematic stories. It is through this process that we can help clients in the construction of new, empowering narratives, where multicultural influences become sources of strength and support.

Unconditional Conversations: Tapping into Social Support Systems

Recall that the largest contributor to therapeutic outcome is what researchers refer to as extratherapeutic factors. Part of this client matrix is the contribution of the client's world outside of therapy. In particular, we have found the role of social support systems to be significant. This includes significant others (e.g., family, partner, friends, spiritual advisors, teachers, coworkers, classmates, scout leaders, coaches) in the lives of clients and community. We have found this to be extremely important in the lives of many clients. In exploring existing and potential support systems with clients, therapists can ask:

- Who helps you in your day-to-day life?
- How or what do those people do to be of help to you?
- Who has been helpful to you in the past in facing daily challenges?
- How have they been helpful to you?

- What did the assistance of these people allow you to do that you might not have done otherwise?

When important people in the lives of clients have been identified, we can use the questions listed previously to find in what way they have been helpful. We then search for ways of tapping into these support systems in the present and the future. Sometimes this means, with the permission of clients, inviting such persons to participate in the therapy or assisting with referring and connecting clients with further community-based resources. Case Example 7.5 demonstrates this idea.

Case Example 7.5 *The Purple Truck*

Fourteen-year-old Sean and his family had moved three times to different states, within a period of two years. According to his mother, each time Sean entered a new school he would have enemies within five minutes. Sean had been in numerous fights with classmates and with neighborhood youth, he argued with his teachers and had poor grades, he had been caught stealing, and he would frequently come in after curfew. He had been suspended from school eleven times in two years, and his parents felt hopeless that things would change.

When Bob met the family, he learned that they had elicited the help of many mental health professionals, including psychiatrists, psychologists, and counselors. They had been through traditional office-based family therapy and intensive home-based services and case management. Not even contacts with local law enforcement and the juvenile court made a difference.

Bob explored many different avenues for creating change with the family. At times, Sean appeared to have turned the corner and would do better for short periods. However, it seemed to be one step forward and two steps backward as just when things had improved, Sean would get into a fight or some other type of serious trouble. The situation was very perplexing to Bob.

As time passed, Bob continued to work with the family together as well as Sean and his mother separately in an effort to obtain lasting change. One day Bob and Sean were sitting on the front porch of Sean's home and a purple truck pulled into the driveway across the street. This clearly sparked Sean's attention. As a man stepped out of the truck, Sean yelled, "Hey Mark, what's up?" The man turned, waved, and replied, "Not much. Come on by later." Bob asked Sean who the man was, and he answered, "He's cool. He helps me out sometimes. I just like hanging out at his house."

When Sean revealed little more, Bob asked his mother about Mark. He learned that Mark was in his mid-thirties, was married, and had a young child. Sean's mother said, "He spends a lot of time over there and Mark doesn't seem to mind. It's weird, but Sean really listens to him and respects him." Bob asked the mother if he could have permission to talk with Mark. He made it clear that Mark did not have to know the details of Sean's trouble, but Bob suggested that since Sean seemed to respond well to Mark, he might be a good resource. Sean's mother readily agreed, and signed a consent form giving Bob permission to talk with Mark.

The next day, Bob met Mark as he arrived home from work. He introduced himself and said, "I've been working with Sean and his family because things haven't been going so well lately. And the reason I've come to you is because I understand that Sean really looks up to you." Mark smiled and added, "Well, he does spent a lot of time over here and we like having him here." Bob continued, "It seems to me that he really gets something from his relationship with you, and even though I have no idea what that is, I think it could be a calming resource for Sean. And what I'd like to know is, would you be willing to continue to spend time with him and perhaps teach him what you know about dealing with trouble and conflict?" Bob was not any more specific and Mark smiled and replied, "I'd be happy to."

What happened over the next few weeks was truly astounding. Sean's behavior changed dramatically. His fighting stopped completely and he seemed to make more of an effort at school and even began helping out with his younger sister. Bob closed the case with the family six weeks after eliciting Mark's help with Sean.

In other cases we can learn from clients what the relationship with significant others symbolizes for them. For example, if you ask people about their experiences growing up, many will cite at least one person whom they felt unconditionally accepted them for who they were, and perhaps helped them through a tough time or two. Sometimes these people were family members or longtime friends. Other times they were only acquaintances. To find out about these people we can ask some of the following questions:

- Who have you met in your life that knows exactly what you've been going through? How do they know that about you? How has that been helpful for you to know they understood?
- Who do you look up to?
- Who has helped you through tough times? How so?
- Who do you feel you can count on?
- When you're struggling, who knows just what to say or do to help you to get back on track?
- Who has the right idea about you?
- (To another family member) Who in your ______'s life seems to be able to get through to him or her? How do they do that?
- Who seems to get through to or is able to have an impact on ______? How so?
- Who do you know that ______ responds to, and would be willing to help out?

If clients have a hard time coming up with names of people, sometimes it's helpful to say something like, "When things were going better for you, who helped you out or made a difference in your life?" Then ask, "What did they say or do?" and "How did that make a difference for you?" Another possibility is to say, "Tell me about a time when things weren't going too well and someone helped you get through it."

Oftentimes the people that clients identify will not be physically available as a resource. However, it may be possible to find a way of replicating what that relationship symbolized for the client. Case Example 7.6 illustrates this point.

Case Example 7.6 *She Knew Me Best*

Bob was working with a young woman, Julie, who was experiencing a variety of psychosomatic concerns. She was having stomach problems and occasional migraine-like headaches. Her medical doctor had been unable to find any physical connection and suggested that she see a therapist. During the third session with Julie, Bob learned that she felt at her best when she was eighteen years old and a freshman at college. It was at this time that she had a sociology professor who spent extra time with her to learn the material, and subsequently used her as a teaching assistant in the second semester. Now twenty-seven years of age, Julie stated that she felt her sociology professor was behind her all the way.

Bob asked Julie what seemed to be most helpful about her relationship with her former professor. She informed him that it was perhaps the only time she really felt supported and valued as a person—like she was intelligent and capable. Bob also asked Julie what difference that made for her. She said that feeling supported helped her feel stronger, and therefore she was more productive. Although the whereabouts of her former professor were unknown, Bob asked Julie if that's what she wanted to experience again—feeling supported and valued. To this she nodded and began to cry.

Over the next two sessions, Bob and Julie talked about other times that she felt even mildly supported and valued. She recalled a friend who she used to talk with on the phone weekly, but who had moved away after getting married. Julie explained that she would like to call her but didn't have her new phone number. When asked what her next step might be, the woman stated that she should investigate trying to find her. So Bob and Julie mapped out an action plan where Julie would make some phone calls and scan the Internet to try and find her old friend.

At the next session, Julie came in elated. She told Bob that he wouldn't believe what happened. Through the Internet she had not only found her old friend, who was now in Arizona, but had also found another friend from college whom she had forgotten about. It was hard for Julie to contain her excitement and she explained how she had already corresponded with her friend in Arizona who was also excited that they were able to reconnect. In fact, they made plans to meet during the summer and correspond through e-mail and by phone in between. Consequently, Julie's stomach problems subsided and her occasional headaches were treated with standard ibuprofen.

Through these inquiries the therapist can get an idea of what made a difference for clients and can work to facilitate possibilities in other areas. In Case Example 7.6, Julie was able to find another source of support that she did not notice at first. Although the initial person she identified as being helpful to her was not found, she found someone else who supported and valued her.

We sometimes say that clients will develop amnesia in times of pain and suffering. They will forget about their resources. Oftentimes it's not that these resources have disappeared, they just aren't being used. Therefore, as therapists, we help clients reorient toward those resources and reconnect with them, or identify new ones that may fulfill the same needs. Another way of doing this is to suggest that clients become involved in activities that they previously enjoyed or might enjoy (sports, clubs, hobbies, arts, support groups, etc.). Engaging in activities that they enjoy may help clients have more energy and feel better. Their chances of meeting others who will be supportive also increases.

Experiencing Spirituality: Contexts of Connection and Disconnection

Another element of context that we can use as both a resource and to examine contextual contributions to the problem is that of spirituality. We define spirituality broadly, so that it can refer to religious practices and rituals as well as a wider context of activities that we group under the rubric of connectedness.

Often people have been traumatized, shamed, controlled, or hurt in the name of some doctrine, and they disconnect from their sense of spirituality. But some yearning for connection may remain. Without imposing any particular form of spirituality on clients, we often investigate where they are connected or disconnected from themselves and their wider contexts. To aid in this inquiry, we search through seven pathways for places where people have disconnected or connected with something beyond their isolated personalities. Spirituality for us refers to what is beyond the *little self*, or the personality. Anything that gives one an experience of the *bigger self*, or what is beyond the limited personality, can be a component of spirituality. We think that there are seven pathways that people go through to connect to something bigger in their lives. The nice part about these pathways is that some of them do not even seem religious or what many consider to be spiritual, so even clients who have experienced religious trauma or think that spirituality is all a new-age claptrap can relate to one or more of these pathways.

Seven Pathways to Spirituality through Connection

1. *Connection to the soul, the deeper self, the spirit.* This involves having a connection with oneself that is beyond the rational, logical, or even the emotional. Many people find that meditating, journaling, or just spending time alone helps them find this connection.

2. *Connection to the body.* This may come through dancing, sex, athletics, yoga, eating fine foods, and so on. Seeing Michael Jordan in the air about to make a basket or other great athletes in action can show spirituality through the body—they seem to do things that are beyond usual human abilities and that seem transcendent.
3. *Connection to another.* This involves intimate one to one relationships. Martin Buber calls this the I–Thou relationship. This pathway does not always need to refer to a relationship with another person; it could be with a pet.
4. *Connection to community.* This pathway involves one's relationship to one's group. If you have ever felt part of a family, extended family group, neighborhood, church group, or workplace, you have taken this pathway.
5. *Connection through nature.* This involves being in and noticing nature and the physical environment. Many of us need to spend time in the outdoors every so often or we begin to feel small and disconnected. One may also experience this sense of connection through a deep understanding and appreciation of the laws of nature, such as physics and mathematics.
6. *Connection by participating in making or appreciating art.* Have you ever seen someone standing in front of a painting in a museum and being moved to tears, or listened to a piece of music and feeling energized or moved? Depending on one's preferences, this may come through literature, painting, sculpture, theater, movies, photography, dance, and so on. Many artists refer to a sense that they are not making the art they produce, but that it is coming to or through them.
7. *Connection to the Universe or a higher power.* This can be a God or cosmic consciousness or whatever word one uses for the sense that there is a greater being or intelligence than oneself at work in life. This connection can happen through prayer, conversion, meditating, and so on.

At times, clients are overwhelmed by their problems and feel as if their personal resources are not adequate to cope with or resolve the problem. Spiritual resources can help them find the strength and energy to meet or overcome problems.

We can ask a series of questions to connect people to their spiritual resources. These questions are designed to illuminate both past traumas that may have blocked access to these resources, as well as to point to the ways that the person or family is connected to something beyond personal limited resources. We search in the past, the present, and the future.

Spiritual History

- Have you ever had religious or spiritual beliefs or practices?
- Have those been helpful in any way?
- Have they been harmful in any way?
- Have you had any traumas connected with religion or spirituality?
- Have you ever felt connected to something more than yourself, like nature, humanity, the Universe, God, or something else?
- Have you had any profound spiritual experiences?

Spiritual Resources and Solutions

- What do you do, or where do you go, to recharge your batteries when you get a chance?
- What kind of artistic activities do you enjoy?
- How do you connect with other people?
- Do you think you have a purpose for being alive? If so, what is it?
- Is there any religious or spiritual figure or activity that you think would be helpful for you in this situation?

Spiritual Hopes and Intentions

- Are there any spiritual or religious activities you would like to do in the future?
- Is there any area of your inner or spiritual life you would like to develop more?
- Is there any spiritual or religious figure that you would like to use as a personal model? In what way?

Case Example 7.7 illustrates how we can help clients use their spiritual resources to facilitate change.

Case Example 7.7 *A God Thing*

A twenty-year-old woman, Sally, came to see Bob. Among her concerns were becoming sober, healing from the breakup with her boyfriend, and securing employment. In the second session of therapy, she came in and said, "A God thing happened to me today. You know, I lost my job a few weeks ago and today I got a call from a temp agency that I applied at five months ago. At AA (Alcoholics Anonymous) they say 'give it to God' and I did and look at what happened." To this Bob replied, "That's terrific. And I wonder, some people would say, 'God helps those who help themselves.' Do you think that's true for you?" "I hope so," answered Sally. Bob inquired, "If that is true for you, what is the next step?" To this Sally responded, "Well, I think it's to go to the interview and see what happens."

In this particular case, Sally's faith was an influential resource that elevated her spirit and allowed her to move forward toward her goal of securing employment. To reiterate, elements of context do not cause problems, they influence them. With this in mind, we learn from clients what contextual propensities allow them to do that they might not otherwise be able to accomplish.

Internalized Medication: Who's Driving the Bus?

Therapists seem to be in the precarious situation of being for or against the use of psychotropic medication. We find it unnecessary and disrespectful to advocate solely for one or the other. We have worked with many clients who have benefited from the use of medication for their emotional concerns, and we have worked with many who have not. No one thing works for everyone. Our concern lies with the degree to which psychotropic medications are used as a first choice with clients. We find this to be unethical and inconsistent with the empirical data on the effectiveness of psychotropic medication. Duncan and Miller (2000) stated that there is little support for:

- The idea that emotional suffering is caused by a biochemical imbalance in the brain
- The superiority of drug treatment over psychotherapy (even for severe depression)
- Better outcomes when therapy is combined with drugs (pp. 20–21)

We are also reminded that clients' theories of change will influence the effectiveness of medication. If clients believe that their problems are organic or biochemical, they are more likely to take their medication regularly and experience some benefit of that treatment. However, if clients believe that their problems are relational, behavioral, psychological, spiritual, or are related to anything other than biology, they are less likely to benefit from medication because it runs counter to their theories of change.

In our experience, when clients are on medication there are two considerations. First, we want to make sure that they understand what the medication is supposed to do. We frequently work with clients who either have no idea of how their medication is supposed to help them, or they have an inaccurate perception of its intended effect. In such cases we make sure that clients are clear on what the medication is designed to do.

Many clients experience positive change while on medication, and attribute the bulk of that change to the medication. However, when they experience further difficulty, or the effectiveness of the medication diminishes in their eyes, clients will blame the medication, deny accountability for their actions, and continue the never-ending search for the right medication. We are amazed at the number of times we hear, "We just haven't found the right medication yet."

When clients are benefiting from medication and experiencing change in the direction of their goals and preferred outcomes, we want to help them to recognize *their* contributions to that change. We have found the following questions to be useful with this process:

- You mentioned that you think that the medication you're taking is helping. How are you working with the medication to better your life?
- In your mind, what does the medication you're taking allow you to do that you might not otherwise be able to do?
- What percentage of the change you've experienced is a result of the medication and what percentage do you think is your own doing?
- What are you able to do as a result of feeling better from taking medication?

Case Example 7.8 shows how to put this idea to work.

Case Example 7.8 *Playing the Percentages*

Seven sessions into his therapy, Todd had his medication changed and informed his therapist that it was working.

THERAPIST: How do you know that it is working?

TODD: I'm not as depressed now.

THERAPIST: I see. And how have you noticed that you're less depressed?

TODD: I've been going out more and getting to work on time.

THERAPIST: Okay. What percentage of this change do you attribute to the medication, and what percentage do you think is related to your own doing?

TODD: I'd say about 60 percent medication and 40 percent me.

THERAPIST: Tell me about the 40 percent. What have you been doing differently?

TODD: Well, I have been going out and I wouldn't have done that before.

THERAPIST: Great. And how have you managed to get yourself to do that?

TODD: Well, for one, I started exercising again so I'm feeling better about my body. I don't feel like such a slob.

THERAPIST: So you've been exercising?

TODD: Yep.

THERAPIST: That's terrific! That really does sound like a "you" thing. It's as if you've prescribed your own medication—exercise.

TODD: I think so.

THERAPIST: So even though you're on medication that you feel is helping you, you've also personally taken some action in your life.

TODD: Definitely.

THERAPIST: What will it take for you to feel that you are more responsible for your changes than your medication is?

TODD: I think that it already is me.

THERAPIST: So it's more than 40 percent?

TODD: Yeah, I think it's more like 80 percent me.

THERAPIST: How so?

TODD: The medication can only do so much. If I don't get my butt in gear it all goes for naught.

THERAPIST: I see. So the medication helps you to feel a little better, but ultimately it's up to you to do something to get the changes you want.

TODD: Exactly.

We agree with clients when they think that medication has helped them in some way. What we want to be clear on is that while medication can help clients feel better, it does not get them up off of the couch, get them to work, complete their work, and so on. Therefore, we work with clients to attribute the bulk of the change that they experience to themselves.

Again, problems do not occur in a vacuum. They exist in specific times, places, cultural and familial contexts, and may have cultural, racial, spiritual, economic, biochemical, physiological, genetic, and gender components as influences. When therapists cannot find personal resources to help resolve the problem, it may be helpful to cast a wider net to these contextual areas to search for negative influences or resources. This may help provide a different and less self-blaming view of the situation or may illuminate unseen solutions or possibilities. Although what we have discussed in this chapter is by no means exhaustive, in Table 7.1 we offer a summary of the extrapersonal, contextual aspects of life that influence clients' problems and solutions.

In Part Four, we will discuss ways of evaluating progress, planning next steps, and ending therapy.

TABLE 7.1 Elements of Context

Community connections to others (church, neighborhood, clubs)
Physical environment or location
Cultural/racial background and propensities
Familial/historical background and propensities
Biochemical/genetic background and propensities
Gender training and propensities
Spirituality

Summary Points for Chapter Seven

- ♦ Contextual propensities do not cause problems, they influence them.
- ♦ We explore and work with contextual influences in two ways:
  1. To help clients to recognize unhelpful patterns and elements from their context—ones that contribute to problems and make them worse.
  2. To search for helpful contextual patterns and influences.
- ♦ Ways of changing aspects of context:
  - ■ Explore generations and patterns of resiliency and competency.
  - ■ Explore multicultural influences.
  - ■ Tap into social support systems.
  - ■ Explore spiritual influences.
- ♦ When working with internalized medication, assist clients in attributing the significant portion of change to their own efforts as opposed to the influence of psychotropic medication.

PART FOUR

Evaluating Progress, Planning Next Steps, and Ending Therapy

Part Four is composed of two chapters. In Chapter 8 we will explore ways of approaching second and subsequent sessions. This includes identifying and amplifying change, evaluating progress in relation to established goals, and extending change into the future. We'll also discuss how to work with clients who seems to remain stuck. Chapter 9 follows with ideas for managing setbacks, growing new stories, and sharing those new stories and changes with larger social contexts. We'll also discuss ways of building on change and helping clients maintain those changes once therapy has ended.

CHAPTER

8 Identifying, Amplifying, and Extending Change in Future Sessions

Whether we are counselors, therapists, psychologists, social workers, psychiatrists, marital and family therapists, case managers, or some other form of mental health professional, we are facilitating processes associated with change. In each and every session we are searching for examples of change in the direction of established goals. In this chapter we'll explore how therapists can approach subsequent sessions with a change-focus. This will include how to evaluate progress, identify, amplify, and anchor change, and plan next steps. We'll also explore creative ways that therapists can negotiate therapeutic logjams and work through difficult situations.

Revisiting Conversational and Relational Preferences, Goals, and Preferred Outcomes

As discussed with initial sessions, we periodically check with clients to make sure that we are in sync with their views of the therapeutic relationship and what they want to see different in their lives. This can occur at any point during a session. Let's briefly look at ways of doing this in all sessions.

There are at least two ways of learning about clients' perceptions of the therapeutic relationship. One is to ask clients questions related to their conversational and relational preferences. In Chapter 4 we offered several questions that can assist with this process. Another method is to use a pencil and paper instrument to measure outcome. One possibility is the Session Rating Scale (SRS) (see Appendix I). The SRS is a self-report that clients can complete quickly. Information from this and similar tools can help therapists learn what clients need more or less of from the therapeutic relationship. They also inform therapists how to work more effectively with clients.

Next, it's important to remember that a lack of clarity regarding what clients want, including their goals and outcomes, can drive therapists and clients apart. Without clear goals, attempts at intervention can be misguided contributing to frustration and negative outcome. Therefore, we advocate for gaining clarity as soon as possible. To inquire about goals and preferred outcomes we simply summarize the goals that were established previously and inquire as to whether they are the same or have changed. The following story illustrates the importance of orienting toward goals for both clients and therapists:

> Bill was once supervising a therapist who felt stymied by the lack of progress in a particular case. When she began describing some of the difficult issues they were dealing with in the therapy, Bill interrupted and asked the therapist what the original presenting concern and goal for therapy were. Since it had been six months or so, the therapist couldn't recall those. Bill suggested that she begin the next session by asking the client what she had entered therapy for and whether she thought she was any closer to her original goal(s). If she had made progress toward those goals, had there been new goals that she had developed during the course of therapy?
>
> After the next session, the therapist reported to Bill that the therapy had terminated. Bill was surprised and asked what had happened. The client had told the therapist, in response to the inquiry, that they had accomplished her original therapy goal several sessions before that one. She had continued on with therapy because she was under the impression that the therapist thought that she had other important issues she (the client) needed to work on. The therapist assured the client that she didn't think the client needed to work on any other issues. The client assured the therapist that she was satisfied with the results, and they agreed that the therapy was over. The therapist, who had been feeling lost and a bit like a failure, instantly had a sense of success and competence from this report.

Second and Subsequent Sessions

Future sessions begin in much the same way as initial sessions. Therapists allow clients to begin where they feel most comfortable. We strive to help clients to feel heard and understood as they tell their stories. In addition to continuing to create a climate that promotes change, therapists listen for words, statements, and phrases that suggest impossibility, and they offer subtle changes in language to introduce the notion of possibility. Future sessions also provide continuing opportunities to change the viewing, actions, and contextual propensities associated with problems and to learn from clients whether or not change is occurring in the direction of previously established goals.

When asked about what has transpired between sessions, clients will respond in a variety of ways. In our experience, these responses can be collapsed into the following five categories:

1. New concerns or problems that have arisen between sessions or were not previously discussed

2. Vague responses that do not indicate any particular direction in change (e.g., "I'm not sure")
3. Things are better
4. Things are so-so
5. Things are the same or worse

Now we'll look more closely at each of these.

When Clients Report New Concerns or Problems That Have Arisen between Sessions

By allowing clients to begin where they feel comfortable, some will respond by describing an entirely new concern or problem that was not part of the problem description in previous sessions. It is not uncommon for clients to move from one problem to another, depending on what transpired between sessions or what is looming largely on their minds. Above all, we are sure to acknowledge all concerns and make sure clients feel that we understand their concerns, whether they are related to the past, present, or future.

When clients have new concerns sometimes acknowledgment will be all that is necessary. However, other clients will need more than acknowledgment. In addition, some clients will be unclear as to whether the concerns they are describing are more significant than the ones discussed in previous sessions. In these cases it is imperative that therapists talk with clients to determine the weight of the present concerns. One way to do this is to summarize both the goals that were previously set and the current complaints, and then ask the client which ones are most concerning. Case Example 8.1 shows a way to do this.

Case Example 8.1 *What Should We Talk About?*

During the initial session, a man named Isaac voiced his concern about being overwhelmed with his workload at his place of employment. Isaac stated that he wanted to be able to manage his work better and be more efficient. At the start of the next session, he said that he was having trouble with his marital relationship. As the therapist listened, Isaac described how he felt that his spouse didn't value his opinion and therefore didn't involve him in important decisions. The therapist acknowledged this new concern and then inquired, "If it's all right with you, I'd just like to make sure we're focusing on what you feel like is most important at this time. I can see that you have a few concerns. Would you rather spend this time talking about your sense of being undervalued and left out of important decisions in your marriage or being able to manage your work better and be more efficient, as we discussed last week?"

As discussed earlier, for some clients, acknowledging their current concerns will be enough for them to return to previously established goals. For example, one client might say, "Well, I am concerned about my marriage, but I'm more concerned about work. Let's talk about that." A different client might respond with, "I'm really not worried about work now. How could I be? My marriage is a mess. I think we should talk about that." Yet another possibility is for a client to say, "I want to work on them both." In this case the therapist would acknowledge this modification in goals and expand it to include the man's marital problems. However, when there are multiple concerns that will likely be addressed over the length of treatment, or when there has been a change in goals, it is a good idea for the therapist to go a step further and ask the client, "Which of these concerns would you like to work on first?" Clients often choose directions for treatment that can and do periodically shift. Therefore, if clients choose to go in a new direction, we follow them. This sometimes means establishing new goals and preferred outcomes.

Although directions in treatment can and often do change, whenever there are new problem reports we find it important to at least inquire as to what has transpired in relation to previously established goals. If we don't, we may overlook positive change that may have occurred. Identifying such change can indicate to clients that change is always happening and can serve as a source of empowerment for future change. What the client did to bring about the change may also be helpful with other concerns in the present or the future. Case Example 8.2 illustrates how therapists might utilize this idea.

Case Example 8.2 *A Brief Update*

Roger's father had expressed his concern over his son's staying out until three or four o'clock in the morning. In the initial session he indicated that this is what brought him and Roger to therapy, and this was what he wanted to see change. During the next session, the father reported that Roger had been truant from school during the previous week. After acknowledging this concern and learning more about it, Bob asked the father if he was most concerned with Roger's staying out late or having been truant. To this the father responded that the truancy was a bigger concern. Before proceeding, Bob inquired, "Before we talk about this further, could you give me a brief update on what's happened with the situation of Roger coming in late?" To this the father replied, "Well, he didn't stay out late this past week, so that's better." Bob followed, "Really? Were you surprised?" "A little," answered the father. Before moving onto the concern of truancy Bob was able to identify and amplify positive change by asking Roger and his father a series of questions including: "Roger, what did you do differently? "Even though you thought about coming in late a few times, how did you get yourself to come in when you were supposed to?" and "What did you do when you found that Roger was coming in on time each night?"

Even if goals have changed or clients choose to shift the conversation for a session or two, it is important that therapists continue to search for evidence of positive change. If there is no exploration of change in relation to previous goals, examples of positive change might be overlooked and clients might become overwhelmed—feeling as if their lives are only problematic and unmanageable. In addition, without the identification of progress and positive change, therapists can begin to feel hopeless—as if clients cannot be helped. In contrast, by identifying change that may have occurred between sessions, therapists can promote hope and facilitate future change in other areas of clients' lives.

When Clients Give Vague Reports That Do Not Indicate Any Particular Direction of Change

Another way that clients sometimes respond is with vague reports. These are situations where it is not clear whether things have improved or become worse. For example, a client might say, "I'm not really sure" or "Well, I guess it's been... I guess I don't really know how it's been. It's hard to tell." In such instances it can be helpful to summarize what transpired in the previous session or series of sessions and then ask the client what has happened since. Here are a couple of ways of doing this:

> The last time we met you told me that you were feeling very upset by the way you felt you had been treated at work. In fact, you commented that being upset had led you to have stomachaches and headaches. Can you tell me about what has happened since our last session?
>
> Last week you mentioned that things had been very tense around the house. Part of this was because Carla had been home just three days from her latest run. You mentioned that that was your biggest concern. You were worried that she might take off again and it was like being on pins and needles, waiting to see what would happen. Your sense was that maybe she was beginning to see things differently because, over the three days that she was home, she was talking to you more openly than before; but because it had only been a few days, you were still apprehensive. So, how have things been since then?

It can also be helpful to ask one or more of the following questions:

- Can you tell me a little bit about how things are in relation to the last time we met?
- What's been different since the last time we met?
- What's your sense about how things are going now, as compared to last time?
- The last time we met, you mentioned that on a scale of one to ten, things were at a five. Where would you say things are today?

Questions such as these can reorient clients toward their goals and help therapists learn about any changes that may have occurred. Another way of determining change from session to session is to use the first session formula task (de Shazer, 1985). At the end of the first session the client is told:

> Between now and the next time we meet, we [I] would like you to observe, so that you can describe to us [me] next time, what happens in your [pick one: family, life, marriage, relationship] that you want to continue to have happen. (p. 137)

At the next session, the therapist asks the client what he or she noticed happening that he or she would like to have continue. This can help to identify what has been working in the client's life. The therapist can then ask the client about how the positive virtue came about, what difference it made or makes for him or her, and what it will take to have it continue to happen in the future. This can provide momentum in the direction of established goals and preferred outcomes.

The methods described can help therapists learn from clients which direction change has occurred in. While the first session task and other change-oriented questions are very useful tools for therapists, we want to pose the reminder that such inquiries are best used after clients have had the opportunity to share their current concerns, views, and stories. Otherwise treatment becomes more therapist directed than client directed and informed. Thus we first help clients feel heard and understood before moving along to questions that identify change. Now let's explore some common ways that clients describe change in second and subsequent sessions.

When Clients Report That Things Are Better

Identifying and Amplifying Change

When clients report that things have improved, we want to identify and amplify these changes. In identifying change we learn from clients what specifically has improved. Amplifying change relates to how the change came about and the difference that it makes or has made in relation to problems clients have described. Let's first look at how to identify change. Here are some questions that therapists can ask clients to assist with this process:

- What have you noticed that has changed with your (concern, problem, self, situation)?
- What specifically seems to be going better?
- Who first noticed that things had changed?
- Who else noticed the change?
- When did you first notice that things had changed?
- What did you notice happening?

Once change has been identified, we begin to amplify it. As discussed, this involves determining how the change occurred and what difference it makes in clients' lives and in relation to their goals. To amplify change we ask clients the following questions:

- How did the change happen?
- What did you find worked for you?
- What did you do?
- How did you do that?
- How did you get that to happen?
- How was that different than before?
- How did that help you?
- Where did you get the idea to do it that way?
- What did you tell yourself?

If clients respond to any of the aforementioned questions with vague answers, it's important that therapists work to translate them into clear, observable ones. For example, if a client responds to the question, "How did the change happen?" with "I just acted different" or "It just did," it is important that the therapist ask the client what specifically was done differently. At other times clients will respond with, "I don't know." In seeking clear descriptions we also accept that some clients may need assistance articulating what they did differently and what their contributions were to the change process.

In some cases, even with the assistance of therapists, clients will be unable to identify specifics regarding what brought about the change. We accept this and consider what speculative theories clients might have about the change. That is, we ask clients to guess what led or contributed to the change. We might ask, "If you had to guess and there were no wrong answers, what would you say made a difference for you?" or "If your ______ were here, what would he/she say has contributed to the change you've experienced?"

What is most important is what clients attribute the change to. If they attribute the significant portion of positive change to the therapist, the actions of others, medication, or some other external entity, the likelihood that the change will last decreases. This is partly because accountability is lost once external factors are removed or diminish. Whether change happens before or during therapy, whether it results from clients' own actions or by happenstance, we want to enhance the effects of change by helping clients see change, and the maintenance of it, as a consequence of their own efforts (Duncan & Miller, 2000; Miller, Duncan, & Hubble, 1997). Therefore, we work toward helping clients attribute the major part of the change to their internal qualities and actions. Next we'll look at two ways of doing this: attributing change to client qualities and speculation.

Attributing Change to Client Qualities

One of the ways that we attribute change to clients is by inquiring about their internal qualities. Whereas many of the questions we offered earlier explore how and what clients' have done to get the change to occur, these questions relate to aspects of personhood. We consider our root question to be, "Who are you?", and assume that clients possess positive characteristics that they can tap into when needed. Here some questions that we use to assist with this process and to help clients internalize change:

- Who are you such that you've been able to ______?
- Who are you such that you've been able to stand up to ______?
- Who are you such that you've been able to get the upper hand with ______?
- What does it say about you that you've been able to face up to adversity?
- What kind of person are you since you've been able to overcome ______?
- Where did you find the means to ______?
- What kinds of inner strengths do you draw on in moments of difficulty?
- What kinds of inner qualities do you possess that allow you to manage adversity?
- What would others say are those qualities that you possess that help you when you need them?

By helping clients attribute change to internal qualities we contribute to the idea that even though external factors may be helpful in producing change, it is clients who are in charge of their lives.

Speculation

Similar to clients speculating about how change came about, therapists also can speculate on what the change can be attributed to. We speculate about internal changes that suggest that clients might be viewing or acting differently and evolving in ways that support new stories of growth, resiliency, and hope. This can be particularly useful with clients who aren't really sure as to what to attribute positive change. To do this, we again use conjecture, and speculate from a position of curiosity. In this way clients have the space to either accept or reject the speculations depending on whether or not they fit for them. Here are a couple of examples of how we usually do this:

THERAPIST: So you've managed to get yourself to work on time for the last week?

CLIENT: Yeah, I have.

THERAPIST: How have you done that?

CLIENT: I don't know. I just did it.

THERAPIST: I'm wondering if perhaps part of it is because you are becoming more responsible, beginning to grow into the type of employee that you are capable of, and learning new ways of managing your life.

THERAPIST: The changes that you've made over the past few months amaze me. You've improved your grades, stayed away from fighting, and have become more responsible at home by completing things your mother has asked of you. How have you done all that?

CLIENT: Well, I'm not sure.

THERAPIST: Do you think that any of it might be because you're getting older, a little wiser, smarter, and more mature?

CLIENT: **(Smiling)** Yeah. I think that's part of it. And I also know that some things just have to be done, so I'm doing them.

Here are some specific questions that can assist with using speculation:

- Do you think the change you have experienced might be related to your gaining wisdom?
- Do you think the change you have experienced might be related to your learning more about yourself?
- Do you think the change you have experienced might be related to your wanting to lead a different life?
- Do you think the change you have experienced might be related to your becoming more mature in dealing with life's circumstances?
- Do you think that the change you have experienced might be an indication that you're taking back control of your life?
- Do you think that the change you have experienced might be an indication that you've turned the corner with ______?
- Do you think that the change you've experienced might be a sign of a new, preferred direction for you?

Speculation can have multiple effects. First, it attributes change to clients. Since we speculate about things that are positive qualities or actions, they are less likely to be rejected. We don't typically hear from clients, "No, I'm not getting smarter and more mature. I'm getting dumber and more immature." Next, even if our speculations are off target, clients will at least ponder them because they highlight competencies. Therapist speculations can be a starting point from which clients can add. In effect, we have found that by using speculation we can help clients grow new stories that run counter to the problem-saturated ones that brought them to therapy, thereby anchoring the change. This can further the change in the direction of their goals and preferred outcomes.

Move to an Experiential Level

As another way of amplifying and anchoring change, we've found it useful to invite clients to move to an experiential level. For some, being able to connect with their internal experiences, including feelings and sensory perceptions, can make their change more profound (Bertolino, 1998). Although many theorists who claim to be solution- or competency-based do not lend much attention to the importance of internal experience, we believe that with some clients this will provide them with another pathway for internalizing change. To do this we ask questions such as:

- When you were able to ______, what did that feel like?
- When you saw your son/daughter ______, what did that feel like?
- How did you experience that change inside?
- How was that feeling similar or different than before?
- What does it feel like to know that others may also benefit from the changes you've made?

We also want to consider that even in the worst of times, many clients will have stored away feelings that once made them feel joy, comfort, reassurance, and hope. Therefore we can also try to re-evoke such feelings from the past as a way of reorienting clients to previous positive experiences. Case Example 8.3 illustrates this idea.

Case Example 8.3 *An A Feels Better than an F*

Bob was working with a fifteen-year-old, Alex, who had been experiencing very poor grades at school—all Fs and one D. As with most teenagers, he did well in school in his early years. Through the sixth grade he was an A and B student. However, when he hit the seventh grade this changed for him. Over the course of about six months, Alex significantly raised his grades. In fact, in two classes he was able to go from Fs to As. He finished his final quarter of the ninth grade with 2 As, 3 Bs, and 2 Cs—enough to pass for the entire year.

As he was raising his grades, Bob asked Alex what it was like for him to have raised them. Alex replied, "It's okay." Bob then reminded him that even though it had been a few years since he had received the type of grades he was capable of, he hadn't forgotten what it felt like to get As, Bs, and even Cs. The feelings associated with those grades were very different than the ones he experienced while getting Ds and Fs. Bob then suggested to Alex that he might even be able to remember those feelings now; what it was like to have his mother put one of his papers with a smiley face on it on the refrigerator, or the favorable reactions of his teachers when he did well. After Bob finished, Alex smiled and said, "Yeah, I remember how proud of me my mom used to be. I liked that. I felt real happy. She can be proud of me again. I like getting good grades. It makes me and my mom feel better."

Although some clients will not be feeling-oriented and will respond from a cognitive perspective, this process can help others experience change at a different and perhaps deeper level.

What Else Is Different? Searching for Change in Other Areas of Clients' Lives

When change has occurred we've found it important that therapists explore the possibility of other changes. Many times a change in one area of an individual's life or in the relationships of couples or family members will lead to further changes. In fact, small changes can lead to bigger changes. This process has been referred to as the *ripple effect*. Others have likened this to the *snowball effect* or the *domino effect*.

If change occurs in one area of a client's life, the therapist should ask about other changes that may have occurred as well. Try questions such as:

- What else have you noticed that has changed?
- What else is different?
- What difference has that made for you?
- What difference has that made with (employment, school, home) life?
- Who else has benefited from these changes?
- What difference has that made for him/her/them?

In the process of identifying and amplifying change in relation to primary goals, it's not uncommon to learn from clients that other goals that were established but perhaps were not formally addressed were also affected in some way. When this is the case, it's important to ask clients to what extent further changes have had an effect on other goals and preferred outcomes previously established in therapy. Last, for some clients, concerns that may not have been addressed in treatment or discussed in terms of goals may have lessened in severity or been resolved. Therefore, we've found it helpful to ask clients about other positive changes or benefits that may have occurred in their lives as a result of the initial change.

Situating Change in Relation to Goals and Preferred Outcomes

When change has been identified and amplified it's important that therapists collaborate with clients to determine how that change relates to the goals that have been established. To what degree does the change that has occurred indicate progress toward established goals? Has the problem been resolved? What else needs to happen for therapy to be deemed successful and for goals to be met? We want to know how the change relates to the overall goals and preferred outcomes of therapy. The following questions can be of assistance in determining this:

- How are you benefiting from the change you've experienced?
- How does the change that's happened relate to the goals that we set?
- What difference has this change made in relation to your goals for treatment?

- To what degree have things improved?
- Has the problem that brought you here been resolved?
- What else needs to happen to fade this problem from your life?
- What else, if anything, needs to happen so that you'll feel/think that the problem you came here for is manageable without therapy?
- What else, if anything, needs to happen so that you'll be convinced that the problem is no longer a problem?

In addition to the questions above, here are a couple of examples of how therapists can summarize change that has occurred and inquire as to how that relates to the overall goals of treatment:

> Last time, you indicated that if you were able get three consecutive nights of restful sleep then you would know that things were better. Now that you have achieved this, how do you see things?

> At the start of therapy you told me that things were at a four on a scale of one to ten. You also mentioned that you would know that therapy had been successful when your daughter started coming in on time and when she was completing at least 50 percent of her homework. That would represent an eight. Now that those things have happened, does that indicate to you that things are at an eight? What else, if anything, needs to happen for you to feel like you have met your goals?

Extending Change in the Direction of Preferred Outcomes

In the process of amplifying change, we've found it helpful to ask clients what difference the change will make in the future as they continue toward their preferred outcomes and visions of the future. To do this we ask the following questions:

- What difference has the change made in your life?
- What will be different in the future as these changes continue to occur?
- In the future, what kinds of other changes do you think might occur that might not have otherwise come about?
- Who else might benefit from these changes? How so?
- In the future, what will indicate to you that these changes are continuing to happen?

Many clients will have visions of the future that extend beyond their immediate goals in therapy. By orienting toward continuing changes, a future-focus can be emphasized suggesting to clients that the positive change doesn't have to stop here.

Extending Change through Letter Writing

As treatment progresses, therapists continue to collaborate with clients to determine how changes that have been made can be extended into the future. We've discussed a variety of ways that therapists can ask questions to orient clients toward future change. Here we offer another method that can be useful to amplify and highlight exceptions and build on change between sessions and beyond therapy.

To do this we use letter writing. Letters to clients can be used at any point in therapy when therapists feel that they may be therapeutic. Informal surveys have found that letters to clients can be worth between 3.2 and 4.5 sessions of face-to-face therapy (Freeman, Epston, & Lobovits, 1997; Nylund & Thomas, 1994; White, 1995). In fact, some of the participants in the Nylund and Thomas study reported that letters were worth as much as ten sessions. Further, some clients reported that the letters were the most therapeutic aspect of treatment.

Why are letters so effective for some clients? There are several reasons. First, they highlight client competencies. Next, letters point clients in the direction of what is working. Letters also amplify changes that have been made during therapy, orient clients toward goals, and presuppose future changes. Perhaps what is most compelling is that because letters are in print, clients can refer back to them over and over, recalling those qualities and skills that they have used to stand up to adversity. Case Example 8.4 shows how letter writing can be used as a therapeutic tool.

Case Example 8.4 *Preparing for the Regular Season*

Fourteen-year-old James was referred to therapy by his juvenile officer after he had been arrested for possession of marijuana. During his initial session with Bob, James's father related that his son had been smoking marijuana, sneaking out at night, and failing his classes at school. James said very little during the session.

It was the start of summer when James began therapy, and he was enrolled in summer school. At the second session, Bob and James began talking about the upcoming football season, James being a huge fan and having played football. In between sessions two and three, Bob wrote James the following letter:

> Dear James,
>
> You may be surprised to receive this letter, but I felt compelled to share some thoughts with you after our last meeting.
>
> I've been so impressed with how you've made an effort to make it to summer school on time. I realize that this must be quite a new game for you. It sort of reminds me of a player being traded to a new team. He has new coaches, new teammates, a new stadium or practice field, and even a new playbook. You've accepted this challenge and have been holding your own. I'll be wondering between now and the next time

we meet, what other changes you'll make to prepare for the next school year. See you soon.

Sincerely,
Bob Bertolino

As the therapy continued, and James continued to make progress, Bob began to intersperse further football metaphors, referring to summer school as the preseason and fall as the start of the regular season. Then, in between sessions five and six he wrote James the following letter:

Dear James,

I wanted to drop you a brief note to share some thoughts with you.

At the start of therapy you mentioned that last school year was a tough one. You had a hard time keeping up with your studies and getting your homework handed in, and that hurt you when it came time to play football. But this year has been different. You started off summer school with a bang and used your preseason well to prepare for the regular season. Now that you're on a roll, I wonder how good a shape you'll be in when the regular season starts in the fall. It seems that you've got some momentum going now.

I keep wondering how you're going to use the new knowledge you described to me. I hope that you will let me know somehow. It's exciting to think that I may be reading about both your academic and sports achievements in the newspaper. Keep me posted!

Sincerely,
Bob Bertolino

James attended eleven sessions, which extended therapy into his next school year. Following his last session, Bob sent him this letter:

Dear James,

You've certainly made the transition from the preseason to the regular season. And I keep wondering, what other changes will happen now that you seem to have secure footing? Who else will learn about these changes? Who else will learn about the kind of person that you are—the kind of person that you've demonstrated that you can be over the past few months? Of course, I don't expect you to have the answers off the top of your head. But perhaps the answers to these and other questions will become clearer as time moves on.

I want to mention something that you taught me. I learned from you that sometimes we have to make smaller changes to get to bigger ones. I also learned from you that even if others are skeptical about the changes you make, their ideas about you will change if you keep moving forward. You're proof of that. I don't think I've ever had a teacher tell me that her student was a "hidden gem"!

I want to wish you the best in the future. Please know that we all believe in you and are here if you need us in the future. Take care.

In appreciation of your efforts,
Bob Bertolino

We don't use letters with all of our clients. However, there are instances when it's much easier to highlight competencies, exceptions, and change in writing. Most importantly, the value of letters to clients alone is worth the time and effort.

When Clients Report That Things Are So-So

In second and subsequent sessions some clients will report that things have been up and down or so-so. When clients experience ups and downs they may look to therapists to see if that makes them abnormal, worse than other clients, incapable of achieving lasting change, and so on. Others will appear to be more ambivalent and will say things such as, "Things were a little better, but in some ways they were worse too" or "It's really hard to tell how things are going. One minute they're fine and the next minute all hell breaks loose." In such cases, clients can blame themselves or turn the blame onto others if things don't go the way they expected.

When clients' indicate that things are so-so, it's important that therapists consider several things. First, therapists need to acknowledge clients' internal experiences and views. If this does not occur some clients will feel that they are being blamed or that the therapist does not really understand their situations. Clients who do not feel heard and understood can have a difficult time shifting their perspectives to include possibilities and solutions.

A second thing that can help clients who report that things have been so-so is when therapists further investigate clients' theories of change. Some clients will say things like, "I feel like every time we make progress we have a slip up" or "Even if things get better it just doesn't last." In such cases it can be helpful to normalize clients' experiences and views and say, for example, "Change that lasts can sometimes feel like three steps forward and two steps back at first."

We also continue to listen for words, phrases, and statements that suggest impossibility. For example, we might respond to the statements in the last paragraph with, "It seems like every time you make progress there's a slip up," "You haven't experienced the kind of lasting change you'd like so far," or "One of the things we might focus on here is getting the change you want to last longer." Responses such as these can both acknowledge clients' experiences and perspectives and leave the possibilities open for positive change.

A final thing for therapists to consider and pursue regarding clients with so-so reports is to learn more from them about what specifically has been better and what has not. Once again, an important aspect in finding out this information is how therapists use acknowledgment and validation. We want to acknowledge and validate clients' internal experience and make sure that we understand their pain and suffering. It then becomes more likely that they will explore both sides of the concern.

This includes learning about what concerns have intensified and what hasn't worked to this point, as well as what has gone better in between sessions. This involves searching for subtle changes. To do this we ask questions that search for exceptions—small traces of change that run counter to the problem description. This can help counter all or nothing views. Case Example 8.5 illustrates how a therapist might go about this.

Case Example 8.5 *I Think I'm Sort of Making Progress* (Part I)

THERAPIST: So how have things been since the last time we met?

CLIENT: Well, I think I'm sort of making progress, but I'm really not sure. It's been very up and down.

THERAPIST: Okay, so it seems like it's been up and down. Tell me more about that.

CLIENT: Sometimes I feel like it's going to be okay, but then I have a setback. It's frustrating. Like last week for instance, on Monday, Thursday, and Friday I got up and went to work on time. But Tuesday and Wednesday I was very late. In fact, Wednesday I was so late I got docked two hours' pay.

THERAPIST: I can see how that might be frustrating to you. On three days you made it to work on time and on the other days you were late—and very late on Wednesday.

CLIENT: Right.

THERAPIST: And I'm very curious about something. Is it okay if I ask you a few more questions?

CLIENT: Fire away.

THERAPIST: It seems like you started the week well by making it to work on time on Monday. Now, things didn't pan out so well on Tuesday and Wednesday and yet you were able to rebound on the last two days. How did you do that?

CLIENT: Well, I knew I couldn't afford to be late again.

Once change has been identified, the therapist works to amplify the change. To do this the therapist inquires as to how the change came about and what the client did. It can also be helpful to explore how other factors or persons may have come into play. Let's continue with Case Example 8.5 to see how this might happen.

Case Example 8.5 ***I Think I'm Sort of Making Progress*** **(Part II)**

THERAPIST: I see. So you knew that you couldn't be late again. And yet, it's one thing to tell yourself that and quite another to get yourself to work at all, let alone on time. What did you do to make that happen differently on Monday, Thursday, and Friday?

CLIENT: I just got myself ready earlier and made sure I left on time.

THERAPIST: And how is that different than what you did on Tuesday and Wednesday or on other days that you are late to work?

CLIENT: On those days I got up late and I figured if I was going to be late I might as well just take my time.

THERAPIST: I see. How did you manage to get yourself up on the days you made it to work on time?

CLIENT: I just went to bed earlier and made sure that I had everything ready to go for the next morning.

THERAPIST: Can you be a little more specific about what you got ready for the next morning?

CLIENT: Yeah. I got out the clothes I was going to wear and I filled up the coffee maker.

THERAPIST: Is there anything else that you did differently?

CLIENT: I made sure that there was enough gas in my car so I didn't have to stop on my way to work.

THERAPIST: That's great. How often do you prepare for the next day by doing those things?

CLIENT: Not often enough. Maybe two or three days a week.

THERAPIST: So last week you did that for three days. What would it take for you to go from two or three days to three or four days?

CLIENT: I just need to prepare a little more—just like I do on the days I make it to work on time.

THERAPIST: And what might bring about that extra bit of preparation?

CLIENT: Well, I know that if I get ready for the next day right when I get home then I'm in good shape. So that's what I'll do.

THERAPIST: So you're going to get ready for the next day right when you get home.

CLIENT: Yep.

THERAPIST: And what about on Sundays when you're preparing for Monday and you're not coming home from work?

CLIENT: I have all weekend to get ready, so Sundays aren't really a big deal for me.

THERAPIST: Great. So can you try that until the next time we meet?

CLIENT: Uh huh.

When working with clients who offer reports of things being so-so, it is important that we remain persistent in identifying small traces of change. Then, when change is identified, we can amplify it in the ways previously discussed.

When Clients Report That Things Are the Same or Worse

When attending second and subsequent sessions, some clients will report that things are the same, unchanged, worse, or some variation thereof. They will say things like, "I haven't noticed anything different," "Seems like the same old thing we've been going through all along," or "Things were even worse this week." As with all concerns, it is important to acknowledge and validate clients' internal experiences and views. Clients will need to feel that therapists understand their pain and suffering. At the same time, it's also important that therapists not buy into clients' stories of impossibility, blame, invalidation, and nonaccountability. Specifically, we make a distinction between what people feel inside and their stories. Stories represent clients' views and are changeable.

When hearing clients' descriptions of all that has gone wrong between sessions it's imperative that therapists do not become blind to small changes that may have occurred. While we are mindful to acknowledge the difficulties that clients face, we want to do this in ways that keep the possibilities open for positive change. It's very easy to become part of the problem-saturated story and become less effective with clients. For clients who report that things are the same or worse there are a few ways of acknowledging their concerns and simultaneously keeping possibilities open. These include *coping sequence questions, sharing the credit for change, joining the pessimism, attending to and altering therapist patterns,* and *reflecting consultations.*

Coping Sequence Questions

When clients indicate that things are not improving or are getting worse it is important to consider that there are often qualities and actions that keep them going. The same can be said for clients who seem more ambivalent or pessimistic about change and say, "Yes, but...." In Chapter 5 we discussed this with regard to resilience and Chapter 6 with regard to finding out why the problem isn't worse. With same or worse reports we can ask clients what it is that has kept things from bottoming out. Here are some coping sequence questions (Berg & Gallagher, 1991) that can assist with this process:

- Why aren't things worse with your situation?
- What steps have you taken to keep things from getting worse?
- What has helped things from getting worse?
- How has that made a difference for you/with your situation?
- What is the smallest thing that you could do that might make a difference in your situation?
- What could others do?
- How could we get that to happen a little now?

Case Example 8.6 indicates how using coping sequence questions can help in shifting the direction of change.

Case Example 8.6 *Going Down the Drain*

A family, consisting of a father, his wife, a mother, her boyfriend, and two boys, fourteen and nine years of age, came to therapy. The fourteen-year-old had been stealing car stereos, breaking curfew, and doing poorly in school. Along with two other clinicians, Bob was part of a reflecting team that worked with the family during a stuck point. During the initial part of the session, the mother stated that she felt as if things were "going down the drain." During the conversation between members of the reflecting team, Bob responded to this comment by saying, "You know those sticky things they put in bathtubs to keep people from slipping and falling? I wonder what those sticky things are in this family that even though they fall down sometimes things keep from going down the drain?" After switching back, the mother responded, "I know what keeps things from going down the drain. We love each other." To this the therapist asked, "That's so nice to hear. And I'm curious, what difference does that make that you love each other?" "We can't give up," replied the mother, "so we pull together when things get rough." The therapist was then able to explore with the family members how they pull together during rough times and what they do differently when things start to get slippery. Then, in a later session, they were able to discuss how the family members can use that more in the future.

By using coping sequence questions, therapists can identify and amplify very small changes that represent what is working in clients' lives. These can then be used as starting points for changing the momentum of treatment and for working toward more significant changes.

Sharing Credit for Change

As discussed with coping sequence questions, some clients, particularly families, will appear to be more ambivalent or pessimistic about change. In our experience, this can sometimes be attributed to clients not feeling as if they have made a valued or positive contribution to change processes. Consider the following situations as examples:

- Family members can become adept at blaming one another or feeling blamed by others for causing problems, but they don't always get credit for their individual contributions when things go better.
- Parents who bring their children or adolescents to therapy and experience success will sometimes have feelings of inadequacy reinforced. They will say things to themselves such as, "I raised my (son, daughter) for fourteen years and couldn't help (him, her). Then I take (him, her) to a therapist and things change in a week. I must be a lousy parent."

The result of these scenarios and similar scenarios is that family members will make comments such as, "Yeah, it's been better, but it won't last. It never does," or "You haven't seen the real Joe yet." Our sense is that such persons tend to experience a double whammy of negativity. First, they feel like a failure for not being able to fix the problem that led to therapy. Second, they feel invalidated when a stranger fixes the situation. Therefore, we recommend that therapists identify the contributions that significant others have made in the lives of those experiencing problems and share the credit for change (Bertolino, 1999).

It is important to note that this idea is not in conflict with attributing change to the qualities and actions of individuals. It's a situation of both/and as opposed to either/or. We still want to attribute the major portion of significant change to the individual to which the change has occurred. We all have qualities and take actions that improve our lives. At the same time, we have had many experiences in life that have shaped who we are as individuals. These experiences do not cause change, they influence it. As discussed in Chapter 5, these include interactions and relationships with others. Such interactions and relationships vary in terms of the influence they have had on us.

We are helping clients identify the contribution and influence of external factors—in this case other people. There are a variety of ways of doing this. One way is to openly give the person credit by saying:

- I'm impressed with how you instilled in ______ the value of ______.
- I've noticed that ______ holds the same value of ______ that you do, and I can't help thinking that he/she learned it from you.
- It seems to me that ______ has learned the value of ______ from you.

Another possibility is to evoke from clients something that they feel contributed to the change process:

- What part of your parenting do you think contributed most to ______'s ability to ______?
- In what ways do you think you have been able to help ______ stand up to adversity?
- In what ways do you think you were of assistance in helping ______ stand up to ______ and get back on track?

A final way is to ask the main client what contributions other people have made to his or her life:

- What did you learn from ______ about how to overcome ______?
- Who taught you the value of ______?

By sharing the credit for change, much negativity can be defused. Furthermore, it is not uncommon for clients to experience a new sense of togetherness or spirit of family.

Joining the Pessimism

Regardless of the approach used, some clients will seem extremely pessimistic. They will say things like, "We've already tried everything and nothing works" or "There is no hope for us. Why do we even bother?" We don't consider these clients resistant. Recall that as therapists we can either promote the expectancy and hope for change or dampen it by how we respond to such clients. Oftentimes clients are simply communicating to us that we still need to learn more about their concerns and theories and that our ways of relating to them are not working. They may be at a precontemplative stage of change and will need us to interact differently with them.

In such cases, we sometimes find it helpful to join clients' pessimism as a way of negotiating tough situations. For example, if we have tried different things and nothing has worked and clients continue to seem very negative, we might say, "You've convinced me just how bad things really are. I don't think I understood at first. And even though I think things can get better, I really don't have a clue as to what to do to help you. I'm sitting here wondering what I must be missing about your situation and where to go with this."

Our colleague Michele Weiner-Davis will sometimes use a similar tack. She will say to the couples with whom she works, "You've convinced me that you probably shouldn't be together." Inevitably, one member of the couple will say, "Well, it's not that bad. I mean, sometimes we get along." By joining the pessimism and working to gain a deeper understanding of clients' experiences, some clients will reverse gears and an exception to the problematic story will become evident. That exception can then be amplified and built upon. In Chapter 6 we discussed this idea and the importance of acknowledging and focusing on small changes to change the momentum. Let's revisit this idea and a further example of working backward before going forward in Case Example 8.7.

Case Example 8.7 ***Escaping Depresso-Land***

CLIENT: Nothing has improved. I still feel like crap. I'm just always depressed.

THERAPIST: You've been quite depressed.

CLIENT: Yep, and nothing has worked for me—it's bringing me down.

THERAPIST: Nothing's worked so far... I can see why that would bring you down.

CLIENT: I just want to feel better.

THERAPIST: Okay. Tell me about a time in the recent past when you felt a little bit less depressed.

CLIENT: There hasn't been a time. I'm always depressed. It's really bad.

THERAPIST: It sounds that way.

CLIENT: I've been depressed for so long—it has always been that way.

THERAPIST: Okay. Tell me about last week. On which day were you the *most* depressed?

CLIENT: Saturday. I was really depressed on Saturday.

THERAPIST: Tell me about that.

CLIENT: I couldn't get out of bed until real late... the phone rang, I don't know how many times... but I didn't answer it. I also didn't eat until that night... it was a wasted day.

THERAPIST: I see. Not the kind of day that you want to repeat too often.

CLIENT: Definitely not.

THERAPIST: Okay, then tell me about Friday or Sunday because even though you were depressed on those days they weren't as bad as Saturday. What was different during those other times?

CLIENT: On Sunday I slept too long too.

THERAPIST: I see. How was Sunday different than Saturday?

CLIENT: Well, I did eventually get up at one o'clock in the afternoon. Saturday I didn't get up until six in the evening.

THERAPIST: How did you manage to get yourself up earlier on Sunday?

CLIENT: I just knew that I had to function at least a little on Sunday so that I could get to work on Monday.

By joining the client in Depresso-Land the therapist was able to learn that she experienced shades of depression. Acknowledgment of the client's experience with the problem was essential in learning about times when it was very bad and times when it was a shade or two removed from being very bad. These differences in the shades of depression represent a starting point for finding what works for the client.

Attending to and Altering Therapist Patterns

Recall that most change occurs early on in treatment. Therefore, if things are not improving or are deteriorating with clients, or if as a therapist you are stuck, there are several ways that can help in becoming unstuck. A first way is to ask clients questions related to their conversational and relational preferences. Find out what their perceptions are of what is working and what is not. It is not uncommon for therapists to get stuck in repeating unhelpful patterns that are unnoticeable to them. In addition to those listed in Chapter 4, here are some questions that can assist with this process:

- How has the way that we've worked toward resolving your concerns been helpful to you?
- What specifically has been helpful?
- How has the way that we've worked toward resolving your concerns been unhelpful to you?
- What specifically has been unhelpful?
- What, if anything, should I do differently?
- What, if anything, have I not done that I should be doing?
- What difference might it make for you if I did that?
- What do you think I've missed about your situation?
- What do you think I haven't understood about you or your concerns?

It's important to note that at times therapists may feel or think that they are working with clients in ways that are completely ineffective or unhelpful. In such cases, what we need to remember is that clients often have different perspectives. For example, in an effort to get things going in a better direction, some therapists will make changes based on gut feelings. However, therapists' ideas and internal guidance systems about what needs to change may or may not be consistent with clients' views. The best way to determine what is working, what is not, and what needs to change is to ask clients about their perceptions and preferences. Case Example 8.8 illustrates another way of learning from the client what the therapist is doing that is helpful or unhelpful.

Case Example 8.8 *Going Nowhere Fast*

Bob was working with a family, including a father, a mother, and their seventeen-year-old son. The parents had divorced three years prior, but both continued to be invested in the welfare and well-being of their son, and attended all sessions together. The parents had several concerns regarding their son, including failing grades, smoking marijuana, coming in very late each evening, and not getting a job to help pay for his car insurance, which he had agreed to do months earlier.

Although there had been small indications of change over the course of about four months, Bob felt he was stuck in quicksand with the family. It seemed to him that even when change occurred, it was minimal, and was often overridden by some sort of crisis that happened between sessions. Finally, Bob said aloud in a session, "I just wanted to share something with all of you. I've been thinking about it for a couple of weeks now. I don't really feel like I've been helpful to you. It seems to me that things seem to get a little better, but then they slip back. It feels to me like quicksand in some ways."

Following Bob's statement, the mother remarked, "I think you've been very helpful." Bob inquired, "In what way?" She responded, "Jake has been doing much better in English and Math and it looks like he has a chance of graduating now. We couldn't have said that before." Jake added, "Yeah, I am going to pass and I've got a job interview next week." The father then followed, "And he does at least tell me when he's going to be late now. That's a miracle in and of itself." It then became clear to Bob that the family members had different ideas about how the therapy had been proceeding and the changes that had occurred. This, in turn, taught Bob about what he needed to do more of to be helpful to the family. Had he not asked, he might have made changes that were unhelpful in the eyes of the family members.

When clients provide little or no feedback about conversational and relational preferences, or when a therapist remains stuck, a second possibility for attending to and altering therapist patterns is to videotape sessions. Because therapists don't always recognize when they are working in ways that are helpful or unhelpful, taping can reveal aspects of sessions that therapists might not otherwise notice. Once a tape has been made, the therapist reviews the tape and considers some or all of the following questions:

- What did I do well?
- How do I know it was helpful to the client?
- What should I consider doing more of in the next session?
- What should I consider doing differently in the future?
- What changes should I consider making in the next session?
- What difference might that make?

By reviewing a videotaped session the therapist can watch the therapeutic discourse unfold from a different position. This can help to generate new ideas and possibilities for future sessions. Another tack that can be helpful is to get a second perspective from another colleague or supervisor. Using the same or a similar set of questions, the person offering the second perspective can help generate other ideas about what might be helpful in future sessions.

Whether reviewing videotape on your own or getting other perspectives, we recommend that new ideas that are generated be shared with the individual, couple, or family. We do this for two reasons. First, we do not want to privilege the ideas of mental health professionals over clients. In other words, we want clients to decide for themselves what fits and what does not. Just because mental health professionals believe in an idea does not mean that clients will feel or think the same. Next, we share many different ideas with clients as opposed to one or two that the therapist has selected. This way clients are not just hearing the idea that the therapist likes the best. Instead, they are hearing a number of ideas with the room to determine what makes most sense and fits best with them.

To offer the ideas that have been generated to clients we typically say, "I reviewed the videotape last week and had some new thoughts that I would like to share with you, if that's okay." If we consult a colleague or supervisor we might say, "I reviewed the tape from last week with a colleague/supervisor and he/she had a few ideas that I would like to share with you, if that's okay." The following questions can then assist therapists in offering clients new ideas that were generated through the aforementioned processes:

- Do any of these ideas stand out for you?
- Which one(s) specifically seems to stand out the most for you?
- What thoughts or ideas do you have as a result of hearing that/those idea(s)?
- What else comes to mind?
- How might these ideas be helpful to you?
- Are there other ideas you have as a result of listening to the ideas I offered?

Reflecting Consultations

In Chapter 5 we discussed ways of using reflecting, consultation, and conversational teams as a way of helping clients to develop new perspectives, take new actions, and become unstuck. The same concept can be used as a way of helping therapists to make changes in the ways they work with clients. To use this idea, the therapist verbally gives a case summary to at least two other clinicians. The clinicians who are forming the consultation team use the same rationale and operational ideas discussed in Chapter 5. They listen to the therapist from a not-knowing position and assume no prior knowledge about the client. Their task is to generate new ideas from their own experience as a way of helping move the therapy along.

After the case summary has been given, the consulting therapists have a conversation with one another. During this process, the therapist whose case it is listens to the conversation. This allows the therapist to choose which reflections fit best with him or her. Following this, another therapist who has not been involved to this point, interviews the therapist whose case it is and asks questions such as:

- What stuck out for you?
- What was new to you? What else was new for you?
- What did you hear? What else did you hear?
- What new ideas do you have as a result of listening to the conversation?
- What will you consider doing differently as a result of having these new ideas?

It is hopeful that this process will help therapists to generate new ideas, and hence new possibilities and directions for treatment. We also encourage you to experiment with this process and adapt it to fit your specific needs.

When to Meet Again

We focus on clients' goals, not therapists' goals. Therefore, clients determine how to proceed in future sessions. If clients feel that the goals of therapy have been met, therapy may end at that point. In the event that goals have not been met we have conversations with clients about how they would like to proceed in regard to future meetings.

The first involves inviting clients back. Although this may sound strange, we've found it important to make no assumptions about clients' preferences. Therefore we say, "Would you like to schedule another appointment?" Therapists can also ask, "How would you like to proceed?" In any regard, we let clients decide what the next moves are. As a result of these questions clients will tell us their preferences or say, "What do you think we should do?" or "What do you usually do?" With the former, we schedule an appointment that is consistent with the client's preferred time frame. In the event that we are not available within the client's preferred time frame we offer a couple of options and ask them what will work best. This usually means scheduling for the next available time and informing the client that he or she can call and talk with us in between sessions if necessary. In our experience, when told that they can call if needed, most clients do not call. Just knowing that they are still connected and have a backup plan is enough for them.

If clients ask us for our opinions as to how to proceed we will usually say, "My sense is that we should go with what makes most sense for you. Would you like to come back next week or the week after, or ...?" In most cases clients already have an idea and want to see if what they're thinking is okay. We also let them know that adjustments can be made at any time by putting more or less time in between sessions.

We've found that spreading out sessions can be an excellent way of measuring change over time and of helping clients feel connected. For example, we might meet with a client for three consecutive weeks and then put more space in between sessions and meet two or three weeks later. In fact, we've had clients that we've seen once a month or once every six or eight weeks.

Particularly when change has occurred in the direction of goals, lengthening times between sessions can be useful in observing changes over an extended period of time. In our experience it also helps clients to stay on track and hold course with the changes they've made, as they know they will be returning in the future. In the first chapter we referred to the general practitioner model for medical doctors. This is also appropriate here because future sessions are sometimes referred to as "checkups."

In this chapter we explored a multitude of ways of approaching second and subsequent sessions. In the next chapter we'll discuss further aspects of future sessions and ideas related to terminating treatment.

Summary Points for Chapter Eight

- In subsequent sessions it's important to make sure that therapists are in sync with clients' conversational and relational preferences, goals, and preferred outcomes.
- In future sessions, clients' initial reports will typically fall into one of five categories:
  - New concerns or problems that have arisen between sessions
  - Vague responses that do not indicate any particular direction in change
  - Things are better
  - Things are so-so
  - Things are the same or worse
- When there has been evidence of change, therapists:
  - Identify and amplify change
  - Attribute change to clients' efforts and actions
  - Attribute change to clients' qualities
  - Use speculation
  - Move to an experiential level
  - Search for change in other areas of clients' lives
  - Situate change in relation to goals and preferred outcomes
  - Extend change in the direction of preferred outcomes
  - Extend change through letter writing
- When clients indicate that things are so-so, the same, or worse:
  - Be sure to acknowledge and validate
  - Search for evidence of small changes
  - Use coping sequence questions
  - Share credit for change
  - Join the pessimism
  - Attend and alter therapist patterns
  - Use reflecting consultations
- Consult with clients regarding how, when, and if to meet for future sessions.

CHAPTER

9 Planning for the End from the Beginning

Through the first eight chapters of this book we have described ways in which therapists can be client- and outcome-informed. Our practices involve therapist–client collaboration in virtually every aspect of treatment. From the beginning we plan for the end. We do this by keeping an eye on the goals that have been established and by engaging clients in conversations to learn when progress is being made and when goals have been met or need to be changed or modified. In this chapter we will discuss ways of managing setbacks, sharing change with larger communities, keeping the ball rolling after therapy has ended, and ending therapy.

Managing Setbacks

As discussed with regard to stages of change, when clients have achieved some degree of change, many will experience temporary setbacks or challenges in maintaining those changes. We tell clients they may experience some ups and downs, but that these fluctuations do not have to knock them off course. In the event that clients experience some difficulty or setbacks, we find out about those difficulties and help them to orient toward exceptions and differences. We explore each setback in an effort to learn about what worked and what did not. We do not consider setbacks to be relapses. Setbacks are part of what some clients will experience in achieving their goals and preferred outcomes. Case Example 9.1 illustrates one way we work with setbacks.

Case Example 9.1 *Everything Has Changed*

At her sixth session of therapy Gina told her therapist, "I feel like my old self again. I'm doing so much better." At one time Gina had been mutilating herself by cutting on her arms with broken glass or scissors, putting herself down, not attending her university classes, and lying to her parents about how she was doing. Now it seemed to her that things had finally turned the corner for the better.

Two weeks later, Gina showed for her next session in tears. As she sat down she seemed to be struggling to tell her therapist what she was experiencing:

THERAPIST: It's okay to cry, Gina.

GINA: **(Sobbing)** I know. I just can't believe it.

THERAPIST: Tell me about that.

GINA: Everything's changed.

THERAPIST: Something's changed....

GINA: ...Yeah, I was doing so good and now... I'm back to where I was.

THERAPIST: I don't understand, can you tell me what has given you the idea that you're back to where you were?

GINA: Everything was going fine, then yesterday I found out that there was no way to pass my communications class because I've missed too many classes. Why should I even bother?

THERAPIST: Your professor told you that?

GINA: Yeah.

THERAPIST: I'm sorry to hear that. What did you do when you got the news?

GINA: I had to go to my next class.

THERAPIST: You went to your next class? How did you muster up the strength to do that after what you had been told?

GINA: **(Wiping her tears)** Well, I can still pass my other two classes.

THERAPIST: Okay. What's confusing to me is that before you would have just gone home and given up.

GINA: I would have.

THERAPIST: So after class what did you do?

GINA: I went home and called my mom.

THERAPIST: What happened?

GINA: She told me not to worry about it. I was doing better and that I could retake the class. But it still hurts; I feel like I failed.

THERAPIST: I can see how you would feel that way.

GINA: I do.

THERAPIST: Do you mind if I ask you another question?

GINA: Go ahead.

THERAPIST: When you called your mom, did you lie to her?

GINA: No.

THERAPIST: Really? Did you cut on your arms?

GINA: No.

THERAPIST: So as upset as you were, you went to class and called your mom and were honest with her. You took care of yourself in good ways and didn't cut on yourself.

GINA: That's true. I did take care of myself and didn't slip back.

THERAPIST: Right. Somehow, even though you were rightfully upset, you kept things from becoming worse. Can you tell me more about what you did that helped you?

GINA: I went to bed early. I felt a little better this morning, but then got sad again later.

THERAPIST: So sleep helped a little. What else?

GINA: Just talking to my mom. I'm going to call her again after this.

THERAPIST: It sounds like you and your mom have been getting along better lately.

GINA: We have. I think because I'm more honest with her now.

THERAPIST: So, getting sleep and talking with your mom helped. If you were to face another obstacle what will you do?

GINA: I guess call my mom, and I know I can talk to my sister too.

In working with clients experiencing setbacks, there are a number of different questions that can be helpful in learning about exceptions to those setbacks. Here is a list of these questions:

- When you hit that rough spot, what kept things from going downhill any further?
- How did you manage to bring things to a halt?
- What did you do?
- What helped you to bring it to an end?
- Who else helped you?
- How were they helpful to you?
- How might they be helpful to you in the future?
- What signs were present that things were beginning to slip?
- What can you do differently in the future if things begin to slip?
- What have you learned about this setback?
- What will you do differently in the future as a result of this knowledge?
- What do you suppose ______ would say that you will do differently as a result of this knowledge?
- What do you suppose will be different as a result of you doing things differently?
- What might be some signs that you are getting back on track?
- How will you know when you're out of the woods with this setback?

It's important to make sure that clients' expectations are realistic. Again, people's lives are not problem free. Therefore, we aim to help clients recognize those occurrences that signify setbacks and those that they don't like but aren't necessarily setbacks. In addition, setbacks can be helpful for clients in building their resiliency muscles.

Documenting Change and New Stories

As clients' stories begin to change, we have found it helpful to document that change. This is a way of orienting clients toward what is working, tracking change over time, and extending those changes into the future (Bertolino, 1999). To do this we will sometimes say to clients:

> Down the road, others may be curious as to how you went about overcoming ______ (fill in the blank). Sometimes people write letters to themselves, others keep journals, diaries, or scrapbooks, or create new ways of keeping track of the changes they've made. What might help you document this journey that you have been on?

Case Example 9.2 illustrates how this might be utilized with clients.

Case Example 9.2 *Everything That Glows*

Bob consulted with a therapist who was working with a client named Nakia who had been severely physically abused when she was younger. Nakia had come to therapy because she had been feeling depressed and isolated. She was also an aspiring musician who, according to her therapist, tended to write "deeply somber" songs. When Nakia began to experience a lifting of her depression, her therapist stated that she saw "a side of her that she did not know existed." She described her client as warm and glowing. Bob suggested that the therapist talk with Nakia about how this warm, glowing presence and new sense of self might be reflected in her music. About two weeks later, Nakia brought her guitar to the session and played her new song, "Everything that Glows." She then went on to record the song so that it would be a reminder to her of "what can be."

We use the idea of documentation not to remind clients of their pasts and the difficulties they have faced, but as a way of orienting them toward the changes they've made and can continue to make in the future. This can be especially helpful with younger clients. For example, for many people, when they were growing up their parents kept scrapbooks or when they got a good grade on a paper it was posted on the refrigerator. Similar to the use of therapeutic letters, clients can review these representations of change and progress and be reminded of what they have accomplished and where they are headed in the future.

Although the actual process of documenting change will not be for everyone, there are questions that therapists can ask clients to assist with shifting their attention to what they have done that has worked. This can be a resource if they need an emotional boost in the event that they encounter turbulence on the ways to their preferred futures. Here are some questions to consider asking clients:

- What have you done in the past to remind you of what's important in your life?
- What can you do to remind yourself of the progress that you've made?
- What will help to remind you of where you're heading in the future?
- What will help you reorient to what has worked for you should you hit some turbulence in the future?
- How will that help you?

Growing New Identity Stories

As clients' identity stories change from being problem-laden to stories of hope and possibilities, we often create a context where they can experience these new stories within themselves. In essence, we help clients experience themselves in new ways and create a new sense of self. To do this, we invite clients to consider the following questions:

- What does your decision to stand up to ______ tell you about yourself?
- Now that you've taken your life back from ______, what does that say about the kind of person you are?
- How would you describe yourself now as opposed to when you began therapy?
- What's it like to hear you describe yourself as ______?
- What effect does knowing that you've put ______ to rest have on your view of yourself?
- Can you speculate about how this view of yourself as ______ is changing how you're relating to me right now?
- What do you think your friends would say about you now that you can stand up for yourself?
- How do you think my view of you has changed since hearing you describe yourself as ______?
- How do you think ______ will treat you now that he/she/they know you see yourself as a person who is capable of getting the upper hand with ______?

We can also incorporate those who are immediately involved with clients and ask them to share their views regarding changes clients have made. We can do this through the following questions:

- What do you think ______'s decision to stand up to ______ tells you about (him, her) that you wouldn't have otherwise known?
- What effect is hearing that ______ views himself/herself as ______ having on your relationship with him/her?
- How do you think ______'s new sense of himself/herself as ______ will affect your relationship with him?

We invite clients and those close to them to experience new stories and expand on them. We grow these stories through further social interactions. This way both clients' identity stories and others' stories about clients continue to evolve and take hold in other relationships.

Sharing Change with Larger Social Contexts

In the last chapter we discussed ways that therapists can work with clients to identify, amplify, and solidify gains, and extend change toward goals and preferred outcomes. As clients' stories change we also move toward sharing these new narratives of hope and possibility in larger contexts. We view this as a way of strengthening the valued stories that have been created.

We have found that when others outside of the therapeutic system become part of newly created narratives, individual changes can contribute to social change. This extending of change beyond immediate, individual systems actually happens each and every day. For example, Bob lives just outside of St. Louis, Missouri. In St. Louis, there is a valued story about St. Louis Cardinals baseball player Mark McGwire. Although most people cannot attest to having met McGwire, they nonetheless have a story about him. Where do these stories come from? They begin with individuals who lead their lives in ways that are consistent with their self-narratives. Then, these stories are carried forth by others. In McGwire's case, the media has highlighted his on-field performance as well as his many contributions to charitable causes off the field. In addition, people who have met him create their own stories and share them with others.

The result of this is that most people hold the story that Mark McGwire is a great athlete, a nice guy, he cares about others, and so on. Because this story is socially entrenched in not only St. Louis, but in many other parts of the United States and the world, he is in turn affected by his *own* story. He is more aware of his actions and the implications of them. In turn, if something negative were to happen, as was the case with a story about McGwire's use of a natural supplement that was considered to be a steroid, the effects are typically limited. This is because of the strength of his valued story. For the vast majority it does not change how they perceive him.

Another example involving the sharing of a valued story is that of 23-year-old Shannon Broom, who lost her life in a car accident while returning home from spending two weeks with her grandmother. Shannon kept a gratitude journal in which she wrote down five things every night for which she was thankful. After she passed away, her parents found it in the suitcase she had taken with her. As a way of healing from their loss, to celebrate Shannon's life, and to share her story with others, her family began to create bookmarks with her statements of gratitude on them. Through this process, more than 15,000 bookmarks were distributed. More importantly, thousands of people who never knew Shannon Broom learned how truly wonderful she was.

People live extraordinary lives and their stories can make a difference in the lives of others and can help to anchor the changes they've made in their own lives. Our clients don't have to be athletes or celebrities to share their new stories. They don't have to be on *60 Minutes*, *20/20*, or *Oprah*. We can help them in other ways. The first thing we do is ask clients some or all of the following questions:

- Who else needs to know about the changes that you've made?
- What difference do you think it would make in others' attitudes toward you if they had this news?
- Who else could benefit from these changes? How so?
- Would it be better to go along with others' old views about you or to update them on these new developments?
- What ideas do you have about letting others know about the changes that you've made?
- What might be a first step toward making this happen?

We then search for how clients' new stories can be shared with others. If clients have identified ways of sharing change with larger social contexts then we investigate how to put those ideas into action. If clients don't have ideas we can offer suggestions on different levels. For example, with younger clients we might suggest that they show their scrapbooks to others—extended family, friends, teachers, and so on. Oftentimes younger clients will be excited about showing their collections of competence to others.

Clients can also become consultants to others who have experienced similar difficulties. Freeman et al. (1997) wrote that when a child, in their example, has taken significant steps toward revising his or her relationship with the problem, he or she "has gained knowledge and expertise that may assist others grappling with similar concerns" (p. 126). Consistent with this idea, David Epston and Michael White (& Ben, 1995) have discussed the idea of *consulting your consultant.* They state:

> When persons are established as consultants to themselves, they experience themselves as more of an authority on their own lives, their problems, and the solution to these problems. This authority takes the form of a kind of knowledge or expertise which is recorded in a popular medium so that it is accessible to the consultant, therapist, and potential others. (pp. 282–283)

One way we use clients as consultants is to audiotape or videotape conversations (with their consent) in which they describe how they've managed to overcome their problems. These tapes can then be shared with other clients. The effects of viewing these tapes can be numerous. As discussed in Chapter 5 with stories and metaphors, they can acknowledge realities and experiences; offer hope, new perspectives and possibilities; and remind clients of previous solutions and resources. Another possibility is to ask clients some of the following questions:

- We periodically meet with others who are experiencing the same or a similar problem to the one you've faced. From what you now know, what advice might I give them about facing their concerns?
- If new clients were to ask me to tell them how previous clients have solved similar problems in the past, what would you suggest that I say to them?
- What suggestions would you have for therapists or other mental health professionals who in the future might work with clients who have experienced the same or similar problems?

Another way of sharing change and knowledge with larger social contexts is to suggest that clients volunteer with other organizations. Former clients are often among those who use their personal experience and the training they receive to help others. They provide conversation, companionship, and support to others. This certainly is not a new idea, just an underutilized one. In fact, many years ago, Alfred Adler (1956) wrote about the importance of *social interest.* Although Adler spoke about this concept in a broader sense, he essentially conveyed the idea that it's not enough for people to make personal changes; most must also make contributions to society.

Every End Is the Beginning of Something New: Ending Therapy

As goals are met and destinations are reached, treatment ends. In the first chapter we stated that therapy takes as long as it takes. We've seen clients for a variety of different lengths of time. The length of therapy is dependent on conversations with clients about what will constitute successful outcome, including the construction of goals, ways of accomplishing those goals, and recognizing when progress is being made. As therapy begins to wind down, we find it important—whether it's the first or fiftieth session—to consider the following:

- Keeping the ball rolling through future-oriented questions
- Anticipating hurdles and perceived barriers
- Using transition and celebratory rituals
- Attending to client satisfaction
- Keeping an open door policy

We'll discuss each of these in this section.

Keeping the Ball Rolling through Future-Oriented Questions

We've found it helpful to talk with clients about how they will continue to extend the changes they've made into the future once therapy has ended. Earlier in this book we discussed the idea of the ripple effect, and how small changes can lead to bigger ones. Therefore, we help orient clients toward positive change in the future. In addition, even though changes have been made and goals have been met in therapy, there are preferred directions that clients will continue to move toward. This is the proverbial "big picture." To assist with this process, we ask clients questions including:

- How can you put your new knowledge to work in the future?
- What have you been doing that you will continue to do once therapy has ended?
- How will you continue to solidify and build on the changes that you've made?
- What will you be doing differently that you might not have otherwise been able to do?
- After you leave here, what will you be doing to keep things going in the direction you prefer? What else?
- How will you keep things moving forward? How will you make sure that you will do that?
- How will you keep your eyes on the road ahead instead of staring into the rearview mirror?
- What do you need from others?
- How might they be of help to you?

Anticipating Hurdles and Perceived Barriers

In between sessions, and as therapy comes to a close, some clients will identify hurdles or perceive barriers that may pose a threat to maintaining the changes that they've made. In other cases, therapists will want to talk with clients about these entities. We never tell clients that they will hit roadblocks, we only suggest that they might experience challenges in the future. In fact, this is typically not news to clients, as they don't expect their lives to be perfect. However, bringing up this idea can serve to normalize their apprehension and fear. In addition, by discussing possible future concerns, we can increase the likelihood that changes will continue (O'Hanlon & Weiner-Davis, 1989).

To discuss the idea of hurdles or perceived barriers we sometimes ask clients, "Is there anything that might come up between now and the next time we meet that could pose a threat to the changes you've made?" or "Can you think of anything that might come up over the next few weeks or months that could present a challenge for you in staying on track?" If the client answers "Yes," we explore in detail what those challenges may be and then explore how the client will handle these challenges. Here are some questions to assist with this:

- What have you learned about your ability to stand up to ______?
- What might be an indication to you that the problem was attempting to resurface?

- What might be the first sign?
- What will you do differently in the future if faced with the same or a similar problem?
- How can what you've learned be of help to you in solving future problems?
- If you feel yourself slipping, what's one thing that can stop that slipping and get you back on track?
- What's one thing that can bring a slippage under control or to an end?

We consider these types of questions to be preventative. In fact, we believe that therapists should help clients use their new knowledge and skills wherever they may be helpful. Therefore, we suggest to clients that they transfer their new learnings and abilities to other contexts.

Transition and Celebratory Rituals

In Chapter 6 we discussed different types and uses of rituals. We also found that transition and celebratory rituals in particular can be helpful in signifying either the achievement of goals or the ending of therapy. In addition, they can help clients accentuate the changes they have made and make the transition out of therapy a positive one. In our experience, rituals are more personal than a handshake and a message of good luck from therapists. In determining whether to use a ritual we ask clients. We sometimes say:

> Oftentimes it helps people to mark the changes they've made or the ending of therapy with something that symbolizes that they're moving on into the future. Is there anything that we might do here to put an exclamation point on the changes you've made or your transition out of therapy?

Although many clients will just want to bring things to a close without the use of any form of ritual, some will want to have a cake. Others will request exchanging cards or sharing stories. If you've used therapeutic letters during therapy clients may request one.

One of the ways that we've marked transitions is by using certificates. This is not a new idea as people have received certificates and awards for years for academics, sports, business, good citizenship, heroism, and so on. With younger clients in particular, certificates can help to build the scrapbooks we referred to earlier as well as a better sense of self and accomplishment. Tables 9.1 and 9.2 offer a couple examples of certificates that we have used.

The context in which you work will have a significant impact on how and to what degree you use these types of transition rituals. For example, if you work with clients who are suffering the aftereffects of sexual abuse you may use them more often and in particular ways. The same goes for therapists who do family therapy where celebrations sometimes take place. Further, transition rituals, as well as rituals indicating rites of passage, will be more common in residential

TABLE 9.1

Certificate of Excellence

in

Tantrum Taming

This certificate is hereby awarded to

____

On this day, ____________________, ______

For demonstrating his/her ability to tame tantrums

Signed: ____________________

placement facilities (Bertolino & Thompson, 1999). In any case, what is important is engaging clients in conversations where they can determine if a ritual will help their transition.

Attending to Client Satisfaction

As clients transition out of therapy we ask them about their therapy experiences to ensure collaboration, quality, and client satisfaction. Research has demonstrated that clients' perceptions of therapists' attitudes are a better predictor of outcome than therapists' perceptions (Bachelor, 1991). Therefore, we invite clients to share

TABLE 9.2

Certificate of Change

This certificate is hereby awarded to

____

On this day, ______________________ , ________

for success in standing up to ____________________

and for reclaiming his/her life

Signed: ____________________

with us what worked and did not work for them. We do this by asking some or all of the following questions:

- Did you feel you were heard and understood by our staff?
- Did you feel accepted for who you are as a person?
- Did you feel understood by our staff?
- Did you think your concerns were taken seriously?
- Did you think that your strengths, resources, and wisdom were acknowledged and honored by our staff? If so, in what ways?
- Did you feel that you were an active participant in our work together?
- Were you given the opportunity to give feedback during the process of treatment? About goals? Tasks?
- Did you think that you were treated respectfully?

- Did you think that an effort was made by our staff to understand your uniqueness?

We encourage therapists to ask questions and create tools to elicit feedback from clients. It's important to maintain accountability and to promote respectful and effective methods. This, in turn, informs our future practices and ways of working with clients.

The Open Door Policy

Somewhere along the way an extremely disrespectful and dangerous line was drawn in the field of mental health. Essentially this line indicated that when treatment ended, the therapist–client relationship ceased at that moment. For example, Bob once had a student who told him that he had been given written warnings on two occasions after he had taken phone calls from former clients who had been in the residential facility at which he worked. He was told that once the youth left the facility, staff were to have no contact with them as it might keep them from moving on or hurt them therapeutically.

The student was extremely upset because he had not violated boundaries and met with the youth without permission. He merely made himself available to these teenagers who knew that they could talk with him and trust him in a time of need. All they wanted was a few minutes of his time, and he gave it to them.

We believe that the ideas that some so-called professionals developed and continue to use are more damaging than anything else. When client relationships are formed, those relationships often continue even after formal therapy has ended. We remain a part of clients' lives and in turn, they are forever a part of ours. This does not mean that we continue being their therapists until the end of time. Instead, we communicate to clients that if they need to contact us after therapy has ended they can do so. We don't guarantee our availability in terms of being able to see them again in the future. We simply let them know that if they need to talk or are considering coming back, we will help them in whatever ways we can. Sometimes this means talking on the phone, starting up therapy again, or referring the client elsewhere.

People and their problems are not static. People experience different problems at different times in their lives (Carter & McGoldrick, 1989). Since we aren't in the business of trying to help clients to live problem-free lives, we realize that they need programs that are flexible enough to meet their needs. Further, we want clients to know that we value our relationships with them and will do what we can as they encounter the challenges of life. Case Example 9.3 illustrates this idea.

Case Example 9.3 *I'm Getting a Complex*

A fourteen-year-old, Cory, was referred to Bob after shooting another teenager in the face with a BB gun. Although Cory was not mandated to therapy, it was strongly suggested that he attend. Cory's mother brought him to see Bob. At the end of the fourth session, Bob asked Cory and his mother how they would like to proceed. His mother suggested that they meet in two weeks. All agreed and an appointment was set for two weeks later.

When Cory and his mother didn't show up for their next scheduled appointment, Bob tried contacting the family by phone. When there was no response he sent a letter to the family. After a few weeks had passed, Bob closed the case and didn't think too much about it.

About six months later, Cory's mother telephoned Bob and asked if she could bring him back. Bob agreed. At their appointment, Bob asked if Cory had been staying out of trouble and he stated that he had. Both Cory and his mother reported that he had been doing well but that recently he had met his biological father for the first time. As a result he was angry and was having difficulty with this new relationship.

During this second stint, Bob saw Cory for three sessions. Then, just as with the first series of sessions, he and his mother disappeared. Once again, there was no response when Bob attempted to contact them.

Approximately one year later, Bob again heard from Cory's mother. She confided in Bob that Cory had been struggling with his grades and seemed apathetic about school. She asked to bring him in and Bob agreed. At the start of the appointment Bob said to Cory and his mother, "I have to tell you that I'm a bit confused here. This is the third round of sessions that we've had. After each of the previous rounds, you disappeared. And I'm still wondering if I did something wrong or just what happened." To this the mother replied, "Oh no. You've been great. That's why we keep coming back. What happens is we come for a few sessions until we can handle things better. Then we come back if we need to." "Okay. I would greatly appreciate it if you could do me a favor," said Bob. "The next time you feel like things are where you think you can handle them, will you let me know so that I don't get a complex?" The mother laughed and replied, "Sure. I'll be sure to remember this time."

So Bob, Cory, and his mother met for six sessions. Oddly enough, what happened in the first two trials of therapy also happened with the third. The family disappeared after the sixth session.

Another year passed, and once again, Cory's mother contacted Bob for an appointment. Cory was now seventeen years old. This time, he explained that his girlfriend had broken up with him and he was bummed out and that he had to decide what to do after graduating. Once again, Bob asked Cory and his mother to please let him know when they felt that they had a better handle on things. So Bob and Cory met, with his mother sitting in occasionally, for three sessions. This time, the mother said, "We're doing well. Thanks again and we'll see you down the road if we need to."

Cory's and his mother's approach to therapy were similar to the general practitioner model referred to in the first chapter. More and more people are coming to therapy to straighten a few things out and then move on. They then return in the future if necessary. They're not in it for the long haul. Therefore, we recognize the importance of brief trials of therapy as opposed to ongoing, year after year treatment. Although some will need long-term therapy, recall that research indicates that most of the significant change in therapy typically occurs in the first handful of sessions.

Given this, we are mindful of maximizing our effectiveness in each and every session and letting clients know that we will keep an open door policy whenever and wherever possible. We strive to let clients know that we do not expect them to live problem-free lives once they have finished therapy with us and it's okay if they need to seek help in the future.

In this chapter we discussed ways of managing setbacks, sharing change with larger communities, keeping the ball rolling in the future once therapy has ended, and ending therapy. These ideas, as with the rest that have been presented throughout this book, are by no means inclusive, but instead represent a point of convergence for collaborative, competency-based counseling and therapy. In the next section we'll discuss future directions for the field of therapy.

Summary Points for Chapter Nine

- Setbacks are common and do not indicate a return to old ways.
- By documenting change and new stories, clients can continue to orient toward what is working, track change over time, and extend changes into the future.
- We can help clients grow their identity stories by asking questions in which they experience themselves in new ways. Those close to clients can also be invited to reflect on clients' new stories.
- Sharing changes with larger social contexts allows for audiences outside of clients' immediate social groups to become part of new stories. Clients can share their new stories by showing documentation of these stories, by becoming consultants to other clients, and by volunteering.
- As treatment comes to an end, therapists attend to the following:
  - Keeping the ball rolling through future-oriented questions
  - Anticipating hurdles and perceived barriers
  - Using transition and celebratory rituals
  - Attending to client satisfaction
  - Keeping an open door policy

EPILOGUE

Toward a Personalized Theory of Counseling and Therapy

The difficulty with writing a book is that there is always something left unsaid. Further, as we learn and interact in the world our ideas evolve and change. We welcome these challenges as we are forever learning. Interestingly, as the field changes, we are learning more and more about the obvious. In fact, it's been said that research has a way of proving the obvious. We've learned that the significant portion of change that clients experience as a result of therapy has little to do with theory. It is very clear that clients are the architects of change. Despite this, therapists continue to hold allegiances to and more faith in their models and theories than in their clients.

The Milan family therapy team that became well known in the 1980s used to warn therapists not to marry their hypotheses. We are even more wary—we suggest you don't even date your hypotheses. Too often, therapists can become enamored of their own ideas and pet theories about people and inadvertently impose these ideas and theories on clients. But clients are always around to give you the information you need; it's a matter of collaborating with them and asking questions to elicit that information. Questions can open or close doors. In fact, Zen philosopher Alan Watts (1966) once wrote, "Problems that remain persistently insolvable should always be suspected as questions asked the wrong way" (p. 55).

This book has been based on a simple but radical premise: people are their own experts and have knowledge and preferences that can guide the therapy process successfully. This premise requires a bit of trust in people, which is not typically provided in most therapy training. But the trust is only required for a short time, because soon, if you work this way, we think you will discover that that trust is warranted. You will learn more from your clients if you are open to that learning than from all the textbooks you could study.

We are reminded of an old Zen story in which the teacher laments that he keeps pointing at the moon and all his students look at his finger. This book has been the finger, but the moon is the amazing capability and resourcefulness of clients.

Therapy That Makes a Difference

One of the risks of teaching new ideas is that emphasis sometimes shifts toward techniques as opposed to utilizing new ideas to facilitate the therapeutic alliance and tap into client factors such as their competencies and social support systems. Yet we know from research that therapeutic techniques make a rather small contribution to positive outcome. What seems to be clear is that methods and techniques enhance change processes when they are consistent with clients' states of readiness to change and their theories about problem formation and problem resolution.

To invite others into this way of thinking, we often ask our students and trainees the following question: "What is the difference between therapy that is effective and helps people to change, and therapy that seems to just be words that go in one ear and out the other?" In our experience, therapy that makes a difference somehow gets into clients' internal experience. Therapy that makes a difference somehow moves clients such that they see things differently and take new action in their lives.

To better understand this we invite you to consider these questions:

- What moves you?
- How do you get into the experience (not merely the intellect) of your clients?
- What do you do that makes a difference for clients in therapy?

We are all moved by different things such as spending time with loved ones, nature, reading poetry, listening to music or a riveting speaker, watching movies, and so on. For most people there are multiple things that move them in different ways. We believe that positive change processes are promoted when methods utilized tap into people's experiential worlds.

Therefore, we encourage you to take the time to get a sense of what moves you. This can help you to better distinguish what it feels like to experience hope for the future and in turn to work with your clients in ways that facilitate hope, expectancy, and individual change processes. We also believe that it can open you up to new ways of working with clients that evolve out of your therapeutic conversations, interactions, and encounters.

We combine this idea with our mission statement that we offered in the Preface. We often find that therapists are already practicing in respectful and effective ways that they should continue. We encourage you to continue to do these things and not abandon what works in lieu of a theoretical overhaul. Instead, we invite you to take from this book that which fits with you and integrate it into your already existing personal theory of change.

Avoiding Flow Charts and Cookbooks

Although we have presented the material in this book in a somewhat methodical way, we hope that you have realized that we do not view therapy in the same way. Therapy is a process that cannot be delineated through flow charts or standardized methods. Therapy and counseling are exquisitely human activities, requiring a meeting of people in human ways. We hope that the ideas we have offered serve as a guide or map, but they certainly are not the territory. In fact, the majority of the ideas we described came from our interactions with clients. Through outcome research and our interactions with them, clients have and will continue to teach us what works.

Smothering the Flames of Burnout

It seems that most every mental health professional will encounter the big B at one point or another. Yes, we are referring to burnout. In our experience, one of the leading causes of burnout is the theories to which therapists hold allegiance. We believe that those theories which focus solely on problems and pathology are, in fact, prescriptions for burnout. If the lenses through which we look at clients only reveal what's wrong, it's not difficult to see how therapists can become disheartened and hopeless—the same as clients.

We have found that a collaborative, competency-based perspective can counter burnout. Instead of looking at our theories to determine what's wrong with people and what's unchangeable, we have offered ways of exploring what's right, what's possible, and what's changeable. To reiterate, we don't ignore the hardships that clients face; we acknowledge and attend to them and simultaneously search for those areas where we can create positive change. As we near the end of our journey together, we'd like to share a couple of personal stories to illustrate the idea of countering burnout:

> Bill was once teaching a workshop on collaborative, competency-based therapy in the Northeast United States. A good friend, a psychiatrist who had worked in this way for many years, decided to attend. After the workshop, as he and Bill were riding to dinner together, he asked Bill if he could give him some feedback on the workshop. Bill readily agreed, always looking to improve his presentation skills.
>
> His friend said, "I really enjoyed the workshop, but I think you missed the most important point of this work." "And what's that?" Bill asked. "You kept telling the participants how effective and respectful this way of working is, but for them the most relevant point is that this way of working is a way to reduce burnout. You see more results, more quickly typically, which helps reduce therapist discouragement. You also get to experience the heroism and resourcefulness of clients instead of seeing them as resistant, pathology-filled people. You should have told them that working this way will be good for them as well as for their clients." Bill had never considered making this explicit before. He just thought that if people got inspired to work this way, they would discover the personal benefit for themselves.

> Bob was teaching a workshop at a mental health center when a woman approached him during an afternoon break. She told him, "I usually sleep through these things because they're so boring and drab. I just go

> because I need the CEUs (continuing education units). But not only am I still awake, I'm feeling reenergized. Isn't that weird?" Bob replied, "I think that's wonderful. What do you suppose has reenergized you?" "It's just the fact that what you've been saying feels right to me. It resonates with every part of me and what I believe. I mean, you're teaching us ideas for working with kids, but it also feels to me like you're teaching us a way of dealing with life in general. I've needed that but didn't realize it until now."

Because we haven't always made it so explicit, we are correcting ourselves. Therapy can be very challenging work. It is sometimes scary, it is sometimes confusing. If you are going through your own personal crisis, you can begin to doubt your abilities or feel like a fake. There are legal worries, ethical rules to master, and a sense of great responsibility at times. Working this way can help lighten some of those burdens because you do not have to be or pretend to be an all-knowing expert who can solve any problem. In addition, we feel that what we have offered is a way of being with people in general. Both in and out of the office we seek an improved quality of life for others and ourselves.

As we were finishing this manuscript, we received an e-mail message from a colleague that we would like to share with you. The message we received speaks to this idea of burnout, and we believe captures the essence of the approach we have described throughout this book. Interestingly, when we asked her for permission to publish the e-mail, she said, "You can use any part of the e-mail I sent you for any purpose you want ... BUT don't you dare change my name." We were delighted that she shared her story with us, and we now share it with a larger social context!

> Dear Bob,
>
> I am writing to thank you for saving what I thought was going to be a very brief career in adolescent psychiatry. I was a critical care nurse for 10 years when I moved to adult psychiatry. I stayed there only a little while until I was offered a position in adolescent psychiatry with great hours (7am–3pm, Monday–Friday). I couldn't turn this offer down, along with the opportunity to develop a pre-adolescent program from the ground up. I took it, but quickly became frustrated and ready to quit. Everyone seemed to have this very hard line approach to dealing with these kids and that just was not me. I was going to throw in the towel when I saw your flyer and told my boss that I needed inspiration or else I was ready to give up.
>
> I came, not really expecting much, but went home thinking "wow." All of a sudden I "got it." It was an approach that I could work with. I spoke to you during the break at that seminar and explained some of my frustrations. You recommended Bill O'Hanlon's book (*Do One Thing Different*) and you said two things to me that I use every day: "just keep your feet moving" and "make a connection."

> I want to thank you so much, and let you know what an impact you made. It is the most gratifying career choice I have ever made. I have even completed what is called the "career ladder II," which is just a test of endurance for advancement in your field. I am currently working on level III, which includes leadership work. I have chosen as my staff education project solution-based therapy: a presentation of my research. I will make sure that all the acknowledgments are proper and hope that just one person will "get it." I have already made a believer out of our psychologist. I found Bill's web site today while researching for this project and ordered waaaaay too much stuff. Just wanted to drop this note and let you know how much I appreciate your enthusiasm for what you do. Now I have the same enthusiasm.
>
> Beverly Crocker, RN
> Gastonia, NC

We hope the pages of this book will somehow resonate with you as well. It is a gift for us when we hear from others that they have made progressive shifts in their personal stories. Not only do we have people feeling better about their work, but we also have clients who are benefiting from mental health professionals who have been reenergized.

We now leave you with a story that we hope will encourage you to keep your feet moving, thereby opening up possibilities for the future.

The Room of 1,000 Demons

Long ago, in Tibet, there was a ceremony held every 100 years that Buddhist seekers could go through in order to attain enlightenment. In the ceremony, all the students would line up in their white robes. The lamas, the Tibetan priests, and the Dalai Lama, would line up before the students. The Dalai Lama would begin the ceremony:

> This is the ceremony of The Room of 1,000 Demons. It is the ceremony for enlightenment and it only happens once every 100 years. You can only go through it now. If you choose not to, you will have to wait another 100 years. To help you make this decision, we'll tell you what The Room of 1,000 Demons ceremony is about.
>
> In order to get into The Room of 1,000 Demons, you just open the door and walk in. The Room of 1,000 Demons is not very big. Once you enter, the door will close behind you. There is no doorknob on the inside of the door. In order to get out, you have to walk all the way through the room, find the doorknob (which is unlocked), open the door, and come out. That's all you have to do to be enlightened.
>
> But it's called The Room of 1,000 Demons because there are 1,000 demons in there. Those demons have the ability to take on the form of

> your worst fears. As soon as you walk in the room, those demons show you your worst fears. If you have a fear of heights, when you walk into the room it will appear as if you are standing on a narrow ledge of a tall building. If you have a fear of spiders, you'll be surrounded by the scariest eight-legged creatures imaginable. Whatever your fears are, the demons take those images from your mind and seem to make them real. In fact, they'll be so compellingly real, it will be very difficult to remember they're not.
>
> We can't come in and rescue you. That is part of the rules. If you go into The Room of 1,000 Demons, you have to make it out on your own. Some people never make it out the other side. They go into The Room of 1,000 Demons and become paralyzed with fright. And they stay trapped in the room until they die. So, if you want to take the risk of entering the room, that's fine. If you don't, if you want to go home, that's fine. You don't *have* to go through it. You can wait until you get incarnated again, come back in another 100 years, and try it again.
>
> If you want to go through, we have two hints for you. The first hint is, as soon as you go into The Room of 1,000 Demons, remember that what they show you isn't real. It's all from your own mind. Don't buy into it, it's an illusion. Of course, most of the people that went into the room before you couldn't remember that. It is very difficult to keep it in mind. The second hint has been more helpful for the people who made it out the other side and became enlightened. Once you go into the room, no matter what you see, no matter what you feel, no matter what you hear, no matter what you think, *keep your feet moving.* If you keep your feet moving, you will eventually get to the other side, find the door and come out.

We hope you make it through your own room of fears and that you can sit and listen respectfully as clients give you the privilege of sharing with them their journeys through their darkest fears and times. This book has been a journey for us, through barriers and challenges. We are excited to be coming out the door to the other side. We are curious to see what the future will bring to therapy and to learning even more ways to be respectful and helpful to people in therapy.

> Somehow I can't believe that there are any heights that can't be scaled by a man who knows the secrets of making dreams come true. This special secret, it seems to me, can be summarized in four Cs. They are curiosity, confidence, courage and constancy, and the greatest of all is confidence. When you believe in a thing, believe in it all the way, implicitly and unquestionably.
>
> —Walt Disney

Please feel free to contact us with suggestions, comments and corrections:

Bob Bertolino, Therapeutic Collaborations Consultation & Training
Phone/fax: 636.441.7779
E-mail: bertolinob@cs.com
Website:
http://www.bobbertolino.com

Bill O'Hanlon, Possibilities
Phone: 505.983.2843
Fax: 505.983.2761
E-mail: PossiBill@aol.com
Website:
http://www.brieftherapy.com

APPENDIX I

Process and Outcome Measures

Session Rating

Name ____________________ Date __________ Session No. ________

Therapist ____________________

Therapy is a cooperative relationship. Please rate today's session. Be honest and frank, to be the most helpful to your counselor. Read each set of descriptions. Circle the number that best describes your reaction, from 0 to 4. Use the rating system below:

AGREE WITH THIS SIDE		NEUTRAL	AGREE WITH THIS SIDE	
4	**3**	**2**	**1**	**0**

(*Under* each set of statements, circle the number that best describes your feelings about today's session)

1. ACCEPTANCE

I felt accepted.			I felt criticized or judged.	
4	3	2	1	0

2. LIKING, POSITIVE REGARD

My therapist liked me.			My therapist pretended to like me or seemed not to like me.	
4	3	2	1	0

3. UNDERSTANDING

My therapist understood me and my feelings.			My therapist didn't understand me or my feelings.	
4	3	2	1	0

4. HONEST AND SINCERITY

My therapist was honest and sincere.			My therapist was not sincere, was pretending.	
4	3	2	1	0

5. AGREEMENT ON GOALS

We worked on my goals; my goals were important.			We worked on my counselor's goals; my goals didn't seem important.	
4	3	2	1	0

6. AGREEMENT ON TASKS

I approved of the things we did in the session or what I was asked to do as a homework assignment.			I didn't like what we did in today's session or what I was asked to do as a homework assignment.	
4	3	2	1	0

7. SMOOTHNESS OF SESSION

The session was smooth; I felt comfortable.			The session was rough; I felt uncomfortable.	
4	3	2	1	0

8. DEPTH OF THE SESSION

The session was deep; we got to the heart of things.			The session was shallow; we stayed on the surface.	
4	3	2	1	0

9. HELPFULNESS, USEFULNESS

I found the session helpful.			The session was not helpful.	
4	3	2	1	0

10. HOPE

I felt hopeful after the session.			I felt hopeless after the session.	
4	3	2	1	0

One more thing: What could help the next session to go better? Please continue on the back if necessary.

REFERENCES

Adler, A. (1956). *The individual psychology of Alfred Adler: A systematic presentation in selections from his writings.* [H. L. Ansbacher & R. R. Ansbacher, Trans.].

American Psychiatric Association. (1994). *Diagnostic and statistical manual of mental disorders* (4th ed.). Washington, DC: American Psychiatric Association.

Andersen, T. (1987). The reflecting team: Dialogue and metadialogue in clinical work. *Family Process, 26,* 415–428.

Andersen, T. (Ed.). (1991). *The reflecting team: Dialogues and dialogues about the dialogues.* New York: Norton.

Andersen, T. (1993). See and hear, and be seen and heard. In S. Friedman (Ed.), *The new language of change: Constructive collaboration in psychotherapy* (pp. 303–322). New York: Guilford.

Anderson, H. (1993). On a roller coaster: A collaborative language systems approach to therapy. In S. Freidman (Ed.), *The new language of change: Constructive collaboration in psychotherapy* (pp. 323–344). New York: Guilford.

Anderson, H. (1997). *Conversation, language, and possibilities: A postmodern approach.* New York: Basic Books.

Anderson, H., & Goolishian, H. (1988). Human systems and linguistic systems: Evolving ideas about the implications for theory and practice. *Family Process, 27,* 371–393.

Anderson, H., & Goolishian, H. (1992). The client is the expert: A not knowing approach to therapy. In S. McNamee & K. J. Gergen (Eds.), *Therapy as social construction* (pp. 25–39). Newbury Park, CA: Sage.

Arredondo, P., & D'Andrea, M. (1995, September). AMCD approved multicultural counseling competency standards. *Counseling Today,* 28–32.

Asay, T. P., & Lambert, M. J. (1999). The empirical case for the common factors in therapy: Quantitative findings. In M. A. Hubble, B. L. Duncan, & S. D. Miller (Eds.), *The heart and soul of change: What works in therapy* (pp. 33–56). Washington, DC: APA Press.

Bachelor, A. (1991). Comparison and relationship to outcome of diverse dimensions of the helping alliance as seen by client and therapist. *Psychotherapy, 28,* 534–549.

Bandler, R., & Grinder, J. (1975). *Patterns of the hypnotic techniques of Milton H. Erickson, M.D.* (Vol. 1). Capitola, CA: Meta.

Barker, S. L., Funk, S. C., & Houston, B. K. (1988). Psychological treatment versus nonspecific factors: A meta-analysis of conditions that engender comparable expectations for improvement. *Clinical Psychology Review, 8,* 579–594.

Becvar, D. S., & Becvar, R. J. (2000). *Family therapy: A systemic integration* (4th ed.). Boston: Allyn & Bacon.

Berg, I. K. (1994). *Family based services: A solution-focused approach.* New York: Norton.

Berg, I. K., & de Shazer, S. (1993). Making numbers talk: Language in therapy. In S. Freidman (Ed.), *The new language of change: Constructive collaboration in psychotherapy* (pp. 5–24). New York: Guilford.

Berg, I. K., & Gallagher, D. (1991). Solution-focused brief treatment with adolescent substance abusers. In T. C. Todd & M. D. Selekman (Eds.), *Family therapy approaches with adolescent substance abusers* (pp. 93–111). Needham Heights, MA: Allyn & Bacon.

Berg, I. K., & Miller, S. D. (1992). *Working with the problem drinker: A solution-focused approach.* New York: Norton.

Berger, P. L., & Luckmann, T. (1966). *The social construction of reality: A treatise in the sociology of knowledge.* New York: Doubleday/Anchor Books.

Bertolino, B. (1998). *An exploration of change: Investigating the experiences of psychotherapy trainees.* Unpublished doctoral dissertation, St. Louis University, St. Louis, Missouri.

Bertolino, B. (1999). *Therapy with troubled teenagers: Rewriting young lives in progress.* New York: Wiley.

Bertolino, B., & Caldwell, K. (2000). Through the doorway: Experiences of psychotherapists in a week-long training intensive. *Journal of Systemic Therapies, 18*(4), 42–57.

Bertolino, B., & O'Hanlon, B. (Eds.). (1998). *Invitation to possibility-land: An intensive teaching seminar with Bill O'Hanlon.* Bristol, PA.: Brunner/Mazel.

Bertolino, B., & Thompson, K. (1999). *The residential youth care worker in action: A collaborative, competency-based approach.* New York: The Haworth Press.

Beutler, L. E. (1989). The misplaced role of theory in psychotherapy integration. *Journal of Integrative and Eclectic Psychotherapy, 8,* 401–406.

Beutler, L. E., & Clarkin, J. (1990). *Systematic treatment selection: Toward targeted therapeutic interventions.* New York: Brunner/Mazel.

Bohart, A., & Tallman, K. (1999). *What clients do to make therapy work.* Washington, DC: American Psychological Association.

Bordin, E. S. (1979). The generalizability of the psychoanalytic concept of the working alliance. *Psychotherapy: Theory, Research, and Practice, 16,* 252–260.

Brown, J., Dreis, S., & Nace, D. K. (1999). What really makes a difference in psychotherapy outcome? Why does managed care want to know? In M. A. Hubble, B. L. Duncan, & S. D. Miller (Eds.), *The heart and soul of change: What works in therapy* (pp. 389–406). Washington DC: APA Press.

Burnham, J. R. (1966). Experiment bias and lesion labeling. Unpublished manuscript, Purdue University.

Carter, B., & McGoldrick, M. (Eds.). (1989). *The changing family life cycle* (2nd ed.). Boston: Allyn & Bacon.

Cleary, T. (Ed. & Trans.). (1993). *The spirit of Tao.* Boston: Shambala.

Cottone, R. R. (1992). *Theories and paradigms in counseling and psychotherapy.* Boston: Allyn & Bacon.

Cummings, N. A., & Follette, W. T. (1976). Brief therapy and medical utilization. In H. Dorken (Ed.), *The professional psychologist today.* San Francisco: Jossey-Bass.

de Shazer, S. (1985). *Keys to solution in brief therapy.* New York: Norton.

de Shazer, S. (1988). *Clues: Investigating solutions in brief therapy.* New York: Norton.

de Shazer, S. (1991). *Putting difference to work.* New York: Norton.

de Shazer, S. (1993). Commentary: de Shazer & White: Vive la différence. In S. Gilligan & R. Price (Eds.), *Therapeutic conversations* (pp. 112–120). New York: Norton.

de Shazer, S. (1994). *Words were originally magic.* New York: Norton.

Doherty, W. J., & Simmons, D. S. (1995). Clinical practice patterns of marriage and family therapy: A national survey of therapists and their clients. *Journal of Marital and Family Therapy, 21*(1), 3–16.

Doherty, W. J., & Simmons, D. S. (1996). Clinical practice patterns of marriage and family therapy: A national survey of therapists and their clients. *Journal of Marital and Family Therapy,* 22(1), 9–26.

Dreikurs, R. (1954). The psychological interview in medicine. *American Journal of Individual Psychology, 10,* 99–122.

Duncan, B. L., Hubble, M. A., & Miller, S. D. (1997). Stepping off the throne. *Family Therapy Networker, 21*(4), 22–31, 33.

Duncan, B. L., & Miller, S. D. (2000). *The heroic client: Doing client-centered, outcome-informed therapy.* San Francisco: Jossey-Bass.

Durrant, M. (1993). *Residential treatment: A cooperative, competency-based approach to therapy and program design.* New York: Norton.

Durrant, M. (1995). *Creative strategies for school problems: Solutions for psychologists and teachers.* New York: Norton.

Efran, J., & Lukens, M. D. (1985). The world according to Humberto Maturana. *Family Therapy Networker, 9*(3), 23–25, 27–28, 72–75.

Epston, D. (1989). *Collected papers.* Adelaide, South Australia: Dulwich Centre Publications.

Epston, D., & White, M. (1992). *Experience, contradiction, narrative, and imagination: Selected papers of David Epston and Michael White 1989–1991.* Adelaide, South Australia: Dulwich Centre Publications.

Epston, D., White, M., & "Ben." (1995). Consulting with your consultants: A means to the co-construction of alternative knowledges. In S. Friedman (Ed.), *The reflecting team in action: Collaborative practice in family therapy* (pp. 277–313). New York: Guilford.

Erickson, M. H. (1954a). Special techniques of brief hypnotherapy. *Journal of Clinical and Experiential Hypnosis, 2,* 109–129.

Erickson, M. H. (1954b). Pseudo-orientation in time as a hypnotherapeutic procedure. *Journal of Clinical and Experiential Hypnosis, 2,* 261–283.

Erickson, M. H. (1980). The use of symptoms as an integral part of hypnotherapy. In E. L. Rossi (Ed.), *Innovative hypnotherapy: The collected papers of Milton H. Erickson on hypnosis* (Volume IV) (pp. 212–223). New York: Irvington.

Erickson, M. H., & Rossi, E. L. (1979). *Hypnotherapy: An exploratory casebook.* New York: Irvington.

Fisch, R., Weakland, J. H., & Segal, L. (1982). *The tactics of change: Doing therapy briefly.* San Francisco: Jossey-Bass.

Fish, J. M. (1997). Paradox or complaints? Strategic thoughts about solution-focused therapy. *Journal of Systemic Therapies, 16*(3), 266–273.

Follette, W. T., & Cummings, N. A. (1967). Psychiatric services and medical utilization in a prepaid health care setting. *Medical Care, 5,* 25–35.

Frank, J. D. (1973). *Persuasion and healing.* Baltimore: Johns Hopkins University Press.

Frank, J. D. (1995). Psychotherapy as rhetoric: Some implications. *Clinical Psychology: Science and Practice, 2,* 90–93.

Frank, J. D., & Frank, J. B. (1991). *Persuasion and healing: A comparative study of psychotherapy* (3rd ed.). Baltimore: Johns Hopkins University Press.

Frankl, V. (1963). *Man's search for meaning: An introduction to logotherapy.* New York: Pocket Books.

Frankl, V. (1969). *Will to meaning: Foundations and applications of logotherapy.* New York: World Publishing.

Freedman, J., & Combs, G. (1996). *Narrative therapy: The social construction of preferred realities.* New York: Norton.

Freeman, J., Epston, D., & Lobovits, D. (1997). *Playful approaches to serious problems: Narrative therapy with children and their families.* New York: Norton.

Friedman, S. (Ed.). (1995). *The reflecting team in action: Collaborative practice in family therapy.* New York: Guilford.

Garfield, S. L. (1982). Eclecticism and integration in psychotherapy. *Behavior Therapy, 13,* 610–623.

Garfield, S. L. (1989). *The practice of brief psychotherapy.* New York: Pergamon.

Garfield, S. L. (1994). Research on client variables in psychotherapy. In A. E. Bergin and S. Garfield (Eds.), *Handbook of psychotherapy and behavior change* (4th ed.) (pp. 190–228). New York: Wiley.

Garfield, S. L., & Bergin, A. E. (1994). Introduction and historical overview. In A. E. Bergin & S. L. Garfield (Eds.), *Handbook of psychotherapy and behavior change* (pp. 3–18). New York: Wiley.

Gentle Spaces News. (1995). Let there be peace. In J. Canfield & M. V. Hansen (Eds.), *A 2nd helping of chicken soup for the soul: 101 more stories to open the heart and rekindle the spirit* (pp. 297–298). Deerfield Beach, FL: Health Communications.

Gergen, K. J. (1982). *Toward transformation in social knowledge.* New York: Springer-Verlag.

Gergen, K. J. (1985). The social constructionist movement in modern psychology. *American Psychologist, 40,* 255–275.

Gergen, K. J. (1994). *Realities and relationships: Soundings in social construction.* Cambridge, MA: Harvard University Press.

Gilligan, S. G. (1987). *Therapeutic trances: The cooperation principle in Ericksonian hypnotherapy.* New York: Brunner/Mazel.

Goldner, V. (1993). Power and hierarchy: Let's talk about it! *Family Process, 24,* 31–47.

Goolishian, H., & Anderson, H. (1987). Language systems and therapy: An evolving idea. *Psychotherapy, 24*(3), 529–538.

Gordon, D., & Meyers-Anderson, M. (1981). *Phoenix: Therapeutic patterns of Milton H. Erickson.* Cupertino, CA: Meta.

Grinder, J., DeLozier, J., & Bandler, R. (1977). *Patterns of the hypnotic techniques of Milton H. Erickson, M.D.* (Vol. 2). Cupertino, CA: Meta.

Gurman, A. S. (1977). The patient's perceptions of the therapeutic relationship. In A. S. Gurman & A. M. Razin (Eds.), *Effective psychotherapy* (pp. 503–545).

Haley, J. (1985). *Conversations with Milton H. Erickson, M.D.: Volume III: Changing children and families.* New York: Triangle Press.

Hare-Mustin, R. T. (1978). A feminist approach to family therapy. *Family Process, 17,* 181–194.

Hare-Mustin, R. T. (1994). Discourses in the mirrored room: A postmodern analysis of family therapy. *Family Process, 33,* 19–35.

Havens, R. A. (Ed.). (1985). *The wisdom of Milton H. Erickson: Human behavior & psychotherapy* (Vol. 2). New York: Irvington.

Held, B. S. (1991). The process/content distinction in psychotherapy revisited. *Psychotherapy, 28*(2), 207–217.

Held, B. S. (1995). *Back to reality: A critique of postmodern theory in psychotherapy.* New York: Norton.

Henrink, R. (Ed.). (1980). *The psychotherapy handbook: The A to Z guide to more than 250 different therapies in use today.* New York: New American Library.

Herman, J. L. (1992). *Trauma and recovery: The aftermath of violence—from domestic abuse to political terror.* New York: Basic Books.

Higgins, G. O. (1994). *Resilient adults: Overcoming a cruel past.* San Francisco: Jossey-Bass.

Hoffman, L. (1990). Constructing realities: An art of lenses. *Family Process, 29,* 1–12.

Hoffman, L. (1995). Forward. In S. Friedman (Ed.), *The reflecting team in action: Collaborative practice in family therapy* (pp. ix–xiv). New York: Guilford Press.

Horvath, A. O., & Luborsky, L. (1993). The role of the therapeutic alliance in psychotherapy. *Journal of Consulting and Clinical Psychology, 61,* 561–573.

Horvath, A. O., & Symonds, B. D. (1991). Relation between working alliance and outcome in psychotherapy: A meta-analysis. *Journal of Consulting and Clinical Psychology, 38,* 139–149.

Howard, K. I., Kopte, S. M., Krause, M. S., & Orlinsky, D. E. (1986). The dose-effect relationship in psychotherapy. *American Psychologist, 41*(2), 159–164.

Howard, K. I., Moras, K., Brill, P. L., Martinovich, Z., & Lutz, W. (1996). Evaluation of psychotherapy: Efficacy, effectiveness, and patient progress. *American Psychologist, 51*(10), 1059–1064.

Hubble, M. A., Duncan, B. L., & Miller, S. D. (Eds.). (1999a). Introduction. In M. A. Hubble, S. D. Miller, & B. L. Duncan (Eds.), *The heart and soul of change: What works in therapy* (pp. 1–19). Washington, D.C.: American Psychological Association.

Hubble, M. A., Duncan, B. L., & Miller, S. D. (Eds.). (1999b). *The heart and soul of change: What works in therapy.* Washington, DC: American Psychological Association.

Hubble, M. A., & O'Hanlon, W. H. (1992). Theory countertransference. *Dulwich Centre Newsletter, 1,* 25–30.

Hudson, P. O., & O'Hanlon, W. H. (1991). *Rewriting love stories: Brief marital therapy.* New York: Norton.

Katz, A. M. (1991). Afterwords: Continuing the dialogue. In T. Andersen (Ed.), *The reflecting team: Dialogues and dialogues about the dialogues* (pp. 98–126). New York: Norton.

Katz, M. (1997). *On playing poor hand well: Insights from the lives of those who have overcome childhood risks and adversities.* New York: Norton.

Kazdin, A. E. (1986). Comparative outcome studies of psychotherapy: Methodological issues and strategies. *Journal of Consulting and Clinical Psychology, 54,* 95–105.

Koss, M. P., & Butcher, J. N. (1986). Research on brief psychotherapy. In A. E. Bergin & S. L.

Garfield (Eds.), *Handbook of psychotherapy and behavior change* (3rd ed.) (pp. 627–663). New York: Wiley.

Kroll, J. (1988). *The challenge of the borderline patient.* New York: Norton.

Kuehl, B. P. (1995). The solution-oriented genogram: A collaborative approach. *Journal of Marital and Family Therapy, 21*(3), 239–250.

Lafferty, P., Beutler, L. E., & Crago, M. (1989). Differences between more and less effective psychotherapists: A study of select therapist variables. *Journal of Consulting and Clinical Psychology, 57,* 76–80.

Lambert, M. J. (1992). Implications of outcome research for psychotherapy integration. In J. C. Norcross & M. R. Goldfried (Eds.), *Handbook of psychotherapy integration.* New York: Basic.

Lambert, M. J., & Bergin, A. E. (1994). The effectiveness of psychotherapy. In A. E. Bergin & S. L. Garfield (Eds.), *Handbook of psychotherapy and behavior change* (4th ed.) (pp. 143–189). New York: Wiley.

Lambert, M. J., Okiishi, J. C., Finch, A. E., & Johnson, L. D. (1998). Outcome assessment: From conceptualization to implementation. *Professional Psychology: Practice and Research, 29*(1), 63–70.

Lambert, M. J., Shapiro, D. A., & Bergin, A. E. (1986). The effectiveness of psychotherapy. In S. L. Garfield & A. E. Bergin (Eds.), *Handbook of psychotherapy and behavior change* (3rd ed.) (pp. 157–211). New York: Wiley.

Lankton, S. R., & Lankton, C. H. (1983). *The answer within: A clinical framework of Ericksonian hypnotherapy.* New York: Brunner/Mazel.

Lankton, S. R., & Lankton, C. H. (1986). *Enchantment and intervention in family therapy: Training in Ericksonian approaches.* New York: Brunner/Mazel.

Lawson, D. (1994). Identifying pretreatment change. *Journal of Counseling and Development, 72,* 244–248.

Lawson, A., McElheran, N., & Slive, A. (1997). Single session walk-in therapy: A model for the 21st century. *Family Therapy News, 30*(4), 15, 25.

Lebow, J. (1997). New science for psychotherapy. *Family Therapy Networker, 21*(2), 85–91.

Levitt, E. E. (1966). Psychotherapy research and the expectation-reality discrepancy. *Psychotherapy, 3,* 163–166.

Lipchik, E. (1988). Purposeful sequences for beginning the solution-focused interview. In E. Lipchik (Ed.), *Interviewing* (pp. 105–116). Rockville, MD: Aspen.

Lipsey, M. W., & Wilson, D. B. (1993). The efficacy of psychological, educational, and behavioral treatment: Confirmation from meta-analysis. *American Psychologist, 48,* 1181–1209.

Lorenz, K. (1997). *King Solomon's ring.* New York: Plume. [Reissue]

Luborsky, L., Singer, B., & Luborsky, L. (1975). Comparative studies of psychotherapies: Is it true that "everyone has won and all must have prizes"? *Archives of General Psychiatry, 32,* 995–1008.

Madsen, W. C. (1999). *Collaborative therapy with multi-stressed families: From old problems to new futures.* New York: Guilford.

Maturana, H. R. (1978). Biology of language: Epistemology of reality. In G. Miller & E. Leneberg (Eds.), *Psychology and biology of language and thought* (pp. 27–63). New York: Academic.

McBride, J. (1997). *Steven Spielberg: A biography.* New York: Simon & Schuster.

McGoldrick, M., & Gerson, R. (1985). *Genograms in family assessment.* New York: Norton.

McKeel, A. J., & Weiner-Davis, M. (1995). *Presuppostional questions and pretreatment change: A further analysis.* Unpublished manuscript.

Miller, S. D. (1994). The solution conspiracy: A mystery in three installments. *Journal of Systemic Therapies, 13*(1), 18–37.

Miller, S. D., Duncan, B. L., & Hubble, M. A. (1997). *Escape from Babel: Toward a unifying language for psychotherapy practice.* New York: Norton.

Mohl, D. C. (1995). Negative outcome in psychotherapy: A critical review. *Clinical Psychology: Science and Practice, 2,* 1–27.

Nylund, D., & Thomas, J. (1994). The economics of narrative. *Family Therapy Networker, 18*(6), 38–39.

O'Hanlon, B. (1994). The third wave. *Family Therapy Networker, 18*(6), 18–26, 28–29.

O'Hanlon, B. (1996). Assessment questions. In B. O'Hanlon (Ed.), *The handout book: Complete handouts from the workshops of Bill O'Hanlon* (p. 3). Omaha, NE: Possibility Press.

O'Hanlon, B. (1999). Possibility therapy: From iatrogenic injury to iatrogenic healing. In S. O'Hanlon & B. Bertolino (Eds.), *Evolving possibilities: Selected papers of Bill O'Hanlon* (pp. 143–157). Philadelphia, PA: Brunner/Mazel.

O'Hanlon, B., & Beadle, S. (1994). *A field guide to possibilityland: Possibility therapy methods.* Omaha, NE.: Possibility Press.

O'Hanlon, B., & Beadle, S. (1999). *A guide to possibility land: Fifty-one methods for doing brief, respectful therapy.* New York: Norton. [Originally published, 1994, as *A field guide to possibilityland: Possibility therapy methods.* Omaha, NE.: Possibility Press.]

O'Hanlon, B., & Bertolino, B. (1998). *Even from a broken web: Brief, respectful solution-oriented therapy for sexual abuse and trauma.* New York: Wiley.

O'Hanlon, B., & Wilk, J. (1987). *Shifting contexts: The generation of effective psychotherapy.* New York: Guilford.

O'Hanlon, W. H. (1987). *Taproots: Underlying principles of Milton Erickson's therapy and hypnosis.* New York: Norton.

O'Hanlon, W. H. (1993). Possibility therapy: From iatrogenic injury to iatrogenic healing. In S. G. Gilligan & R. Price (Eds.), *Therapeutic conversations* (pp. 3–17). New York: Norton.

O'Hanlon, W. H., & Hexum, A. L. (1990). *An uncommon casebook: The complete clinical work of Milton H. Erickson, M.D.* New York: Norton.

O'Hanlon, W. H., & Weiner-Davis, M. (1989). *In search of solutions: A new direction in psychotherapy.* New York: Norton.

O'Hanlon, S., & Bertolino, B. (Eds.). (1999). *Evolving possibilities: The selected papers of Bill O'Hanlon.* Philadelphia, PA: Brunner/Mazel.

O'Hanlon, S., & O'Hanlon, B. (1999). Possibility therapy with families. In S. O'Hanlon & B. Bertolino (Eds.), *Evolving possibilities: Selected papers of Bill O'Hanlon* (pp. 185–204). Philadelphia, PA: Brunner/Mazel.

Orlinsky, D. E., Grawe, K., & Parks, B. K. (1994). Process and outcome in psychotherapy—noch einmal. In A. E. Bergin & S. L. Garfield (Eds.), *Handbook of psychotherapy and behavior change* (4th ed.) (pp. 270–378). New York: Wiley.

Patton, M., & Meara, N. (1982). The analysis of language in psychological treatment. In R. Russell (Ed.), *Spoken interaction in psychotherapy.* New York: Irving.

Payer, L. (1996). *Medicine and culture: Varieties of treatment in the United States, England, West Germany, and France.* New York: Henry Holt and Company.

Penn, P., & Sheinberg, M. (1991). Stories and conversations. *Journal of Strategic and Systemic Therapies, 10,* 30–37.

Prioleau, L., Murdock, M., & Brody, N. (1983). An analysis of psychotherapy versus placebo studies. *The Behavioral and Brain Sciences, 6,* 275–310.

Prochaska, J. O. (1993). Working in harmony with how people change naturally. *The Weight Control Digest, 3,* 249, 252–255.

Prochaska, J. O. (1995). Common problems: Common solutions. *Clinical Psychology: Science and Practice, 2,* 101–105.

Prochaska, J. O. (1999). How do people change, and how can we change to help many more people? In M. A. Hubble, B. L. Duncan, & S. D. Miller (Eds.), *The heart and soul of change: What works in therapy* (pp. 227–255).

Prochaska, J. O., & DiClemente, C. C. (1982). Transtheoretical therapy: Toward a more integrative model of change. *Psychotherapy Theory, Research, and Practice, 19,* 276–288.

Prochaska, J. O., & DiClemente, C. C. (1984). *The transtheoretical approach: Crossing traditional boundaries of therapy.* Homewood, IL: Dow Jones-Irwin.

Prochaska, J. O., & DiClemente, C. C. (1986). The transtheoretical approach. In J. C. Norcross (Ed.), *Handbook of eclectic psychotherapy* (pp. 163–200). New York: Brunner/Mazel.

Prochaska, J. O., DiClemente, C. C., & Norcross, J. C. (1992). In search of how people change: Applications to addictive behaviors. *American Psychologist, 47,* 1102–1114.

Prochaska, J. O., Norcross, J. C., & DiClemente, C. C. (1994). *Changing for good.* New York: Morrow.

Rogers, C. R. (1951). *Client-centered therapy.* Boston: Houghton Mifflin.

Rogers, C. R. (1961). *On becoming a person: A therapist's view of psychotherapy.* Boston: Houghton Mifflin.

Rosen, S. (1982). *My voice will go with you: The teaching tales of Milton H. Erickson.* New York: Norton.

Rosenthal, R. (1966). *Experimenter effects in behavioral research.* New York: Appleton-Century-Crofts.

Rossi, E. L. (Ed.). (1980a). *The collected papers of Milton H. Erickson on hypnosis* (Volumes I–IV). New York: Irvington.

Rossi, E. L. (Ed.). (1980b). *Innovative hypnotherapy: The collected papers of Milton H. Erickson on hypnosis* (Vol. IV). New York: Irvington.

Rossi, E. L., & Ryan, M. O. (Eds.). (1983a). *Life reframing in hypnosis: The seminars, workshops, and lectures of Milton H. Erickson* (Volume II). New York: Irvington.

Rossi, E. L., & Ryan, M. O. (Eds.). (1983b). *Mind-body communication in hypnosis: The seminars, workshops, and lectures of Milton H. Erickson* (Volume III). New York: Irvington.

Rossi, E. L., & Ryan, M. O. (Eds.). (1983c). *Creative choice in hypnosis: The seminars, workshops, and lectures of Milton H. Erickson* (Volume IV). New York: Irvington.

Rossi, E. L., Ryan, M. O., & Sharp, F. A. (Eds.). (1983). *Healing in hypnosis: The seminars, workshops, and lectures of Milton H. Erickson* (Volume I). New York: Irvington.

Rowan, T., & O'Hanlon, B. (1999). *Solution-oriented therapy for chronic and severe mental illness.* New York: Wiley.

Rutter, M. (1987). Psychosocial resilience and protective mechanisms. 1987 meeting of the American Orthopsychiatric Association. *American Journal of Orthopsychiatry, 57* (3), 316–331.

Sachs, J. S. (1983). Negative factors in brief psychotherapy: An empirical assessment. *Journal of Consulting and Clinical Psychology, 51,* 557–564.

Selekman, M. D. (1997). *Solution-focused therapy with children: Harnessing family strengths for systemic change.* New York: Guilford.

Seligman, M. E. P. (1995). Effectiveness of psychotherapy: The *Consumer Reports* study. *American Psychologist, 50,* 965–974.

Sells, S. P., Smith, T. E., Coe, M. J., Yoshioka, M., & Robbins, J. (1994). An ethnography of couple and therapist experiences in reflecting team practice. *Journal of Marital and Family Therapy, 20*(3), 247–266.

Selvini Palazzoli, M., Boscolo, L., Cecchin, G., & Prata, G. (1978). *Paradox and counterparadox.* New York: Jason Aronson.

Selvini Palazzoli, M., Boscolo, L., Cecchin, G., & Prata, G. (1980). Hypothesizing-circularity-neutrality. *Family Process, 19,* 73–85.

Shapiro, D. A., & Shapiro, D. (1982). Meta-analysis of comparative therapy outcome studies: A replication and refinement. *Psychological Bulletin, 92,* 581–604.

Smith, C., & Nylund, D. (Eds.). (1997). *Narrative therapies with children and adolescents.* New York: Guilford.

Smith, M. L., Glass, G. V., & Miller, T. I. (1980). *The benefits of psychotherapy.* Englewood Cliffs, NJ: Prentice-Hall.

Smith, T. E., Yoshioka, M., & Winton, M. (1993). A qualitative understanding of reflecting teams I: Client perspectives. *Journal of Systemic Therapies, 12*(3), 28–43.

Steenbarger, B. N. (1992). Toward science-practice integration in brief counseling and therapy. *The Counseling Psychologist, 20,* 403–450.

Talmon, M. (1990). *Single session therapy: Maximizing the effect of the first (and often only) therapeutic encounter.* San Francisco: Jossey-Bass.

Talmon, M., Hoyt, M. F., & Rosenbaum, R. (1990). Effective single-session therapy: Step-by-step-guidelines. In. M. Talmon, *Single session therapy: Maximizing the effect of the first (and often only) therapeutic encounter* (pp. 34–56). San Francisco: Jossey-Bass.

VandenBos, G. R., & Pino, C. D. (1980). Research on outcome of psychotherapy. In G. R. (Ed.), *Psychotherapy: Practice, research, and policy* (pp. 23–69). Beverly Hills, CA: Sage.

Vaughn, K., Cox Young, B., Webster, D. C., & Thomas, M. R. (1996). Solution-focused work in the hospital: A continuum-of-care model for inpatient psychiatric treatment. In S. D. Miller, M. A. Hubble, & B. L. Duncan (Eds.), *Handbook of solution-focused brief therapy* (pp. 99–127). San Francisco: Jossey-Bass.

von Foerster, H. (1984). On constructing a reality. In P. Watzlawick (Ed.), *The invented reality: How do we know what we believe we know? Contributions to constructivism* (pp. 41–61). New York: Norton.

von Glasersfeld, E. (1984). An introduction to radical constructivism. In P. Watzlawick (Ed.), *The invented reality: How do we know what we believe we know? Contributions to constructivism* (pp. 17–40). New York: Norton.

Waters, D. B., & Lawrence, E. C. (1993). *Competence, courage, and change: An approach to family therapy.* New York: Norton.

Watts, A. (1966). *The book: On the taboo against knowing who you are.* New York Pantheon.

Watzlawick, P. (Ed.). (1984). *The invented reality: How do we know what we believe we know? Contributions to constructivism.* New York: Norton.

Weiner-Davis, M., de Shazer, S., & Gingerich, W. J. (1987). Using pretreatment change to construct a therapeutic solution: An exploratory study. *Journal of Marital and Family Therapy, 13,* 359–363.

White, M. (1989). *Selected papers.* Adelaide, South Australia: Dulwich Centre Publications.

White, M. (1993). Commentary: The histories of the present. In S. Gilligan & R. Price (Eds.), *Therapeutic conversations* (pp. 121–132). New York: Norton.

White, M. (1995). *Re-authoring lives: Interviews and essays.* Adelaide, South Australia: Dulwich Centre Publications.

White, M., & Epston, D. (1990). *Narrative means to therapeutic ends.* New York: Norton.

Williams, J., Gibbons, M., First, M., Spitzer, R., Davies, M., Borus, J., Howes, M., Kane, J., Pope, H., Rounsaville, B., & Wittchen, H. (1992). The structured clinical interview for the DSM IIIR (SCID)II: Multi-site test-retest reliability. *Archives of General Psychiatry.*

Wolfe, B. E. (1993). Psychotherapy research funding for fiscal years 1986–1990. *Psychotherapy and Rehabilitation Research Bulletin, 1,* 7–9.

Wolin, S, J., & Wolin, S. (1993). *The resilient self: How survivors of troubled families rise above adversity.* New York: Villard Books.

Zeig, J. K. (Ed.). (1980). *A teaching seminar with Milton H. Erickson.* New York: Brunner/Mazel.

Zeig, J. K. (1982). (Ed.). *Ericksonian approaches to hypnosis and psychotherapy.* New York: Brunner/Mazel.

Zeig, J. K. (1985a). (Ed.). *Ericksonian psychotherapy: Volume I: Structures.* New York: Brunner/Mazel.

Zeig, J. K. (1985b). (Ed.). *Ericksonian psychotherapy: Volume II: Clinical applications.* New York: Brunner/Mazel.

Zeig, J. K. (Ed.). (1994). *Ericksonian methods: The essence of the story.* New York: Brunner/Mazel.

Zeig, J. K., & Gilligan, S. G. (Eds.). (1990). *Brief therapy: Myths, methods, and metaphors.* New York: Brunner/Mazel.

Zeig, J. K., & Lankton, S. R. (Eds.). (1988). *Developing Ericksonian therapy: State of the art.* New York: Brunner/Mazel.

BIBLIOGRAPHY

Andersen, T. (Ed.). (1991). *The reflecting team: Dialogues and dialogues about the dialogues.* New York: Norton.

Anderson, H. (1997). *Conversation, language, and possibilities: A postmodern approach.* New York: Basic Books.

Bell-Gadsby, C., & Siegenberg, A. L. (1995). *Reclaiming herstory: Ericksonian solution-focused therapy for sexual abuse.* Philadelphia: Brunner/Mazel.

Berg, I. K. (1994). *Family based services: A solution-focused approach.* New York: Norton.

Berg, I. K., & Kelly, S. (2000). *Building solutions in child protective services.* New York: Norton.

Berg, I. K., & Miller, S. D. (1992). *Working with the problem drinker: A solution-focused approach.* New York: Norton.

Berg, I. K., & Reuss, N. H. (1998). *Solutions step by step: A substance abuse treatment manual.* New York: Norton.

Bertolino, B. (1999). *Therapy with troubled teenagers: Rewriting young lives in progress.* New York: Wiley.

Bertolino, B., & O'Hanlon, B. (Eds.). (1998). *Invitation to possibility-land: An intensive teaching seminar with Bill O'Hanlon.* Bristol, PA: Brunner/Mazel.

Bertolino, B., & Schultheis, G. (in press). *The solutions workbook.* New York: The Haworth Press.

Bertolino, B., & Thompson, K. (1999). *The residential youth care worker in action: A collaborative, competency-based approach.* New York: The Haworth Press.

Budman, S. H. (Ed.). (1981). *Forms of brief therapy.* New York: Guilford.

Budman, S. H., Hoyt, M. F., & Friedman, S. (Eds.). (1992). *The first session in brief therapy.* New York: Guilford.

Cade, B., & O'Hanlon, W. H. (1993). *A brief guide to brief therapy.* New York: Norton.

Chevalier, A. J. (1995). *On the client's path: A manual for the practice of solution-focused therapy.* Oakland, CA: New Harbinger Publications.

Chevalier, A. J. (1996). *On the counselor's path: A guide to teaching brief solution-focused therapy.* Oakland, CA: New Harbinger.

Christensen, D. N., Todahl, J., & Barrett, W. C. (1999). *Solution-based casework: An introduction to clinical and case management skills in casework practice.* New York: Aldine de Gruyter.

Cooper, J. F. (1995). *A primer of brief psychotherapy.* New York: Norton.

De Jong, P., & Berg, I. K. (1998). *Interviewing for solutions.* Pacific Grove, CA: Brooks/Cole.

de Shazer, S. (1982). *Patterns of brief family therapy: An ecosystemic approach.* New York: Guilford.

de Shazer, S. (1985). *Keys to solution in brief therapy.* New York: Norton.

de Shazer, S. (1988). *Clues: Investigating solutions in brief therapy.* New York: Norton.

de Shazer, S. (1991). *Putting difference to work.* New York: Norton.

de Shazer, S. (1994). *Words were originally magic.* New York: Norton.

Diamond, J. (2000). *Narrative means to sober ends: Treating addiction and its aftermath.* New York: Guilford.

Duncan, B. L., Hubble, M. A., & Miller, S. D. (1997). *Psychotherapy with "impossible" cases: The efficient treatment of therapy veterans.* New York: Norton.

Duncan, B. L., & Miller, S. D. (2000). *The heroic client: Doing client-centered, outcome-informed therapy.* San Francisco: Jossey-Bass.

Durrant, M. (1993). *Residential treatment: A cooperative, competency-based approach to therapy and program design.* New York: Norton.

Durrant, M. (1995). *Creative strategies for school problems: Solutions for psychologists and teachers.* New York: Norton.

Durrant, M., & White, C. (Eds.). (1990). *Ideas for therapy with sexual abuse.* Adelaide, Australia: Dulwich Centre Publications.

Epston, D. (1989). *Collected papers.* Adelaide, Australia: Dulwich Centre Publications.

Epston, D., & White, M. (1992). *Experience, contradiction, narrative, and imagination: Selected papers of David Epston and Michael White 1989–1991.* Adelaide, Australia: Dulwich Centre Publications.

Eron, J. B., & Lund, T. W. (1996). *Narrative solutions in brief therapy.* New York: Guilford.

Freedman, J., & Combs, G. (1996). *Narrative therapy: The social construction of preferred realities.* New York: Norton.

Freeman, J., Epston, D., & Lobovits, D. (1997). *Playful approaches to serious problems: Narrative therapy with children and their families.* New York: Norton.

Friedman, S. (Ed.). (1995). *The reflecting team in action: Collaborative practice in family therapy.* New York: Guilford.

Friedman, S. (1997). *Time-effective psychotherapy: Maximizing outcomes in an era of minimized resources.* Needham Heights, MA: Allyn and Bacon.

Friedman, S., & Fanger, M. T. (1991). *Expanding therapeutic possibilities: Getting results in brief therapy.* Lexington, MA: DC Heath.

Furman, B., & Ahola, T. (1992). *Solution talk: Hosting therapeutic conversations.* New York: Norton.

Gilligan, S., & Price, R. (Eds.). (1993). *Therapeutic conversations.* New York: Norton.

Hawkes, D., Marsh, T. I., & Wilgosh, R. (1998). *Solution-focused therapy: A handbook for health care professionals.* Woburn, MA: Butterworth-Heinemann Medical.

Hoffman, L. (1993). *Exchanging voices: A collaborative approach to family therapy.* London: Karnac.

Hoyt, M. F. (Ed.). (1994). *Constructive therapies.* New York: Guilford.

Hoyt, M. F. (1995). *Brief therapy and managed care: Readings for contemporary practice.* San Francisco: Jossey-Bass.

Hoyt, M. F. (Ed.). (1996). *Constructive therapies 2.* New York: Guilford.

Hoyt, M. F. (Ed.). (1998). *The handbook of constructive therapies.* San Francisco: Jossey-Bass.

Hoyt, M. F. (2000). *Some stories are better than others: Doing what works in brief therapy and managed care.* Philadelphia: Brunner/Mazel.

Hubble, M. A., Miller, S. D., & Duncan, B. L. (Eds.). (1999). *The heart and soul of change: What works in therapy.* Washington, DC: American Psychological Association.

Johnson, L. D. (1995). *Psychotherapy in the age of accountability.* New York: Norton.

Kollar, C. A. (1997). *Solution-focused pastoral counseling: An effective short-term approach for getting people back on track.* New York: Zonderman.

Lethem, J. (1995). *Moved to tears, moved to action: Solution-focused brief therapy with women and children.* London: BT Press.

Littrell, J. (1998). *Brief counseling in action.* New York: Norton.

Madsen, W. C. (1999). *Collaborative therapy with multi-stressed families: From old problems to new futures.* New York: Guilford.

Matthews, W. J, & Edgette, J. H. (Eds.). (1997). *Current thinking and research in brief therapy: Solutions, strategies, and narratives* (Vol. 1). New York: Brunner/Mazel.

Matthews, W. J, & Edgette, J. H. (Eds.). (1998). *Current thinking and research in brief therapy: Solutions, strategies, and narratives* (Vol. 2). New York: Brunner/Mazel.

Matthews, W. J, & Edgette, J. H. (Eds.). (1999). *Current thinking and research in brief therapy: Solutions, strategies, and narratives* (Vol. 3). New York: Brunner/Mazel.

McFarland, B. (1995). *Brief therapy and eating disorders: A practical guide to solution-focused work with clients.* San Francisco: Jossey-Bass.

McNamee, S., & Gergen, K. J. (Eds.). (1992). *Therapy as social construction: Inquiries in social construction.* Newbury Park, CA: Sage.

McNeilly, R. (2000). *Healing the whole person: A solution-focused approach to using empowering language, emotions, and actions in therapy.* New York: Wiley.

Metcalf, L. (1995). *Counseling toward solutions: A practical solution-focused program for working with students, teachers, and parents.* New York: Simon & Schuster.

Metcalf, L. (1997). *Parenting toward solutions: How parents can use skills they already have to raise responsible, loving kids.* New Jersey: Prentice Hall.

Metcalf, L. (1998). *Teaching toward solutions: Step-by-step strategies for handling academic, behavioral, and family issues in the classroom.* New York: Simon & Schuster.

Metcalf, L. (1998). *Solution-focused group therapy: Ideas for groups in private practice, schools, agencies, and treatment programs.* New York: The Free Press.

Miller, G. (1997). *Becoming miracle workers: Language and meaning in brief therapy.* New York: Aldine de Gruyter.

Miller, S. D., & Berg, I. K. (1995). *The miracle method: A radically new approach to problem drinking.* New York: Norton.

Miller, S. D., Duncan, B. L., & Hubble, M. A. (1997). *Escape from Babel: Toward a unifying language for psychotherapy practice.* New York: Norton.

Miller, S. D., Hubble, M. A., & Duncan, B. L. (Eds.). (1996). *Handbook of solution-focused brief therapy.* San Francisco: Jossey-Bass.

Monk, G., Winslade, J., Crocket, K., & Epston, D. (Eds.). (1997). *Narrative therapy in practice: The archaeology of hope.* San Francisco: Jossey Bass.

Murphy, J. J. (1997). *Solution-focused counseling in middle and high schools.* Alexandria, VA: American Counseling Association.

Murphy, J. J., & Duncan, B. L. (1997). *Brief intervention for school problems: Collaborating for practical solutions.* New York: Guilford.

Nardone, G. (1996). *Brief strategic solution-oriented therapy of phobic and obsessive disorders.* Northvale, NJ: Jason Aronson.

O'Callaghan, J. B. (1993). *School-based collaboration with families: Constructing family-school-agency partnerships that work.* San Francisco: Jossey-Bass.

O'Connell, B. (1998). *Solution-focused therapy.* Newbury Park, CA: Sage.

O'Hanlon, B., & Beadle, S. (1999). *A guide to possibility land: Fifty-one methods for doing brief, respectful therapy.* New York: Norton. [Originally published 1994 as *A field guide to possibilityland: Possibility therapy methods.* Omaha, NE.: Possibility Press.]

O'Hanlon, B., & Bertolino, B. (1998). *Even from a broken web: Brief, respectful solution-oriented therapy for sexual abuse and trauma.* New York: Wiley.

O'Hanlon, B., & Bertolino, B. (Eds.). (1999). *Evolving possibilities: The selected papers of Bill O'Hanlon.* Bristol, PA: Brunner/Mazel.

O'Hanlon, B., & Wilk, J. (1987). *Shifting contexts: The generation of effective psychotherapy.* New York: Guilford.

O'Hanlon, W. H., & Martin, M. (1992). *Solution-oriented hypnosis: An Ericksonian approach.* New York: Norton.

O'Hanlon, W. H., & Weiner-Davis, M. (1989). *In search of solutions: A new direction in psychotherapy.* New York: Norton.

Parry, A., & Doan, R. E. (1994). *Story re-visions: Narrative therapy in the postmodern world.* New York: Guilford.

Quick, E. K. (1996). *Doing what works in brief therapy: A strategic solution-focused approach.* San Diego, CA: Academic Press.

Rowan, T., & O'Hanlon, B. (1999). *Solution-oriented therapy for chronic and severe mental illness.* New York: Wiley.

Schultheis, G. M. (1998). *Brief therapy homework planner.* New York: Wiley.

Schultheis, G. M., O'Hanlon, B., & O'Hanlon, S. (1999). *Brief couples therapy homework planner.* New York: Wiley.

Selekman, M. D. (1993). *Pathways to change: Brief therapy solutions with difficult adolescents.* New York: Guilford.

Selekman, M. D. (1997). *Solution-focused therapy with children: Harnessing family strengths for systemic change.* New York: Guilford.

Sklare, G. (1997). *Brief counseling that works: A solution-focused approach for school counselors.* Newbury Park, CA: Sage.

Smith, C., & Nylund, D. (Eds.). (1997). *Narrative therapies with children and adolescents.* New York: Guilford.

Talmon, M. (1990). *Single session therapy: Maximizing the effect of the first (and often only) therapeutic encounter.* San Francisco: Jossey-Bass.

Thomas, F., & Cockburn, J. (1998). *Competency-based counseling: Building on client strengths.* Minneapolis: Fortress Press.

Turnell, A., & Edwards, S. (1999). *Signs of safety: A solution and safety-oriented approach to child protection casework.* New York: Norton.

Walter, J. L., & Peller, J. E. (1992). *Becoming solution-focused in brief therapy.* New York: Brunner/Mazel.

Walter, J. L., & Peller, J. E. (2000). *Recreating brief therapy: Preferences and possibilities.* New York: Norton.

Waters, D. B., & Lawrence, E. C. (1993). *Competence, courage, and change: An approach to family therapy.* New York: Norton.

Webb, W. H. (1999). *Solutioning: Solution-focused interventions for counselors.* Philadelphia: Accelerated Development.

White, M. (1989). *Selected papers.* Adelaide, Australia: Dulwich Centre Publications.

White, M. (1995). *Re-authoring lives: Interviews and essays.* Adelaide, Australia: Dulwich Centre Publications.

White, M. (1997). *Narratives of therapists' lives.* Adelaide, Australia: Dulwich Centre Publications.

White, M., & Epston, D. (1990). *Narrative means to therapeutic ends.* New York: Norton.

Wilgosh, R., Hawkes, D., & Marsh, T. I. (1998). *Solution-focused therapy: Managing human relationships.* Woburn, MA: Butterworth-Heinemann Medical.

Zimmerman, J., & Dickerson, V. (1996). *If problems talked: Narrative therapy in action.* New York: Guilford.

INDEX